HEALTH CARE FEDERALISM IN CANADA

Health Care Federalism in Canada

in Canada

Critical Junctures and Critical Perspectives

Edited by

KATHERINE FIERLBECK AND WILLIAM LAHEY

McGill-Queen's University Press

Montreal & Kingston · London · Ithaca

© McGill-Queen's University Press 2013

ISBN 978-0-7735-4253-2 (cloth)
ISBN 978-0-7735-4254-9 (paper)
ISBN 978-0-7735-8941-4 (ePDF)
ISBN 978-0-7735-8942-1 (ePUB)

Legal deposit fourth quarter 2013
Bibliothèque nationale du Québec

Printed in Canada on acid-free paper that is 100% ancient forest
free (100% post-consumer recycled), processed chlorine free.

McGill-Queen's University Press acknowledges the support of the
Canada Council for the Arts for our publishing program. We also
acknowledge the financial support of the Government of Canada
through the Canada Book Fund for our publishing activities.

Library and Archives Canada Cataloguing in Publication

  Health care federalism in Canada : critical junctures
and critical perspectives / edited by Katherine Fierlbeck and
William Lahey.

Includes bibliographical references and index.
Issued in print and electronic formats.
ISBN 978-0-7735-4253-2 (bound). – ISBN 978-0-7735-4254-9 (pbk.).
ISBN 978-0-7735-8941-4 (ePDF). – ISBN 978-0-7735-8942-1 (ePUB).

  1. Medical care – Government policy – Canada. 2. Federal
government – Canada. I. Fierlbeck, Katherine, author, writer of
introduction, editor of compilation II. Lahey, William, 1961–, author,
editor of compilation

RA395.C3H42165 2013   362.10971   C2013-905382-4
                                                C2013-905383-2

This book was typeset by True to Type in 10.5/13 Sabon

Contents

Tables and Figures

Acronyms

ACHDHR	Advisory Committee on Health Delivery and Human Resources
A-G	Attorney-General
CDMR	Care Delivery Model Redesign
CHA	Canada Health Act
CHHRN	Pan-Canadian Health Human Resources Network
CHST	Canada Health and Social Transfer
CHT	Canada Health Transfer
CIHI	Canadian Institute for Health Information
CST	Canada Social Transfer
CT	computed tomography
EPF	Established Programs Financing
FMM	First Ministers' Meeting
GDP	gross domestic product
GST	goods and services tax
HHR	health human resources
IT	information technology
MOCINS	Model of Care Initiative in Nova Scotia
MRI	magnetic resonance imaging
OECD	Organisation for Economic Co-operation and Development
RCMP	Royal Canadian Mounted Police
SUFA	Social Union Framework Agreement
UBC	University of British Columbia
VIHA	Vancouver Island Health Authority
WHO	World Health Organization

Preface

STEVEN LEWIS

History is full of what-ifs and longings for a do-over. What if Napoleon and Hitler hadn't invaded Russia or the Lenape Indians had held onto half of Manhattan in 1626 rather than taking the extra $12? Sometimes you get a do-over: the Montreal Alouettes' Damon Duval missed the game-winning field goal on the last play of the 2009 Grey Cup against the Saskatchewan Roughriders but got a do-over because the Riders had 13 men on the field. He made that one. Rider Nation yearned for a do-over to avoid the fatal do-over.

So what do we make of federalism in Canadian health care? Federalism is the result of multiple levels of government co-existing within a common jurisdiction. A federation is a coming together of parties to advance their common interests. Sometimes the union is involuntary, as in the old Soviet Union and Yugoslavia. Such federations break apart at the first opportunity. In Canada, as in the United States, the constituent parts decided that on balance, ceding some autonomy and making common cause with each other was preferable to standing alone. The resulting union is fundamentally a bargain and a trade-off that over time requires adjustments, accommodations, and recalibrations. There are bound to be "if we knew then what we know now" debates about the wisdom of constitutional arrangements and negotiated agreements. Modern health care wasn't even a gleam in the eye of the architects of Confederation in 1864 and 1867. How much simpler matters would be had it found its way into section 91 instead of section 92 of the (then) British North America Act.

Would matters truly have been simpler? Health care is never simple and free of tension. It is just as fractious in England's unitary system as it is in Canada's federalist system. There have been periods of cooperation and periods of conflict between the federal and provincial levels of government throughout the Canadian medicare era, largely but not exclusively correlated with how lavishly or parsimoniously the federal government used its spending power. In the end, all health care is local, and for the patients and other members of the public, the nuances and mechanics of federalism are hardly top of mind when assessing whether the system works well. Access, quality, fairness, and cost will always be contentious issues, and no clarification or reconfiguration of powers, revenue sources, or fiscal arrangements will put an end to the debates or a happy face on every citizen and every provider. It is tempting to conclude that federalism doesn't matter much after all.

As the contributors to this volume demonstrate, we should resist that temptation. Federalism does matter, and governments can change many features of health care finance and delivery without amending the constitution. Improving how federalism works generates both normative and empirical questions. For example, one can debate whether in theory it is more desirable to have one or two levels of government set the health care agenda or whether, all things considered, homogeneity or diversity is more desirable among provincial systems. Questions about whether and where it is more efficient to have Ottawa or the provinces responsible for programs and services are – should be – subject to empirical analysis. One of the most useful constructs explored in the book is the distinction between hard and soft law and between broadly worded commitments and aspirations and contractual obligations. There are endless subtleties in federal-provincial relations, and every government aims to take credit for what works and avoid taking the rap for what doesn't.

The symposium out of which this collection emerged took place in a particular political context. The Harper government favours a highly decentralized view of federalism. Among many useful reminders in this volume is the extent to which Canada was arguably the most decentralized federation in the OECD even before the election of the current regime. To cite just one symbolically powerful example, not a dime of US federal government money goes to the states unconditionally. By contrast, Canada has been a nation of tax point transfers, block grants, and weak and unenforced conditionality, particularly in the domain of social spending.

The other context undergirding these analyses is the last fifteen years of health care spending and what it accomplished. It seems fair to infer that none of the contributors believes that Canada gets good value for money from health care, and all are chagrined, if not alarmed, by how little change we got for the massive and sustained increases in spending. International comparisons do not flatter Canada's performance on access and efficiency. We are laggards in the uptake of health information technology. The workforce has prospered financially but is no happier. It seems impossible to achieve a reasonable distribution of physicians despite the fact that medical school enrolment has been increased by 84% since 1997 and physicians have been offered every conceivable inducement to locate outside urban areas. The result is a perfect storm: more and more doctors are pouring out of medical schools; the fee-for-service system is still largely intact, which means that the new doctors will have to order more tests, prescribe more drugs, and do more procedures to generate incomes; the country is just getting started on the quality improvement and waste reduction agenda; and drug companies and professional lobbies have largely succeeded in creating a nation of the worried well who can't get enough diagnostics. All of these factors drive up costs, just as governments seek to reduce cost escalations to deal with the fiscal problems created by the 2008 worldwide financial meltdown.

In short, the country missed a glorious opportunity to create a less fragmented, better quality system when the money flowed freely. Some of the failures can plausibly be attributed to an inability to cooperate and coordinate combined with a leadership vacuum. In the area of health human resources, two aspects illustrate the extent of the problem. All provinces have faced pressures to increase entry-to-practice credentials. Nursing now requires a baccalaureate degree instead of a diploma. Almost all undergraduate physical and occupational therapy programs have disappeared, making a master's degree the *de facto* entry-to-practice requirement. Each jurisdiction makes its own decisions on these matters, and the common thread is that not a single credential upgrade rested on a solid base of evidence that the existing credential produced graduates unfit for practice. Nor were the upgrades called for by employers; when asked, more often than not they opposed them.

Frustrated by this seemingly unstoppable trend, the governments collectively established a federal-provincial-territorial Coordinating Committee on Entry to Practice Credentials to address the issues and develop a systematic approach to evaluating new proposals. I sat on the committee for six years. The idea was to reject proposals to increase credentials that did not have adequate supporting evidence. But the provinces and territories made no commitment to abandon their right to make a decision, contrary to the recommendation of an independent review process, or to act in concert. Predictably, the committee has been a triumph of information sharing and deliberation and powerless to hold back the tide. Not only have governments essentially lost control of credential requirements, they have shown no interest in evaluating the impact of the changes on costs, access to education, recruitment and retention, or actual health care performance. Don't ask, don't tell, don't learn is hardly a motto that breeds confidence.

A second issue is numbers: how many of each category of professional do we need? The answer depends on how we define "need," how we organize services, and what levers exist to encourage the practices we desire. Notably, the multiple and mostly independent decisions to increase the number of seats in medical and nursing programs took place without addressing the important issue of scope of practice. If primary care clinics led by nurse practitioners are just as effective as traditional physician-led practices, how many of each of these two types of professional should we educate? If family doctors working with teams of other professionals at the renowned Group Health Cooperative in Seattle have patient rosters of 1800, do provinces like British Columbia have a shortage when the average roster is closer to 1000? All planning and projections are based on assumptions, and all too often we simply accept that current service patterns and divisions of labour are both sensible and immutable.

These and a host of other public policy dilemmas reveal the challenges to health care federalism that go well beyond the division of powers and fiscal imbalance. It is less a debate about which government should be in charge of what and where they should jointly set direction than about whether either level of government has much substantive control over anything that goes on in the system. Put simply, the supply side – the professions, the vendors, the manufacturers – largely runs the show. Governments annually decide how much money to spend on health care, and that amount is consumed in the millions of essentially unsupervised and unevaluated transactions that take place. Clinical practice is much more autonomous in Canada than in high-performing health care systems around the world. There is no requirement to follow clinical practice guidelines and no expectation that major variations in practice will be narrowed. The unstated assumption is that the system is in a perpetual state of scarcity, and the public trusts the professions more than it trusts the people it elects. Governments pretend to manage the system and providers pretend that they are chafing under the jackboot of the state. Remarkably, when things go wrong the public points the finger at governments and lets the real decision-makers off the hook.

None of these phenomena is unknown to governments, and blue-ribbon panels and commissions across the country have recommended similar solutions for decades. Within these pages, the contributors advocate for a much greater federal role in steering the system and for Ottawa getting out of the game entirely. For some the case is instrumental: which arrangement is more likely to result in politically achievable reforms that will make the system better and more efficient? For others it is more ideological: which arrangement is more likely to lead to a greater role for for-profit health care and market-like competition? And for others it is about more than health care – it is about the very nature of the country, an expression of pan-Canadian solidarity, and a core element of our identity.

Whatever one's view, it seems undeniable that the provinces have found it extraordinarily difficult to make any significant changes at a reasonable price when they have acted alone. The logic of provincial autonomy is analogous to the famous prisoner's dilemma problem in game theory. When each person acts on his or her own self-interest and assumes that the others will do likewise, the outcomes are worse for all than had they cooperated. We see this in negotiations with health care unions, where the provinces are whipsawed into races to the top in a competition that benefits the supply side but not necessarily the public interest. Cooperation is, as a rule, painfully hard won – it took a decade to get agreement on something so transparently sensible as the Common Drug Review. It seems clear that the provinces' odds of making real breakthroughs in primary care organization and delivery, payment reform, and effective health human resource deployment will be better if they create and stick to a common front. In theory this could be done without Ottawa, but history suggests that the judicious and negotiated use of the federal spending power would be a key factor in making changes that are sure to elicit interest group resistance. This is the Hobbesian bargain in federalism: the provinces agree to let Ottawa impose conditions in some areas to save themselves from each other. But first they have to think they need saving, and second that Ottawa is a reliable lifeboat.

Getting federalism in health care right implies that we would know whether we had or hadn't done so. The truth of the matter is that we don't have much valid, current, and truly comparable information on the performance of the system and its constituent parts. Our culture is somewhat hostile to transparent and honest reporting on performance. On the few occasions when the Canadian Institute for Health Information has published comparative data such as hospital standardized mortality rates or, more recently, the Canadian Hospital Reporting Project, an all-too-common reaction is to challenge the data rather than seize the opportunity for improvement. Perhaps one reason why we are so interested in intergovernmental issues is that we have so few objective measures of what works and what doesn't in which places. It is thus extremely valuable that the health information and performance metrics agenda is one of the topics covered in these pages.

Needless to say, this book is but the beginning of what we hope will be a thoughtful, deep, and creative series of explorations of the intersection of federalism and health care. Those who read it will be invited to examine their own assumptions and preferences and to assess which prescriptions are more likely to achieve the ends they prefer. The interdisciplinary nature of the contributions ensures that the issues are tackled from a number of perspectives. Those with a taste for history, law, political science, and economics will all find much to admire and think about. Every option has an explicit or implicit agenda, and every analysis is based on assumptions about what we are trying to achieve. The one inescapable conclusion is that how health care federalism evolves will affect how the health care system evolves. Health care federalism is thus a means to an end, and the critical challenge is to assess which means are most compatible with which ends.

HEALTH CARE FEDERALISM IN CANADA

1

Introduction:
Renewing Federalism, Improving Health Care:
Can this Marriage Be Saved?

KATHERINE FIERLBECK

The architects of Canadian federalism could not, in 1867, have considered the possible implications of their design for social policy a century and a half later. They were focused upon ethnic discord, political corruption, insolvency, the threat of republicanism, and military annexation; to be fair, they probably did the best they could. But today we are obliged to address the consequences of this federal structure and, much like our predecessors, we face a critical jumble of obstacles and opportunities. Because of these historical circumstances, the marriage of health care and federalism in Canada has been a marriage based more on convenience than mutual attraction. It is also, as one health minister has noted, both a polygamous and a dysfunctional marriage.

This relationship is at a critical juncture. On 19 December 2011, federal and provincial finance ministers met for what most expected would be the beginning of a discussion of health, social, and equalization transfers, including the first tentative steps to renegotiate the 2003 First Ministers' Accord on Health Care Renewal (appendix 1) and the 2004 10-Year Plan to Strengthen Health Care (appendix 2). To the contrary, federal Finance Minister Jim Flaherty presented the group with a non-negotiable proposal. This offer involved three key changes to the status quo: first, transfers would be limited to Canada's rate of economic growth; second, they would be allocated on a strict per-capita basis, rather than on one that was weighted (to acknowl-

edge that poorer provinces could not take advantage of the tax transfers that had been part of the 1977 health funding deal to the extent
that richer provinces could); and third, the nature of health care provision would be left completely up to the provinces. There would be
no renegotiation of the health care accord, as there would simply be
no health care accord. There would be no statement of common principles, no national vision of what Canadian health care should be, and
no articulation of the way in which essential health care reforms
ought to be pursued.

We thus stand at a critical juncture in Canadian health care federalism, where the nature of health care (and possibly the nature of
Canadian federalism itself) will be redefined for a very long time. The
precarious equilibrium of federal-provincial health care relations has
been decisively punctured: what follows next? This volume examines
this shift in Canadian health care federalism: how did it arise? What
are the consequences? And what are the options now? Pointedly, the
analyses here are presented from a multidisciplinary perspective. Any
comprehensive understanding of this phenomenon requires scrutiny
from a number of critical perspectives. In addition, although the economic, political, legal, and technical issues are tightly intertwined,
each discipline offers a particular insight into what happened and
where to go from here.

THE CONTOURS OF
CANADIAN HEALTH CARE FEDERALISM

Federal systems are not reducible to a single model. Common to all is
the principle that formal political power is dispersed between discrete
jurisdictions; beyond this, the variations are innumerable. Some federal states are "power sharing" or "administrative" in design, characterized by a high degree of interdependence between jurisdictions,
like Germany's federal system; others are "power separating" or "jurisdictional" models, which emphasize a clearer delineation of jurisdictional responsibilities, like Canada's federal system (Jordan 2009).
Many, like the United States, have a congressional system of competing checks and balances; Canada, in contrast, is a hybrid of federal and
parliamentary models. An optimistic view of federal models is that
they are grounded in a desire for the wider accommodation of diversity; a more pessimistic one is that they are founded on the principle
of distrust. Federal states, in contrast to unitary ones, offer both

greater flexibility and a solid fence against the concentration of power; at the same time, and for the same reasons, they are much more likely to experience stalemate and deadlock.

The division of power in federal states is usually articulated through a constitutional document. The problem is that health care changes quite steadily and dramatically over time, and constitutions generally do not. This is one reason that federal debates over health care can be so tricky. The British North America Act and its successor, the 1982 Constitution Act, did not give explicit jurisdiction over health care to the provinces. They gave jurisdiction over *hospitals* to the provinces. If considered in isolation from years of judicial interpretation, this would seem to leave a great deal of modern health care (which exists independently of hospitals) left open to dispute. Provincial jurisdiction over health care was, historically, also inferred from the fact that the provinces were granted jurisdiction over "matters of a merely local or private nature," which, again, seems incoherent to modern sensibilities given that much of Canada's health care system is neither local in scope nor private in nature.

Yet constitutional frameworks are only the starting point, as political objectives and interests often shape their own pathways. The warp and weft of power and institutions produce a policy fabric that is unique to each country; in Canada, the dynamics of nation building and ideology have often sat athwart the formal constitutional divisions of power. Federal involvement in health care, notwithstanding formal provincial jurisdiction, is arguably quite extensive, comprising not only the distribution of funds to provincial health systems but also significant regulation (notably but not exclusively of pharmaceuticals), innovation and infrastructure (including information technology), public health, and the direct delivery of health services for discrete groups. Much federal involvement occurred after the Second World War, in line with the development of welfare state models in a number of western countries. A national program of infrastructure development was introduced in 1948 in the form of national health grants and, after several abortive attempts, Ottawa developed a shared-cost program for hospital insurance, and later medical insurance, that became national in scope when all provinces finally subscribed to it. Although this period is frequently referred to as one of "cooperative federalism," such a label tends to downplay the highly acrimonious nature of much of this "cooperative" activity.

Following the 1957 Hospital Insurance and Diagnostic Services Act and the 1966 Medical Care Act, there are generally seen to be four major benchmarks for health care federalism leading up to the 2003 health accord. The first was the shift from shared-cost funding to block funding formalized in the Established Programs Financing (EPF) program in 1977. The EPF program to a large extent defined three key issues that continue to shape health care federalism. The first is the relationship between flexibility and clarity. Ottawa disliked being locked into an obligation to provide unknown levels of funding in the open-ended shared-cost system; provinces disliked the painstakingly detailed justification of costs that they had to make for specific items (such as which beds were designated either acute care or long-term care). By providing single annual block grants for all hospital and medical services (combined with funds for post-secondary education) and by tying the spending escalator to national economic growth rather than provincial expenditure, the federal government was better able to address its fiscal problems (which were themselves escalating significantly). At the same time, provinces could use federal cash in ways that best suited their particular needs. But this increased flexibility also led to greater confusion. Much of this was driven by Ottawa's decision to distribute half of the EPF transfers in the form of tax points. It became increasingly unclear what Ottawa's contribution to the provinces was, as the federal government continued to claim that the amount of cash it *could* have given was represented by the tax points still within its own jurisdiction rather than in the possession of the provinces. This negative hypothetical calculation was more difficult to assess than simple cash transfers, and it was also a source of major irritation to the provinces, who argued that the distribution of half of the EPF transfers in the form of tax points had been a one-time event and therefore the value of the tax points could not coherently be considered as something still belonging to Ottawa even at a hypothetical level.

This confusion gave rise to another tension: the relationship between conditionality and accountability. Greater flexibility meant less conditionality, but less conditionality meant that there was little reason to account for how funds were spent. Federal health care funds were becoming little more than another generic form of transfer payment, much like equalization funds, and were moving away from serving the purpose for which they had been initially established. Given that the Liberal administration in Ottawa had political capital in these original objectives, the issue of the way in which health transfers were used became increasingly contentious. Indeed, the federal-provincial dialogue on health care funding has increasingly oscillated between the poles of fiscal flexibility (Established Programs Financing and the Canada Health and Social Transfer) and spending accountability (the Canada Health Act, the 2000 and 2003 accords, and the 2004 10-Year Plan to Strengthen Health Care). The issue of accountability in health care spending has generally required a larger federal presence in the health policy arena, although there have been more recent attempts to reconfigure the way in which accountability is exercised. One approach, for example, is citizen accountability, which emphasizes greater transparency to the public at large. This idea was articulated within the 1999 Social Union Framework Agreement (SUFA), but various attempts to operationalize the principle (e.g., with citizens' watchdog organizations) have had mixed success at best (Anderson and Findlay 2010). A different approach altogether to accountability has been pursued by the Harper administration, which has focused on the "clarity of roles and responsibilities" of governments (Lazar 2008, 139).

The third point of contention between provinces following the EPF program was the appropriate process and procedure of health care funding itself. The original set of policies that gave health care a distinctly national form – the 1957 Hospital Insurance and Diagnostic Services Act and the 1966 Medical Care Act – had been secured through the voluntary buy in of provinces over a period of fourteen years. By 1977, however, it became clear that Ottawa's unilateral actions could, and did, directly impact provinces in what was technically their own area of jurisdiction. The federal government's largesse in distributing funds for health care had not, for the most part, come with a clear protocol on how shifts in funding policy would be addressed. As the provinces learned, Ottawa's ability to withdraw funding from established programs (which some called its "dis-spending" power) was a greater cause for concern than its spending power, as it affected provinces once they were already deeply committed to spending their resources in a particular way.

The next benchmark for federal-provincial relations in the field of health care was the establishment of the 1984 Canada Health Act (CHA). Initially an issue raised by the New Democratic Party, the creeping tendency of physicians and hospitals to bill patients above and beyond rates set by provincial insurance plans set in motion a forceful revision of federal health funding policy (Bégin 2002). Buoyed by

positive public feedback, the federal Liberal administration introduced the CHA after ongoing negotiations with the provinces on this
issue proved to be fruitless. The CHA combined the measures contained in both the 1957 Hospital Insurance and Diagnostic Services
Act and the 1966 Medical Care Act, articulated basic principles upon
which federal funding would be provided (including a new principle
of reasonable access), and set out the nature of penalties for non-compliance. Provinces were furious, not only because of the unilateral
nature of the move and because of the increased costs to provincial
treasuries the CHA implied, but also because the public popularity of
the new legislation among their own electorates meant that they were
forced to swallow the changes unchallenged.

For similar reasons, the nadir of federal-provincial relations in
health care was the creation in the 1995 federal budget of a new Canada Health and Social Transfer (CHST), which cut federal transfers to
health, post-secondary education, and social welfare programs by
approximately six billion dollars. The federal budget was presented
without prior consultation with the provinces notwithstanding the
enormous impact the budget was to have on them. It was the introduction of the CHST that provided the main impetus for the provinces
to think seriously about ways of protecting themselves from the vul-
nerabilities that had resulted from their dependence upon federal
funding (see chapter 3). But the CHST was only part of a larger context
of political turmoil in federal-provincial relations that included the
failures of the Meech Lake accord in 1990 and the Charlottetown
accord in 1992, as well as the perilously close Quebec referendum
result in 1995. By the late 1990s, when the dust began to settle and the
federal deficit began to recede, it became clear that a change to the status quo was imperative. The direction of the change, of course, was
much less clear. The provinces desired a return to greater federal
health care funding, a new intergovernmental decision-making protocol, and limits on federal spending power; Ottawa wanted to formalize its spending power and strengthen national health care standards; and Quebec, somewhat awkwardly, also desired the restoration
of federal health care spending while maintaining its principled
opposition to the legitimacy of the federal spending power (see Bakvis et al. 2009, 174–6).

The result of this collective attempt at bridge-building was the
Social Union Framework Agreement (SUFA) of 1999. The SUFA was
notable for three reasons. First, it was at a symbolic level the articula-

tion of a truce between orders of government. Second, it explicitly recognized the very existence of a Canadian "social union," which was understood as a recognition of "the web of rights and obligations between Canadian citizens and governments that give effect and meaning to our shared sense of social purpose and common citizenship" (Biggs 1996, 1). This was, in effect, a formal statement of support for Canada's public health care system without explicit reference to the words "public health care" (which would have raised, among other things, the issue of just who was responsible for what). Third, SUFA attempted to establish a blueprint for a new *modus operandi* between orders of government in the field of health care. The overarching design of the agreement, note Cameron and McCrea-Logie, "reflects an effort to establish a system in which the various relationships between the federal and provincial governments in the social policy field are rendered more stable, more predictable, and more balanced" (2004, 121).

SUFA had seven major components. The document began with a statement of principles, stressing equality, participatory democracy, and adherence to the principles set out in the CHA. The second section, building on the Agreement on Internal Trade, stressed the principle of interprovincial mobility. It stipulated a pan-Canadian recognition of occupational qualification, an area in which substantial progress has in fact been made (although barriers still exist: see, e.g., Brownlee 2011). Much less progress has been made in the third section, on public accountability and transparency, although the simple articulation of these ideas was (and still is) quite radical given the historical context of executive federalism in which it was embedded. The fourth section stresses the principle of intergovernmental collaboration. This was a very general and abstract statement, although one of the few concrete provisions within it was the stipulation that Ottawa would inform the provinces before undertaking substantial policy changes that would affect them in a significant way. The fifth section, which ultimately led Quebec to refuse unanimous ratification of the agreement, formally recognized Ottawa's spending power and specified particular conditions under which Canada-wide programs could be established by the federal government. Dispute avoidance and resolution, the subject of the penultimate section, was sketched out in very general terms, and it discussed public reporting, mediation, third-party involvement, and fact-finding. The potential here for establishing a critical protocol for intergovernmental dispute resolution never materialized into a clearer and more detailed set of co-decision rules. The final section of the agreement called for a review of SUFA after three years.

By 2001, however, the groundbreaking nature of the SUFA was dramatically overshadowed by the announcement that both a Royal Commission (chaired by Roy Romanow) and a Senate committee (chaired by Michael Kirby) would address health care reform. Another major distraction was the 2000 intergovernmental agreement on health renewal, which promised $23.4 billion of additional funding over five years, including $2.2 billion for early childhood development (set aside in the CHST), $1 billion for diagnostic and treatment equipment, $800 million for the development of primary health care reforms, and $500 million (through Canada Health Infoway) to assist in the development of health information technology. The 2000 agreement was the beginning of a brief era of cheque-book federalism in Canadian health care and very much served as the template for the 2003 accord and the 2004 10-year plan. Although the agreements in this period fell far short of becoming the "fix for a generation" anticipated by those negotiating them, one should perhaps not understate the importance of the years of relative peace and grudging concord that they bought. The open animosity and acrimonious hostility of the 1990s was at the very least forestalled, allowing governments to give some thought to the substance of health policy-making that was not completely dominated by political strategizing.

THE 2000 AND 2003 HEALTH CARE AGREEMENTS AND THE 10-YEAR PLAN ON STRENGTHENING HEALTH CARE

The 2000 agreement, considered at the time "the most expensive and possibly the most contentious intergovernmental agreement in recent Canadian history" (Decter 2000, 20), was a clear bridge between SUFA and the 2003 accord. Like SUFA, it began with a discussion of vision and principle: the vision, unsurprisingly, was structured upon a reiteration of the value of public health care and the explicit acknowledgement of provincial jurisdictions' "primary role" in the provision of health care. There was also, promisingly, a clear commitment to greater integration of health care services and to "reasonably timely access" to these services. The specific principles upon which the 2000 agreement was built included not only the standard components of the CHA but also the promotion of "health and wellness," the identification of best practices, the stipulation of regular reporting, and a partnership with Aboriginal stakeholders. It is in the eight-point action plan of the 2000 agreement that one can make out the armature for later intergovernmental agreements. Although these action points are (not surprisingly) articulated at a very general level, they do indicate priority areas for governments, including access to care, health promotion (especially early childhood development and public health), primary health care, health human resources, home care and long-term care, pharmaceuticals, health information technology, and health infrastructure. What was remarkable in the 2000 agreement was the explicit articulation of a framework for accountability on the part of all governments. This provision required all health ministers to provide "regular and comprehensive" public reporting on the scope and performance of the services they delivered as well as updates on the progress they made on specific priorities. To this end, health ministers were directed to work with third parties to collaborate in the development of a number of comparative health indicators in the areas of health status, health outcomes, and quality of service.

To a large extent, the 2003 accord is an expanded (and more expensive) version of the 2000 agreement. Beginning with a statement observing "a great convergence on the value of our publicly funded health system, the need for reform, and on the priorities for reform," the 2003 document yet again reiterates the principles of the CHA, and then describes the accord as a "covenant" to ensure that:

- all Canadians have timely access to health services on the basis of need, not ability to pay, regardless of where they live or move in Canada;
- the health care services available to Canadians are of high quality, effective, patient-centred, and safe; and
- our health care system is sustainable and affordable and will be here for Canadians and their children in the future.

The vision articulated by the accord is more of an ideal model than policy target, and it sets out a heath care system in which Canadians:

- have access to a health care provider 24 hours a day, 7 days a week;
- have timely access to diagnostic procedures and treatments;
- do not have to repeat their health histories or undergo the same tests for every provider they see;

- have access to quality home and community care services;
- have access to the drugs they need without undue financial hardship;
- are able to access quality care no matter where they live; and
- see their health care system as efficient, responsive, and adapting to their changing needs, and those of their families and communities, now and in the future.

In more concrete terms, the accord comprised a Health Reform Fund worth $16 billion targeting three areas (primary health care, home care, and catastrophic drug coverage) and a Diagnostic and Medical Equipment Fund worth $1.5 billion. These monies were distributed directly to the provinces, although, as these funds went directly to provinces' general operating budgets, there developed some uncertainly in the short term over whether the funds were in fact used for the purposes for which they were designated. The accord also promised an increase of $14 billion in CHST transfers above existing funding levels and declared a commitment by Ottawa to provide funding to support collaborative work in the areas of patient safety, health human resources, technology assessment, innovative research, and a "healthy living strategy" for Canadians. Finally, $5.3 billion was committed to direct federal spending in health care improvement, including target areas such as information technology (especially through Canadian Health Infoway) and Aboriginal health.

But the 2003 accord was particularly notable for two other reasons. First, it determined that the CHST was by April 2003 to be split into two separate payment streams, the Canada Health Transfer (CHT), and the Canada Social Transfer (CST), which was to be used for post-secondary education, social assistance, and social services. Again, both forms of transfers went directly into the provinces' general coffers, but because the amount given by Ottawa to each province was clearly specified, it became easier to calculate what percentage of provinces' health spending was comprised of federal money and whether the amounts given by Ottawa were reflected in the amounts spent by the provinces in these two areas. The second remarkable feature of the 2003 accord was the detailed discussion of performance indicators. Indicators were divided into three sections: "timely access indicators" consisted of fourteen specific indicators in three subcategories; "quality indicators" consisted of nine indicators divided between a further three subsections; and "sustainability" (efficiency and effectiveness) indicators comprised nineteen indicators within five categories.

In addition to the $36.8 billion over five years in health care spending outlined in the 2003 accord, the 2004 10-Year Plan to Strengthen Health Care committed an additional $41.3 billion over ten years. The 10-year plan gave explicit recognition to the problem of wait times and designated $5.5 billion as a Wait Times Reduction Transfer. Wait times were also to be addressed through further investment in strategic health human resources action plans, home care, health promotion, and primary care reform. A further $500 million in the first year went toward additional funding for medical and diagnostic equipment, while $35.3 billion was used to increase the CHT base the following year. In the third year of the plan a 6% escalator was added to the transfers (later to become the subject of some political discussion in the 2011 federal election). The principles articulated in the preamble of the document again reinforced support for the concept of public health care and included not only the CHA principles but also an explicit statement that Canadians ought to have access on the basis of need rather than ability to pay. Three points set out the vision of federalism encapsulated in the document: intergovernmental collaboration, jurisdictional flexibility, and asymmetrical federalism (allowing Quebec to implement its own plan). Two points – the sharing of best practices and a continued commitment to transparency and accountability – set out the principles of governance endorsed in the document. It is important to point out that federal funding initiatives have continued throughout the life of the 10-year plan. The 2007 budget, for example, directed over $1 billion to be used to help provinces and territories develop and implement wait-time guarantees, while additional payments to Canada Health Infoway (including $500 million in both the 2009 and 2010 budgets) have been made to accelerate the implementation and integration of electronic medical records.

How well have the 2003 accord and the 2004 10-year plan succeeded? Unsurprisingly, the results are mixed. In the wake of the Romanow and Kirby reports, with the momentum provided by the 2003 and 2004 funding agreements, a number of key agencies and institutions were established. These included the Public Health Agency of Canada, the Health Council of Canada, the Mental Health Commission of Canada, the Common Drug Review, and the Canadian Patient Safety Institute. Priority areas have been identified and strategies have been developed to address them. The "Romanow gap" – the shortfall in federal funding needed to provide "stable, long-term, predictable, and adequate funding" for Canada's health care system – was effectively closed, at least for the short term. Provincial and territorial governments increased their annual health care spending by an average of 6.7%, from $85 billion in 2004 to about $125 billion in 2010 (Health Council of Canada 2011, 3). Constructive intergovernmental dialogue has resumed in a number of areas, with some notable successes (e.g., in the area of the training and licensing of health care professionals). A new regime of public reporting and accountability in the field of health care has gradually been developing over the past decade (see chapter 7). Funding for innovative health care research through the Canadian Institutes of Health Research has increased from $668.2 million in 2003–04 to almost $1 billion currently (Health Council of Canada 2011, 23).

But there have also been considerable limitations on success. Much of the focus of the 2004 10-year plan when it was launched, for example, was on wait times. Overall, 80% of Canadians were treated within the benchmark times established for five priority areas (hip and knee replacement, cataract surgery, radiation treatment, and cardiac surgery) in 2005, and some provinces (including Saskatchewan, Ontario, British Columbia, and New Brunswick) have even broadened their wait-times policies to include other health services. Since 2008, however, improvements in wait-time reductions (with some exceptions) have been static, and significant wait times for some diagnostic services still remain (Health Council of Canada 2011, 7–8). Many programs billed as important components of a new health care regime have simply fallen off the map. The most notorious is the National Pharmaceuticals Strategy announced in the 10-year plan, although the focus upon healthy living and health promotion has also dissolved as priority is being given to disease surveillance as the dominant pan-Canadian public health objective. The restructuring of primary health care has also been sluggish: although the 10-year plan anticipated that half of all Canadians would have access to a collaborative health care team by 2011, less than 32% of Canadians currently do. Likewise, progress in the reconfiguration of long-term care and home care has been limited and piecemeal, with significant domino effects on hospital wards. Compared with many OECD states, Canada's embrace of electronic health care systems is quite weak (Davis et al. 2010). "Although there is electronic health record infrastructure for half of Canadians," notes the Health Council of Canada, "many physicians are not using it in their clinical decision-making and patients can't benefit fully from the technology until they do" (2011, 17).

Interestingly, the area of public reporting and accountability has at once seen the most progress and received the most criticism. In 2000 it was difficult to evaluate health care provision in Canada simply because so little useful data existed (the Canadian Institute for Health Information, CIHI, was only established in 1994). The development of evidence-based benchmarks based upon comparable indicators has advanced considerably in the past decade, and most provinces routinely produce information on health service performance. Nonetheless, data alone cannot provide an adequate accounting of performance; much depends upon how the data are interpreted, presented, and used. "There remains," states Fafard (2013), "a mishmash of 'indicators,' 'targets,' and 'benchmarks' suggesting confusion over the nature and goals of the performance management regime." The way in which performance indicators are used to secure the goals of accountability through public reporting is equally ambiguous. How, exactly, do Canadians know how well their health care system is working? They must be prepared to dig deeply and search widely. Although the intergovernmental agreements of 2000, 2003, and 2004 called for the publication of comparable health indicators, not all governments have done so. Although some preliminary reports were published by all jurisdictions in 2002 and 2004, by 2006 only Ottawa had published a report on comparable health indicators. While provinces do produce performance reports, there is no pan-Canadian agreement on comparable indicators that could provide a comprehensive survey of health care performance across jurisdictions.

It is equally difficult to determine how well Ottawa has accomplished its stated goal of public reporting. Health Canada, with the assistance of CIHI and Statistics Canada, publishes a federal report entitled *Healthy Canadians* on comparable health indicators every two years. It addresses issues such wait times, patient satisfaction, readmission rates for specific conditions, life expectancy, and so on. This document can be found by searching Health Canada's website under "Reports and Publications." Somewhat confusingly, however, Health Canada also runs a website called "Healthy Canadians," which gives no access to the document *Healthy Canadians*. Two other documents, each published annually, also give a cross-country snapshot of the state of health care by using comparable health indicators. *Health Indicators* is a joint effort by CIHI and Statistics Canada that highlights over forty comparable measures of health and health system performance by health region, province, and territory. *Health Care in Canada* is produced by CIHI and is a review of key analytic works produced by CIHI over the year. It is a somewhat more synthetic document with an interpretive focus. In January 2011, the Health Council of Canada published *A Citizen's Guide to Health Indicators* to make some of the findings originally designed for professionals more accessible to the rest of Canadians. Health Canada has noted (in a response to a query posed by the auditor general) that it has also been fulfilling its public reporting duty through documents including its report on plans and priorities, departmental performance report, and Canada Health Act annual report. Notwithstanding this, however, the auditor general's report concluded that Health Canada, while meeting specific commitments on health indicator reporting, had not fulfilled "the broader intent of the agreements" in informing Canadians on the progress of health care renewal (Auditor General Canada 2008, sect. 8:34).

If Health Canada has not achieved the aims set for Ottawa by the agreements of 2000, 2003, and 2004, the provinces have shown even less compliance. This is not to say that the provinces have not been willing to develop and disseminate information on how well their respective systems have accomplished specific health care goals: to the contrary, progress in numerous areas is now more easily tracked than ever. But the attempt to synthesize this information in a more comprehensive national format has stalled. Indeed, as Fafard (2013) argues, 2007 "may have marked the end of the pan-Canadian public discussion of wait times and indeed of the broader questions of measuring the overall performance of health care service delivery." This observation underlies a more problematic evaluation of the health care agreements: for all the cash provided and progress made, the nature of health care federalism itself has not improved.

SUFA was a promising exception to the inveterate bitterness underlying health care federalism in the 1990s. It made hopeful references to collaborative governance, public accountability, and a "partnership with Canadians," themes that were echoed in the 2003 accord and the 2004 10-year plan. But the decade that followed saw very little progress on concerted "collaborative" efforts in many areas identified by the agreements as important complements of an effective national health care system. For example, both the National Immunization Strategy noted in the 2003 accord and the National Pharmaceuticals Strategy outlined in the 2004 10-year plan have completely faded away. The Health Council of Canada was initially expected to serve as an arm's-length body that could conceivably "resolve some of the most difficult intergovernmental disputes that have bedeviled the provinces and Ottawa in recent memory" (Marchildon 2003, 2). But neither Alberta nor Quebec accepted any form of third-party oversight, and the mandate of the council became much more restricted than originally anticipated. Rather than an independent watchdog monitoring governments' compliance with negotiated agreements, the Health Council of Canada has become more of "a vehicle to showcase and disseminate information about innovation and best practices" (Fafard 2013). This is not in itself a bad thing, but the council has been far less effective than it was conceived to be in preventing the political gamesmanship that undermines the utility of negotiated agreements such as the accord and the 10-year plan.[1]

The philosophical limitations on third-party oversight in Canadian health care federalism have been noted, among others, by Marchildon (2003, 6), who writes that "[a]t the end of the day, each partner in the federation is responsible to the people through its own legislature … For this reason, intergovernmental bodies must remain non-legal and consensual instruments." This is certainly a key feature of a political system that attempts to incorporate the concept of responsible parliamentary government into a federal system. But it may also be overstating the need to ring fence sovereignty so tightly. Any sovereign state that negotiates agreements with other nation states must be prepared to concede a certain amount of autonomy for the advantages that membership confers. Member states of the World Trade Organization, the North American Free Trade Agreement, or the European Union, for example, can be (and are) penalized (by fines or sanctions that bite) for transgressing agreements that they have formally accepted. While these penalties, and often the bodies imposing them, are usually viewed as annoyances, neither are generally seen by these states as perilous threats to overall self-government.

In sum, while the billions of dollars distributed in the agreements of 2003 and 2004 have certainly resulted in a number of remarkable improvements in the provision of health care services in Canada, they have not substantially changed the nature of Canadian health care federalism. There is much debate over whether the structural and institutional characteristics of Canadian federalism can in fact provide any real opportunity for substantial change to intergovernmental relations governing health care. But the point of faith for the

Romanow report – that increased federal funding could lead to a different way of doing things – has been tried and found wanting. This is one of the key lessons of the 2003 and 2004 agreements and became the starting point for Ottawa in 2011. If conditionality was producing neither constructive change nor gains in productivity, then the discipline of the market might. The critical juncture in health care federalism, then, is a shift away from hierarchical conditionality and toward a competitive form of federalism that employs the market as a hard constraint. A number of contributors to this volume examine the move toward "market-preserving federalism," investigating the theoretical force and integrity of the concept and analyzing the application of the theory to the Canadian context.

THINKING ABOUT HEALTH CARE FEDERALISM FROM A MULTIDISCIPLINARY PERSPECTIVE

The study of health care as a discipline closely reflects the health care system itself: a series of relatively self-contained silos more inward looking than focused upon their relationship with other cognate units. There are very good reasons why this is the case: for health care institutions, for example, there is the requirement of vertical accountability; for academic disciplines, there is a discursive logic that establishes research agendas according to discipline-specific intellectual frameworks. But reality often fails to respect these arbitrary boundaries, and this is especially true for the study both of health care and of federalism as discrete subjects of analysis. Federalism, viewed through the prism of political science, looks at how the relations of power are channelled between levels of government, how actors take advantage of (or are restricted by) the structure of federal governance, and how the conflicts resulting from the federal division of power affect political relationships more broadly. Legal scholars not only interpret how existing constitutional stipulations ought to be understood but also examine the way in which institutions and processes themselves can be formally constructed or modified to respond more positively to the exigencies of federalism. Economists, unsurprisingly, look at the economic effects of federal structures: economic efficiency is the most common focal point for economists specializing in the area of federalism, but economists are also especially well qualified to analyze the way in which federal structures produce externalities that are often both unexpected and undesirable.

In chapters 2–4, this volume compares the ways in which the disciplines of economics, political science, and law view not just federalism but, more specifically, the phenomenon of *health care* federalism. While health care federalism is only a tiny corner of these disciplines, researchers within each of these intellectual approaches are able effectively to use the tools of their discipline to produce an analysis of how federalism has affected health care in general terms and, more specifically, in the decade that promised the "fix for a generation." Health care federalism is perhaps most clearly an economic issue, as so much of the debate over health care revolves around the provision of "efficiencies," cost containment, economies of scale, and so on.

In chapter 2, Haardt presents a synthesis of theoretical and empirical research on health care federalism from within the discipline of economics. While many discussions of health care are situated within classic questions of economic federalism (does a federal system exacerbate or mitigate cost expansion?), Haardt addresses the claim in much current economics literature that competition between federal units leads to greater economic efficiency. He argues, rather, that such a competitive approach leads to a number of damaging externalities and that a more coordinated approach, especially in the area of health care, is much more efficient. The problem, he concludes, is that the federal leadership necessary to obtain these efficiencies is simply not forthcoming.

This is the starting point for my argument in chapter 3: if, in fact, competitive federalism is disadvantageous, and if the federal government is nonetheless disinterested in pursuing a coordinating role, what options are left? I look to the policy literature on soft governance and argue that the attempt by Ottawa to construct an arena of competitive federalism is being resisted by the provinces through the use of soft, or voluntary, modes of horizontal coordination in health care.

In chapter 4, Lahey pushes this analysis further and explains how the legal realities of Canadian federalism make the need for soft instruments of governance "absolutely essential if Canada is to achieve a more comprehensive and cohesive approach to health care system governance." He argues that the weakness of Canadian health care federalism is not the need for governments to cooperate per se, but rather the way in which the concept of accountability in health care governance has been relatively neglected.

What is interesting about the chapters in this first section is that they seem to be characterized by a certain synchronicity. While each chapter is situated within its own literature, with remarkably little overlap, there is a clear understanding in all of these chapters (and in their supporting literature) that health care federalism must be under-stood with reference to a legal institution (the constitution) and the legal processes that are interwoven with it; the economic demands imposed upon health care governance both by the structure of service delivery and its funding models and by wider economic phenomena; and the active involvement of political actors who use legal institu-tions, economic arguments, and even health care itself as resources to achieve their own interests. The contributors representing each intel-lectual discipline focus upon a different aspect of the issue, but each recognizes the integral aspect of the others' focus. There is a sense of a real discussion occurring, with each interlocutor having a slightly different take on the issue.

But the picture changes noticeably in the second section. Here is where the discussion about health care federalism takes place on the front lines, and the notion of what is relevant changes considerably. This is because health care federalism, rather than being the subject of the investigation, is something very abstract that has to be factored into a more clearly defined policy area. Haardt's second chapter (chapter 5) serves as a segue between the disciplines that look at the system of health care formulation (consisting of connections between policy players, or these actors and their environment) and those dis-ciplines that are responsible for developing policies in much more detail. In this instance, Haardt looks at the challenge faced by health policy administrators in balancing efficiency concerns with those of equity. In particular, he explores some of the problems caused, or rein-forced, by interprovincial competition. Here the lessons of econom-ics, politics, and law are still quite clear, even if the attempt to apply them is considerably more difficult.

Chapters 6 and 7 look at two of the most pressing issues Canada is facing in thinking about how to restructure key features of its health care system. The first issue is the effective provision of health care pro-fessionals. In its 2011 report, the Health Council of Canada "urges governments over the remaining years of the accords" to focus, in the first place, on "health human resource planning and the development of concrete action plans" (25). In its December 2010 report entitled *Health Care in Canada 2010*, CIHI points out that this debate over health human resources planning became so intractable not simply because of the horizontal tensions between jurisdictions (such as the "poaching" of health care professionals) and the overlapping vertical jurisdiction of governments (although a quarter of Canada's doctors are foreign trained, Ottawa has clear jurisdiction over immigration). The problem is more complicated still because, while there are increasing numbers of health professionals, there are "continued declarations of shortages" yet no clear idea of what the optimal number of health care professionals is "and how and where and when they can be best utilized to deliver the most appropriate care" (82). The most promising approach to addressing these problems is a *needs-based* health human resources strategy. "Historically," notes Tomblin Murphy in chapter 6, "planning approaches have been hampered as each province and territory in Canada has worked independently to design its service system, develop service delivery models and plan health human resources. This has often resulted in competition between jurisdictions for limited health human resources." Moreover, these planning approaches were based upon historical patterns of funding and service provision rather than upon the actual needs of a changing population. The goal, then, is to have orders of government working collaboratively to implement a new kind of health human resources planning model. Tomblin Murphy outlines a new framework adopted by the Federal/Provincial/Territorial Advisory Committee on Health Delivery and Human Resources (ACHDHR) that is based upon the principle of needs-based planning. She then discusses the challenges of implementing this approach within the current context of health care federalism.

The second issue is that of health care performance measurement. As the CIHI report *Health Care in Canada 2010* notes, a critical aspect of health care renewal across jurisdictions is in "aligning care with evidence": currently, not only does provided care often leave a great deal of room for improvement, but often the care provided is not the appropriate care. The issue, as Levy and Sobolev observe in chapter 7, is precisely how to measure, and report on, the performance of the Canadian health care system at both the federal and provincial levels. The issues are much more complex than would appear from a casual understanding of the problem. Although Canada has made great strides in collecting data from and about the health care system, there remain many unresolved issues about how to systematically choose, implement, and interpret performance data. Again, we are obliged to think about issues of accountability in health care governance: as

early as 1999, the accountability of the provinces for their conditional grants was grounded upon the existence of performance indicators
and benchmarks. Exactly how these performance indicators were to
be designed and interpreted was assumed to be a small, technical, and
unproblematic issue. Health policy analysts still assume this to be the
case (with the notable exception of Fafard 2013). Yet health practitioners understand that this assumption is dangerously misinformed.
As Levy and Sobolev explain, the process of determining what performance measures to use (and how to interpret them) is a highly difficult and contentious one, with a number of conceptual, political,
and technical issues that must be carefully navigated. Regardless of
whether performance indicators are used to ground accountability
through conditional spending (as, for example, Marchildon argues in
this volume) or through soft horizontal governance (as Fierlbeck and
Lahey suggest), policy-makers must understand that the development
of these performance measures is an ambitious and problematic
(although essential) exercise that *itself* requires a high level of intergovernmental coordination.

The curious distinction between the first section of the book and
the second section is that the first section illustrates disciplines that
have sophisticated accounts of how and why health care federalism
operates in general terms. The theoretical strengths of these disciplines, however, are undermined by a paucity of the considerable but
highly technical details involved in discrete fields (such as needs-
based HHR resource modelling or performance assessment). At the
same time, however, the disciplines that produce experts who have a
clear and detailed sense of exactly what is needed in these very specific fields lack a thoroughgoing sense of how to see that their approaches get implemented, what the political and institutional barriers to
implementation are, and what kinds of windows of opportunity may
be available to help them operationalize their proposed strategies in
the current attempt to rethink how health care is provided across and
between jurisdictions. This same observation is true for a number of
policy areas: a national pharmaceutical strategy, vaccination policy,
healthy living strategies, and so on. Thinking much more carefully
about health care federalism from a multidisciplinary perspective
may begin to help us narrow the current chasm between those who
know what should be done and those who know how to do it. The
contributors to this volume are attempting not only to offer their own
perspectives on health care federalism but also to incorporate insights

about the constraints and opportunities identified by colleagues from different vantage points throughout the health care system.

If the distance between system experts and policy experts is still disconcertingly wide, perhaps an even greater gulf remains between experts (of all stripes) and the officials who make policy decisions in light of (and, at times, despite) the best explanations and advice that experts can provide. The last word in this volume belongs to two individuals who have each had one foot in academia and one in government. In chapter 8, Boessenkool makes the case for firmly uncoupling the tangled relationship between federal and provincial governments in the field of health care; in chapter 9, Marchildon argues precisely the opposite. These arguments, made with a broader sweep of the brush, are much more intelligible to all of us (regardless of how much we tend to favour or dispute them) than are the more detailed accounts of what ought to be done, how we ought to get them done, and why. But the multidisciplinary reflections on some of the challenges and promises in health care federalism presented in this volume should, at the very least, oblige us to think harder about the nuances and intricacies involved in establishing a new era of health care in Canada.

ACKNOWLEDGMENT

The editors would like to acknowledge the efforts of our indefatigable assistant, Ben Diepeveen, in readying this manuscript for publication.

NOTE

1 In the end, Ottawa announced in April 2013 its intention to abolish the Health Council of Canada.

A Multidisciplinary Overview
of Health Care Federalism

2

The Economics of Health Care Federalism: What Do We Know?

DAVID HAARDT

The economics of federalism has been a relatively small research area, surfacing a few times during the last 80 years but never constituting a major component of the economics literature. The economics of *health care* federalism is a topic that has been studied even less. The purpose of this chapter is to take account of what the literature on the economics of federalism (and, specifically, health care federalism) has taught us. (In chapter 5 I will provide more specific insight into some of the trends and challenges in health care federalism in Canada.) The first section of this chapter addresses the classic economics of federalism of the mid-twentieth century, which was consolidated in the 1970s. The subsequent section discusses the modern economics of federalism that emerged in the 1990s. Next I analyze what we know from the literature on the economics of US health care federalism then discuss the literature on the economics of European health care federalism. The last two sections cover the (small) literature on the economics of Canadian health care federalism and the empirical case for centralization, respectively.

THE CLASSIC ECONOMICS OF FEDERALISM

The economics of federalism is an American-centric literature that has focused for the most part on the efficiency of federalism: on federalism's potential efficiency advantages (or benefits) and disadvantages (or costs). Equity considerations with respect to federalism have been covered by economists only in a cursory manner, perhaps more so in the economics of health care federalism than in the more general literature on the economics of federalism. Hamlin (1991, 193–4) argues that since the 1950s "emphasis has shifted away from the potential equity defects of federalism and towards the potential efficiency advantages of federalism." I would argue that the move toward efficiency took place earlier, during the 1930s. Most economists would agree that the classic economics of federalism is in the literature that emerged in the mid-twentieth century (Weingast 2005, 151), with the triumph of modern economic theory. However, this literature had various predecessors: research that did not yet use the tools of modern economic theory but realized that federalism was a topic that ought to be analyzed by economists.

Incidentally, one of these predecessors, or an example of what could be called the pre-classic economics of federalism, comes from Canada. Vincent Wheeler Bladen argued in his seminal interwar paper that the economics of federalism was deemed unimportant in the nineteenth century, because economic "expansion was general, and mobility of capital ... could be relied on to equalize standards of living" (Bladen 1935, 349). He then went on to argue why this simple view was incorrect, especially in the different economic context of the twentieth century, which presented two types of costs that the nineteenth century view did not take into account. He calls the first of these two types of costs "unpaid social costs of movement," that is, monetary (but social, rather than private) costs, and the second "unpayable costs connected with the break-up of cultural communities," that is, non-monetary costs (Bladen 1935, 350). Bladen felt that the degree of mobility necessary to ensure automatic equalization of standards of living across provinces without government intervention was associated with substantial non-market costs, many of which would be difficult to assess monetarily. This can be observed also today, with very large differences between Canadian provinces with respect to income and health care spending. Bladen concluded by advocating shifting the focus from the economy of individual provinces to the equalization of standards of living across provinces, arguing that this would automatically resolve "conflicting provincial interests" (Bladen 1935, 351). This point is certainly useful for the purposes of this chapter. I would argue that when it comes to health care policy, conflicts between provinces concerning what they want to achieve usually stem from differences in their incomes and hence fiscal resources. Bladen's paper can be seen as one of the last of the era in which the economics of federalism focused on equity. The development of what I call the classic economics of federalism brought about the shift toward efficiency that Hamlin (1991, 193–4) pointed out.

Hamlin (1991) and Weingast (2005) provide a good overview of the classic economics of federalism and of the mechanisms that lead federalism to produce economically desirable or undesirable results. According to Weingast (2005, 151–2), the classic economics of federalism has three roots: the ideas of Hayek, Musgrave, and Tiebout, which were brought together by Oates in 1972. (Hamlin 1991 feels that the contributions of Hayek and Tiebout are the most important and does not cover the ideas of Musgrave.) Weingast (2005, 152) argues that Hayek's main contribution to this literature was his focus on information: according to this idea, regional governments have better information about their constituents than federal governments and are hence better able to assess their constituents' preferences as well as policy options. This is what Hamlin (1991, 194) calls the "decentralization thesis." Weingast (2005, 152) also emphasizes that federal governments often impose a uniform menu and uniform prices when offering subsidies to regional governments, distorting their decisions considerably. However, this does not seem to be the case in health care federalism, where the degree of micromanagement by the federal government is, at least in Canada, much smaller than in other policy areas. Musgrave's most important contribution to the classic economics of federalism was the so-called "assignment principle," which "holds that authority over public goods should be assigned to that level of government that can most efficiently produce it" (Weingast 2005, 153), hence leaving local matters to regional governments and issues such as national defence (where there are large economies of scale) to federal governments. It is important to note here that this research was not specifically about health care – and, at least in today's world, it is clear that there are huge economies of scale and externalities as far as health care decision-making at a sub-national level is concerned. Finally, Tiebout's main contribution to the classic economics of federalism is about competition between regions: regions compete with each other for mobile factors and hence will have to do their best to provide public goods that suit their constituents. Moreover, there will be sorting across regions by preferences – not only by companies but also by individuals. This is what Hamlin (1991, 194) calls the competition thesis. In fact, Ribstein and Kobayashi (2006, 1) argue that "jurisdictional competition between state governments for mobile individuals and resources" is the most important component of the economics of federalism (besides the work on fiscal federalism). An important point that Hamlin (1991, 194) makes is that both the decentralization thesis and the competition thesis are linked to interregional mobility: it is interregional mobility that reinforces the provision of government services that are more closely aligned to the preferences of voters in the different regions, and it is the threat of interregional mobility that is responsible for competition between regional governments over voters and taxpayers. As Hamlin (1991, 194) writes, it is therefore the interregional mobility of voters and taxpayers "which brings the two lines of argument into contact with each other."

Needless to say, the classic economics of federalism is a very North American theory in the sense that it assumes very high mobility (and would be much less useful in a European context), but in the case of health care in Canada it is certainly a quite appropriate one. However, the classic economics of federalism, as is well known today, is very naive in its ignoring of externalities. Because of that, its recommendations are usually strongly in favour of decentralization (Weingast 2005, 153). Federalism as studied in the classic economics of federalism is also called market-preserving federalism. For a detailed explanation of this term, see Weingast (2005, 155). The US literature on tax competition often praises fiscal federalism because of its tendency to lead to low tax rates. However, we also know from the European literature on tax competition that fiscal federalism can (and usually does) lead to inefficiently low tax levels (see Brøchner et al. 2006). This static finding is reflected in the following dynamic argument in Canadian health care financing: each individual province knows that it should raise taxes to cover the rising costs of health care that it is facing, but it does not feel able to do so because it knows that other provinces would benefit from not following suit. It is a classic example of the prisoner's dilemma: because provinces find it difficult to enforce a countrywide political commitment on higher taxes, each province does something that is hurting its own interests.

THE MODERN ECONOMICS OF FEDERALISM

It was only in the 1990s that the modern economics of federalism became mainstream, incorporating for the first time the previously ignored externalities cost of decentralization. I would argue that these externalities (as well as issues of economies of scale) are particularly crucial in health care; hence, someone who would have analyzed the economics of health care federalism in the 1970s would have had a much more positive view of decentralization than somebody who analyzes the economics of federalism today, even more so than in other areas of public policy. Gordon (1983) was perhaps one of the first to analyze problems that arise from decentralized decision-making, even before the triumph of the modern economics of federalism in the 1990s. Gordon (1983) used an optimal taxation model to investigate these problems, assuming that lawmakers were benevolent. In other words, the goal of Gordon (1983, 567) was to give an overview of "the types of externalities that a unit of government can create for nonresidents through both its public goods decisions and its taxation decisions." Gordon (1983, 582) shows that fully coordinated decisions, that is, decisions in a federal system where actors take into account their externalities, are better than centralized and decentralized decisions. This is the case because of the standardization restrictions implied by centralized decisions and because of the externalities implied by decentralized decisions. Gordon (1983, 582) also shows that it is ambiguous whether a decentralized system of decision-making would be better or worse than a centralized system of decision-making. In other words, a federal system is desirable only if it is structured so that most externalities are internalized. Given the vast lack of coordination in Canadian health care federalism, it is doubtful whether this is the case.

Weingast (2005, 153–4) gives several examples of externalities that the modern economics of federalism aims to take into account: first, pollution, second, internal trade barriers, and third, soft versus hard budget constraints. In the economics of health care federalism, subsidies to physicians and pharmaceutical companies can be seen as equivalent to the pollution example. There are some, but only few, internal trade barriers in Canadian health care federalism, and their importance is small because of how rarely health care services are exported across provincial boundaries. Finally, there is the issue of soft versus hard budget constraints, which will become more and more important as some provinces' budgets are starting to feel significant pressures caused by health care expenditures. Weingast (2005, 156) also points out that the classic economics of federalism suffered from a naive view of politicians' behaviour. They were based on the assumption that "men were angels," as James Madison wrote in 1788 in the

Federalist No. 51. As Weingast (2005, 156) writes, "[t]his assumption rules out corruption, rent-seeking, service to interest groups, and generally, manipulation of public policy to serve private instead of public ends." Clearly, this is an unrealistic depiction of policy-making, especially in an area in which as much money is at stake as in health care. However, the question remains whether self-interested lawmakers and public officials are more of a problem in a centralized or in a decentralized system.

I would argue that the classic economics of federalism, having been heavily influenced by libertarian thought, were even more slanted than it may seem from Weingast's (2005, 156) argument. The main idea of much of the classic literature was that a "corrupt" federal government would be forced to behave more appropriately if there is some competition between states, that is, if there is political and fiscal pressure exerted by voters and taxpayers. It is clear that this rather naive traditional theory of federalism is not very helpful when it comes to Canadian health care federalism, where only a miniscule proportion of high costs and high cost increases will be due to corruption. Moreover, this theory fails to provide a rationale for why federal lawmakers are more likely to be corrupt than state/provincial lawmakers.

Weingast (2005, 150) argues that, even though the modern economics of federalism has relaxed the assumption that regional governments take into account the externalities of their decisions, there remain various gaps in standard modern economics of federalism, the most important one being the assumption that regional governments are benevolent (the other one being an incorporation into the model of why the federal government is or is not benevolent). In other words, Weingast (2005, 150) would like to see more research on how an assessment of the economic efficiency of federalism is affected by regional governments acting out of self-interest rather than maximizing the utility of their constituents. This is where the research of Cai and Treisman (2004) comes into play. They argue that this assumption of different corruption levels in different levels of government was fundamentally wrong, and they show that unless there are dramatic differences in the level of corruption between the different levels of governments involved, centralization is beneficial because state governments will waste resources helping companies avoid federal taxation. They argue that such behaviour is most common in developing countries (Cai and Treisman 2004, 821), but one of the three examples they provide comes from the United States (Cai and Treisman 2004, 834–5), where the state government of West Virginia, financially heavily supported by coal companies, spent considerable amounts of time and money helping coal companies avoid federal environmental regulations instead of, as they were meant to do, enforcing them. (Similar things can currently be observed with Tea Party Republicans in the United States trying to fight the Environmental Protection Agency: see Roberts 2011.)

Petretto (2000) argues that regions have to take into account two usually overlooked considerations when they decide whether or not regionalization would raise their residents' utility. Using a Stackelberg game theoretic framework with the federal government being the leader and regional governments being the followers (Petretto 2000, 222), Petretto (2000, 215, 230) shows that regions have to take into account first what he calls the export effect or spillover effect (when regions export health care services to residents of other regions, which in Canada is very rare; see Berger 1996, who states that only approximately 3% of Canadians seek treatment outside their own province or territory; more recent data from 2007–08 show that 2% of hospitalizations in Canada are by out-of-province or out-of-territory patients, see CIHI 2010b, 2) and second what he calls the "self-financing effect of regionalisation." By this, he means that regionalization implies a shift toward a closer alignment between tax collection and public expenditure. Petretto's (2000) model is used to analyze the UK National Health Service but can be used for any health care system with federalist aspects.

The goal of Petretto's (2000) article is to assess whether (and under what conditions) geographical decentralization (or regionalization) would be better or worse from a welfare point of view than a continuation of a centralized health care system. Petretto (2000, 215–6) argues that, from the point of view of society overall (i.e., utility maximization for the entire country), whether or not regionalization is beneficial depends on the importance of redistributional goals. In other words, if society prefers to have the potential for stronger redistribution, or a larger role for equity, then a centralized system is better, whereas if society is willing to give up the potential for stronger redistribution then a decentralized system may be better. This is a very intuitive result that is quite informative for the Canadian policy debate: the gradual move toward stronger regionalization brought about by the ongoing expansion of health care services in Canada has increased interprovincial inequalities (see the section on economies of scale in the Canadian health care system in chapter 5), which is exactly in line with Petretto's argument. Petretto (2000, 231) concludes by arguing that, in a decentralization scenario, regions may produce more health care than efficient if spillover effects are important or in other words if exports of health care services to other regions (or regions' residents) are important. Given the already mentioned observation that such exports are extremely rare in Canada, this is not likely to be a problem in the Canadian health care system.

Keen and Kotsogiannis (2002, 363) argue that the literature on the (modern) economics of federalism has traditionally focused on horizontal externalities (i.e., on the effects of competition and mobility between provinces, regions, or states) and has, until at least the 1980s, neglected vertical externalities (i.e., the effects that changes in tax policy at one level of government have on the other level of government) through the behavioural changes they will have on the taxed. It is well known that taxes will be inefficiently low in the traditional scenario of horizontal externalities: each province, region, or state wants to attract mobile voters and taxpayers, hence undercutting the other provinces, regions, or states, leading to inefficiently low tax levels. Keen and Kotsogiannis (2002, 363) argue that with vertical externalities, the opposite is the case: since each province, region, or state does not care about the effects its taxes have on voters and taxpayers as far as federal tax revenue is concerned, taxes will be inefficiently high. Therefore, the question is whether, in a model of federalism that incorporates both horizontal as well as bottom-up vertical externalities (i.e., vertical externalities in which each province, region, or state ignores the effects of its tax policies on the federal level but not vice versa, see Keen and Kotsogiannis 2002, 365), the horizontal externality or the vertical externality will dominate. In principle it could even happen that the two are of the same absolute amount, leading to the efficient tax level in equilibrium. The model that Keen and Kotsogiannis (2002, 365) use assumes benevolent lawmakers who only care about their own constituency. Put differently, they do not allow for self-interested lawmakers who pursue goals other than maximizing the welfare of their constituents. They show that, in a number of plausible scenarios, the vertical externality dominates, implying that federalism would, contrary to conventional wisdom, cause provincial, regional, or state tax rates to be inefficiently high (see Keen and Kotsogiannis 2002, 367). They also show that, under plausible assumptions, the direction of the inefficiency is the same for the provincial, regional, or state tax rates as well as for the federal tax rate, implying an even greater inefficiency than one may assume from just looking at one level of government (see Keen and Kotsogiannis 2002, 369).

As can be seen from this overview of the economics of federalism, many gaps remain despite decades of research – for the most part due to the fact that research progress has been slow because the field has never attracted a lot of mainstream attention. As to be expected, results depend considerably on which types of externalities are modelled and on the behavioural assumptions being made for lawmakers at different levels of government. In part, the reason why many gaps remain in the economics of federalism literature is because it attempts to explain federalism in every topic area with a single theoretical framework, when in fact federalist arrangements and incentives for, say, health care are often very different from those for, say, education. Therefore, I will now, in the next three sections, discuss what we know from the literature on the economics of health care federalism. I will start with the literature on US health care federalism before turning to the literature on European health care federalism and, last but not least, to the literature on Canadian health care federalism.

THE ECONOMICS OF US HEALTHCARE FEDERALISM

US healthcare federalism has come a long way since the legal battles of the 1980s. Bobinski (1990) gives an excellent overview of these many legal battles between employers and employees, between insurance companies and states, between states and the federal government, and so on. Many of the lessons that we can learn from Bobinski's (1990) analysis of the resistance to US health care reform in the late 1980s also apply to the resistance to US health care reform today.

Bobinski (1990) mentions four reasons why political resistance to health care reform was so strong in the 1980s. The first reason, and this is the focus of her article, is that the Employee Retirement Income Security Act pre-emption provision limits states' ability to design health care plans (see, for instance, Bobinski 1990, 272–8). The second is that, as predicted by the economic theory covered earlier, states fear a loss of their competitiveness if they increase taxation on business and/or individuals (Bobinski 1990, 271, 314–5, 344, 347; because of the same reason, state taxation is generally much less redistributive than federal taxation, see 270–1). The third reason is that states fear that there will be an inflow of unhealthy individuals (Bobinski 1990, 272, 347). The fourth is that there is political resistance from those who feel that they would have to pay; most of this resistance comes from employers, but also from well-off individuals (Bobinski 1990, 271).

Bobinski (1990) also mentions several problems that emerged as states tried to be more active in shaping health care policy. First, states have neither the administrative nor the policy expertise that the federal government has with respect to health care (Bobinski 1990, 270). Second, if each state decides to create a different health care policy environment, employers that operate in several states will face a high administrative burden (Bobinski 1990, 323). I would argue that both these problems can be summarized by the idea of economies of scale: substantial costs emerge if many small administrative units duplicate their efforts. I will discuss the topic of economies of scale and how it relates to health care federalism in Canada in more detail later.

Despite the obvious problems with not exploiting economies of scale, some economists have argued that US federalism allows states to experiment with health care reform, with the "best" ideas eventually being adopted in several states or even nationally. Donahue (1998, 434–5), in the Clinton era, concluded his article by recommending that states be allowed to experiment and then that the federal government pick and choose the most successful experiments. This is also what can be observed right now in the United States with Obama's attempts at health care reform. However, I believe that this 50-fold multiplication of efforts entails enormous legislative and regulatory cost. It also ignores the consequences of more significant experimentation on the supply side, because health care providers and insurance companies always have the option of out-migration to other states. Because of that, state-level experimentation is effectively limited to scenarios that yield little or no cost containment. Federal reform, on the other hand, would presumably entail no out-migration of providers and insurance companies, because the United States would most likely remain the world's most profitable country for health care providers and health insurance companies.

In light of this, it is not surprising that states have always put forward health care reform proposals that entail even higher health care spending. Nathan (2005) analyzes the historical development of Medicaid and argues that it has been states that have been driving Medicaid expansions, both with respect to scope and with respect to spending (see Nathan 2005, 1,459). More specifically he argues that, if there is a conservative federal government, states experiment with Medicaid innovations that then, later, in times of a liberal federal government, become national policies (Nathan 2005, 1,458-60). He also argues that state governments, regardless of their party background, have tended to fight against Medicaid reductions (Nathan 2005, 1,459). Like Donahue (1998, 434-5), Nathan (2005, 1,459) argues that it is easier for state governments to experiment, which then, in turn, if successful, gives lawmakers from other states the confidence to implement similar legislation themselves. Interestingly, Nathan (2005, 1,460-1) argues that it is exactly because federal legislation in the United States only specifies basic minima for service provision that states have carried out expansions, arguing that the service level with this federalist structure is higher than it would be without it. In a way, this can be seen as coming back to the argument of Keen and Kotsogiannis (2002) in the scenario in which the vertical externality is dominant. It also shows that reform tends to be provider friendly (i.e., no cost containment) if states compete with each other for health care providers. Nathan (2005, 1,463) feels that an important reason for this expansive growth path of Medicaid is probably its focus on the elderly and disabled, rather than its original target group of welfare recipients, hence giving most of the benefit to a group that has much more political power.

Given the importance of political power in health care reform, it is unlikely that states will ever be able to exert "the power to impose a global budget," which, according to Donahue (1998, 434), would be perhaps the most important step in reforming the public component of US health care. The importance of political power in shaping health care reform is a recurring theme in the analysis of health care reform, especially in the United States. It is a topic that I will come back to with respect to health care federalism in Canada in chapter 5.

THE ECONOMICS OF
EUROPEAN HEALTH CARE FEDERALISM

European health care federalism is extremely diverse. It ranges from the situation in countries such as Switzerland, which offers cantons substantial autonomy in shaping health care policy, to the situation in countries such as the United Kingdom, where there is some regionalization in decision-making but still very strong central control over the health care system. Because of its unusual degree of health care federalism, Switzerland has often attracted the attention of US health economists and US health care researchers more generally. Incidentally, health care federalism in Switzerland shares many of the problems seen in health care federalism in the United States. Donahue (1998) argues that cost increases have been shaping Swiss health care reform. These cost increases "[have] been more pronounced ... than anywhere else in Europe" (Donahue 1998, 419). As Donahue (1998, 430) reports, in 1994, Switzerland had the second-highest GDP share spent on health care in the world (after the United States) and the second-highest per capita health care costs in the world (again, after the United States). However, Donahue fails to understand why this is the case; the answer lies in the fact that the Swiss health care system, with its federalist structure and its "competitive" set-up, is very different from any other European health care system, making it difficult to enforce cost containment because providers have much more market power in a fragmented health care system in which they always have the option to move to other cantons (especially in a country as small as Switzerland) than in a unified, monopsonistic health care system. Donahue (1998, 420) also briefly mentions the importance of keeping enrolment high in a voluntary enrolment environment because of the dangers of adverse selection, which led to a 1991 policy change in Switzerland. Donahue (1998, 430–1) highlights the fact that health care costs in Switzerland were rising while the federal government's share of health care costs was decreasing. Again, this is not really surprising when one takes the market structure into account: federal governments are more effective at cost control than regional governments (and regional governments, in turn, are more effective at cost control than individual health care "consumers").

Switzerland is also interesting with respect to federal transfers: in 1991, Switzerland introduced subsidies from the federal government to cantons (Donahue 1998, 421). Cantons that adjusted health insurance premiums to cantonal income levels and fulfilled other requirements started receiving subsidies from the federal government. This is quite interesting because these transfers are highly conditional – cantons receive money for fulfilling very specific policy goals set by the federal government. This is quite different from the situation in Canada, where federal health care transfers are usually not conditional and where general federal transfers reward poor fiscal decision-making by provinces. Crivelli et al. (2006, 538) show that Switzerland exhibits a strong and statistically significant link between the percentage of the cantonal population that is older than 75 years and cantonal health care expenditures. A proportion that is 1% (not 1 percentage point!) higher is associated with cantonal health care expenditure that is 0.351% higher. Because of that, Crivelli et al. (2006, 539) conclude that "a more active financial intervention by the central state would be highly desirable in order to avoid fiscal distress at the cantonal level." It seems to me that it would be relatively easy to complement the income-related federal transfers that Donahue (1998, 421) described with age-related federal transfers.

The Swiss case shows that drastic health care reform, which would really reduce providers' incomes, can indeed take place even in a federal health care system, but only if steps are taken at a countrywide level. There are three instances in Switzerland of countrywide drastic reforms that relate to price regulation. First, in 1994, Switzerland introduced price controls on an RPI+X basis, i.e., based on the retail price index plus an allowable real price increase of "X" (see Donahue 1998, 422). As is well known in the industrial economics literature, RPI+X regulation is very inefficient and does not provide any incentive to become more productive. Nonetheless, the introduction of such regulation would have been impossible at the cantonal level because of provider mobility. The second instance of drastic, countrywide health care reform in Switzerland relates to global budgets. The 1994 federal law on health insurance in Switzerland allows cantons and insurance companies to move to a global budget for hospital services if certain conditions are met – the most important one is that cost increases must have been unusually high (Donahue 1998, 428). This recognizes the adverse effects of fee-for-service reimbursement and, at the same time, ensures that cantons operate uniformly, considerably limiting the profitability of provider mobility. The third and final instance of Switzerland-wide drastic health care reform relates to negotiations with providers. As Donahue (1998, 429) points out, the Swiss 1994 federal law on health insurance gives cantons unusual powers in negotiating with providers: if negotiations are unsuccessful, cantons can continue the existing fee schedule for another year and thereafter impose a new fee schedule unilaterally (requiring only "consultation" with the other parties). Again, this significantly limits the bargaining power of monopolistic professional associations and, because it is federal legislation, prevents providers from circumventing the cost-containing policy by moving to another canton.

Switzerland is quite different from Italy, in which the regions have much less fiscal autonomy. Since 2001, Italian regions have been able to increase the regional value added tax and the regional surtax on the national income tax "in order to meet the constraints of their health care budgets" (Petretto 2000, 217–8). However, the bounds within which this is possible are very narrow (see Peretto 2000, 218). Moreover, even if the bounds were wide, regions would of course not want to carry out large increases because of interregional mobility, linking back to the three examples of drastic health care reform in Switzerland.

The regionalization of the Spanish health care system exhibits a number of parallels with US health care federalism (Rico and Costa-Font 2005, 240–3). Just as Nathan (2005) showed for the United States, it was regions in Spain that were the driving force of health care expansion. Needless to say, these were for the most part the wealthy regions of the northeast of Spain. Rico and Costa-Font (2005, 248) argue that "inequalities can decrease if efficient innovations by affluent, dynamic regions can be copied by laggard regions," maintaining that over the relevant time period overall equity with respect to global health outcomes and expenditure levels does not seem to have been affected by these regional initiatives (Rico and Costa-Font 2005, 243). However, at least with respect to the expenditure level, the data they present do not support this argument, since they show that considerable differences with respect to expenditure levels have emerged since the reforms, with the two regions that have full fiscal autonomy having seen the highest increases in health care expenditure (Rico and Costa-Font 2005, 244). As Rico and Costa-Font (2005, 249) explain, "all regions [of Spain] competed with each other and with the central government to increase health care expenditure." The reason for this phenomenon is the political power of (public) health care providers: "in Spain, regions and trade unions managed to increase their collective action resources by defending citizens' preferences for an expanded NHS against the resistance of cost-minded central governments" (Rico and Costa-Font 2005, 250). No explanation is given why the regions that face the hardest budget constraint, namely those with full fiscal autonomy, have experienced the largest increases in health care spending. I would argue that the answer is most likely to lie in differences in willingness to pay. Rico and Costa-Font (2005, 243–4) argue that regionalization has increased efficiency, especially in regions with full fiscal autonomy (these regions, as already mentioned, of course face a much harder budget constraint than regions without full fiscal autonomy). They also argue that decentralization has helped Spain to have higher population satisfaction with health care than its centralized southern European peers that have similar health care expenditure levels (Rico and Costa-Font 2005, 244–5).

To conclude this section I would like to emphasize that many European countries have taken steps to re-centralize their health care systems given fiscal pressures during the past ten years (Saltman 2008, 105).

THE ECONOMICS OF
CANADIAN HEALTH CARE FEDERALISM

Donahue (1998, 433) argues that Canadian lawmakers are less "responsive to local interests" than US lawmakers. He argues that there are two reasons for this phenomenon: "the separation of executive and legislative power, and the frequency with which different parties have controlled one of these two branches of government." Given the research I discussed in the previous sections, this implies that Canadian health care federalism is better able to mitigate the costs of federalism than its US counterpart and that it is more reformable. Donahue (1998, 387–97) gives a good overview of the historical development of health care in Canada, arguing that "highly suspect, though widely shared" fears of high administrative costs were "a driving force" in Canada's decision to adopt provincial single-payer systems rather than allow for competing private insurers (Donahue 1998, 404). However, there is plenty of evidence that the costs of marketing and risk-selection administration by competing private insurers lead to low medical loss ratios, that is, to a low proportion of the total expenditure of health insurers actually being spent on health care services (see Woolhandler et al. 2003). Moreover, there is some recent research from the United States showing that, in an environment with competing private insurers, the medical loss ratio further decreases if there is consolidation, because insurers use their market power (see Abraham and Karaca-Mandic 2011, 19–21). In other words, there are two opposing forces at work in an environment with competing private insurers: it would be good to have many insurers to limit market power, but it would be good to have few insurers because of the costs of marketing and risk-selection administration. Canada's provincial single-payer system avoids this dilemma altogether.

One of the reform steps that Donahue (1998, 407–8) recommends for the Canadian health care system is the introduction of managed care (health maintenance organizations), which he feels would be allowable under the Canada Health Act. He argues that such a step could lead to further cost containment. However, I would like to note here that the introduction of managed care, which would contain costs because it would reduce providers' incomes, would be much more difficult in a federalist system in which providers can much more credibly threaten to move elsewhere than in a national system in which providers would have to move much further, and indeed to a different country, to circumvent cost containment. In the first of a series of articles published in the *Canadian Medical Association Journal* in 2002 on the future of the Canadian health care system, Lewis (2002) argues for "renewing federalism in health care." He understands such renewal to mean a higher and more sustained financial commitment of the federal government with respect to health care spending (Lewis 2002, 1421). He correctly diagnoses several problems: too little federal involvement is inefficient and expensive, the provinces are not able to deal with the increasing financial burden of health care themselves, and the provinces are too close to their voters and thus susceptible to day-to-day political pressures (Lewis 2002, 1422). However, his call for a more equal sharing of the financial burden, with a continued focus of the federal government on overarching strategic issues, ignores several issues. It ignores the fact that because two levels of government are potential payers spending is driven up as it is always possible to shift costs to the other level of government. It also ignores the fact that many of the benefits of coordination can only be reaped if the federal government takes a bigger role than just focusing on strategic issues: it must start to shape pharmaceutical purchasing and health human resource planning. Lewis (2002) provides many arguments for a strong federal role in health care but does not provide any arguments for a strong provincial role in health care, except for constitutional issues that are taken as unalterable (and that, as I will discuss in chapter 5, are based on an interpretation that would be very difficult to maintain in twenty-first century health care).

THE EMPIRICAL CASE FOR CENTRALIZATION

The fact that Switzerland, as discussed earlier in this chapter, has a very fragmented health care system and by far the highest GDP share of health care expenditure in Europe can be seen as an indication that decentralization is costly, but it is not a very satisfying proof. Similarly, the fact that the health care recentralization efforts that many European countries have undertaken during the past ten years have often been driven by fears of inefficient duplication (Saltman 2008, 105) can be seen as an indication but not as a clear proof.

Mosca (2007) studied 20 OECD countries, consisting of 17 European ones plus Australia, Canada, and New Zealand, and shows that even when one controls for a number of demographic variables and variables that relate to the density of health care resources, per capita health care expenditure is significantly higher in countries with a decentralized health care system than in countries with a centralized one. Mosca (2007, 513) also shows that countries with social health insurance spend more on health care than countries with a national health system, which is not surprising given that the former are less unified than the latter. The paper has limitations, such as relying on a four-category typology of health care systems rather than measuring the degree of (de)centralization in a more comprehensive way, but it is perhaps the first paper that assesses the impact of health care (de)centralization on health care costs in a rigorous way.

CONCLUSION

In this chapter I aimed to give an overview of the economics of federalism and the economics of health care federalism, covering theoretical research as well as applied research about Canada, Europe, and the United States. One important observation that can be made from the comparison of the European experience with health care federalism to the North American experience with health care federalism is that the European experience seems to be considerably more positive: the examples that I presented from Italy, Spain, and Switzerland all paint a more positive picture of federalism than the examples I presented from Canada and the United States. Why is that the case? I believe that the answer is very simple: most European countries have a much lower degree of federalism than Canada or the United States, and hence regionalization of the health care system helps to strengthen the bond between the health care system and voters. In Canada and the United States, on the other hand, there is a very extensive degree of federalism, which is very costly and makes reform very difficult; this is why the negative consequences of health care federalism become more apparent. One could hypothesize, perhaps, an "ideal" degree of health care federalism, which would be (somewhat) higher than in most European countries and (considerably) lower than in Canada or the United States. Moreover, out-of-pocket health care expenditures are lower in virtually every European country than in the United States (with the notable exception of Switzerland; see OECD 2011) and lower in most European countries than in Canada, and "medical bankruptcy" is an unheard-of term in Canada and Europe, hence any negative effect of regionalization on cost containment will be met with less voter resistance. The Swiss case clearly shows that effective health care reform in a federal system must take place using federal legislation. The problem is that such federal legislation seems very difficult to enact in North America.

3

The Political Dynamics
of Health Care Federalism

KATHERINE FIERLBECK

The federal system itself appears to highlight and encourage some types of political debate and sidetrack others. In our present straitened financial circumstances, it appears to suppress or muffle social policy debate at the national level, while fostering national public discussion of fiscal policy and inciting a good deal of political conflict about the operation of federalism itself. It is in this fashion that our national social programs may be dismantled – as an apparently indirect consequence of decisions taken in another policy realm.

David R. Cameron (1994, 440–1)

One could be forgiven for thinking that the design and implementation of health care institutions, processes, and agreements are all about improving health care. At best they are the product of the political zeitgeist: a reflection of what goals political actors deem to be important and the resources they have at their disposal to achieve them. At worst health care reforms are not really about health care at all but merely serve as a means of achieving other political objectives. This chapter describes how the nature of health care federalism (and federalism writ large) in Canada is changing dramatically. My argument in this chapter is that the attempt by Ottawa to impose a regime of market-preserving federalism has in fact resulted in the development of a dialectical tension between two very distinct kinds of federalism. On the one hand, *competitive federalism* holds that economic growth in a federal system depends upon subnational units competing among themselves for business development within an environment in which both labour and capital are highly mobile. On the other hand, *soft federalism* is the attempt by provinces to use soft governance mechanisms to achieve a form of horizontal collaboration that can sustain public heath care in a highly market-oriented environment. The clash between these two approaches has been most clearly exemplified within the field of health care federalism in Canada, although similar developments have taken place within other federal units (particularly the European Union).

To understand (or even, more rashly, to predict) the overarching patterns of change in Canadian health care federalism, one must identify three interrelated elements. The first is the set of power dynamics between the provincial, territorial, and federal governments. Health care federalism, for example, is irreducibly interwoven with fiscal federalism. Thus one must consider the armature of laws and institutions upon which political action is structured; the fiscal capacity of each government; and the pressures each administration faces from the electorate and political interest groups to achieve particular goals. Federalism, like hemlines, has been subject to discernable trends: the disentangled federalism of the "watertight compartments" era gave way to the collaborative federalism of the postwar years; the breakdown of collaborative federalism in the 1990s led to discussions of interprovincial federalism; and the bilateral or "hourglass" federalism of the Martin years was superseded by declarations of "open federalism" under the Harper administration. The other two elements are much less constant. One is the set of political or ideological goals of each government. These include the type and amount of nation building a government may wish to pursue (most notably in the case of Ottawa and Quebec) and the degree to which it chooses to embrace either market- or solidarity-inspired policies. The other is the way in which all of these political tensions intersect with the nature of health care provision itself. Technology has manifestly changed the way in which health care is used (e.g., outpatient drug therapy has largely replaced care in convalescent institutions) and has facilitated the management of health care delivery (such as the collection of health care data or the use of electronic health care records). The complexity of modern health care demands both greater collaboration and integration between sectors and a system that ensures the efficient use of health care resources. Even the world around us changes the way we structure health care: this includes demographic shifts (aging, rural depopulation, immigration); globalization (greater risk of cross-border illnesses such as pandemics or food-borne diseases, greater mobility of service providers); and, somewhat more ephemerally, broader social values (to what extent can collective responsibility for health care be maintained in the context of greater health care costs within a shrinking economy?). A reasonably accurate understanding of the political dynamics of health care federalism, in sum, rests upon the clear identification of all three elements: the institutions and laws underlying national governance; the political objectives of key actors; and the nature of health care itself.

These variables have always been relevant in determining the way in which health care federalism has manifest itself in Canada. But rarely have so many factors coalesced so dramatically that a clear critical juncture has been so evident. The renegotiation of the 2003 First Ministers' Accord on Health Care Renewal at the end of 2011 was expected to have been an occasion to think deeply and carefully about the provision of health care in Canada. However, by this time, a perfect storm was brewing that began to push the established political context off its moorings. What resulted was a tectonic shift not only in the way the country would be thinking about health care but also in the way in which federalism itself would be reconfigured.

THE ESTABLISHED ORTHODOXY: OTTAWA, HEALTH CARE, AND NATION BUILDING

The 2003 accord was the culmination of a long-standing policy strategy that, like many previous national health care initiatives before it, focused upon the federal government's role in infrastructure building, bridge building (of a more political nature), and nation building. The 1995 federal budget, which had removed over six billion dollars in transfer payments to the provinces, led to a period of retrenchment and cutbacks in health services provision at the provincial level. While the provinces rallied to ensure that federal cuts did not undermine the existing quality of service provision, "the gap between Canada and other G7 countries widened significantly" throughout the 1990s in such areas as the development and use of new technologies (Saulnier et al. 2004, vii). By 2002 the high-profile Romanow report (*Building on Values: The Future of Health Care in Canada*) noted quite emphatically the importance of directing more federal resources into health care across the country to achieve structural changes that would permit a more efficient and sustainable system to emerge. But no concerted national effort at systemic reform could be accomplished by hostile parties lacking mutual respect and trust. Thus, the period between 1998 and 2003 was characterized by a sustained attempt by the Liberal administration in Ottawa both to mollify the provinces and to reinforce a *national* focus upon health care.

One must recall that 1995 was the nadir of federal-provincial relations not only because of the draconian federal budget but also because of the dramatically close results of the Quebec referendum seven months later. Thus, the fiscal bridge building with individual provinces was inextricably linked with the attempt to cultivate a greater sense of pan-Canadian nationalism, a job that the federal Liberal party viewed (when strategically useful) as its traditional mandate. The decision by the Martin administration to engage in remedial nation building was more reactive than proactive, and the observation that Canada was unravelling was underscored not only by vituperous federal-provincial relations and a close call with separatism but also by the decision by many provinces to construct a confederal relationship that did not involve Ottawa.

Politically, this simmering resentment solidified a resolve between provinces to minimize the federal presence in social policy-making. At the annual premiers' conference in St. John's in 1995, the provinces agreed to establish the Ministerial Council on Social Policy, Reform, and Renewal. The council's report, released in March 1996, called for negotiation between the federal and provincial and territorial governments and consultation on federal spending, a limit on unilateral federal action in social policy, the clearer delineation of federal and provincial and territorial responsibility, and the transfer of federal resources to provinces where necessary. Also in 1996, Ontario released a report it had commissioned from Thomas Courchene (*ACCESS: A Convention on the Canadian Economic and Social Systems*) that set out a road map for provinces to manage social programs without the involvement of the federal government. ACCESS received a great deal of discussion (see Cameron 1997) but did not receive widespread support (especially from the smaller provinces). In contrast, the ministerial council's report was endorsed (except by Quebec) in 1997 as part of the Calgary Declaration. Interestingly, this process was the starting point for both a more national institution (the Social Union Framework Agreement) and a far more confederal one (the Council of the Federation).

From 1991 to 1996, the growth rate of average annual health expenditure per capita was -0.2%; from 1996 to 2009 it had increased to an average of 3.5% (CIHI 2011a, 5). Certainly the increase in federal spending in the late 1990s was not in and of itself any more contentious than it had been for the previous sixty years. It was, after all, not the application of federal spending but rather the arbitrary and unexpected withdrawal of it that had exacerbated tensions between governments. Reaction to increased federal spending by the provinces was viewed with ambiguity: it was a short-term solution to their fiscal crises, but it was also a symptom of the deeper structural issue of vertical fiscal imbalance between levels of government. Vertical fiscal imbalance referred to the gap that was created because Ottawa was able to collect more revenue than it needed to maintain its own constitutional responsibilities, while the social programs run by the provinces became increasingly difficult for them to maintain. Adding to the tension was the skepticism regarding the very legitimacy of the federal spending power, a position that Quebec emphatically maintained and that other provinces after 1995 began to see as an increasingly sensible one. While a large body of jurisprudence addresses the issue of the legitimacy of the federal spending power, the debate is generally split between those who argue that federal expenditure to the provinces is a "gift" that they are free to accept or refuse (and thus legitimate), and those who hold that the "choice" provinces have to refuse is more an abstract than a practical one, as shared-cost programs not only commit provinces to expenditures they might not otherwise make but also undermine their capacity to levy taxes for their own purposes.

At the annual premiers' conference in Saskatoon in 1998, Quebec finally joined the other provinces to create a united front when they agreed to adopt Quebec's position that provinces had a right to opt out of federally supported social programs under provincial jurisdiction with full financial compensation. This position and principles articulated in the Calgary Declaration were formalized in a 1999 document entitled *Securing Canada's Social Union into the 21st Century* (also known as the Victoria Proposal). The Victoria Proposal differed slightly from the Saskatoon Consensus (it contained, for example, a more detailed dispute resolution mechanism: see Tremblay 2000). But the "opting-out" principle that had secured Quebec's support was to be a casualty in the ensuing negotiations between the provinces and the federal government, a circumstance that (along with the provinces' de facto recognition of the federal spending power) led to Quebec's refusal to sign the final product of these talks: the Social Union Framework Agreement (SUFA). To sweeten the pot and secure agreement by the remaining provinces, Ottawa included a "health care side-deal" promising additional funding for the Canada Health Social Transfer (CHST) and a reallocation formula based upon equal per capita shares of the CHST for all provinces, an incentive that many hold was crucial to the success of SUFA (Bakvis et al. 2009, 178).

SUFA will probably be remembered more as a treaty that ended overt hostilities than as a document establishing a new intergovernmental protocol. Many studies have analyzed the fate of SUFA (e.g., Lazar 2000; Noel 2000; Lazar 2003; Facal 2005; Bakvis et al. 2009) and few have found much of an influence of SUFA's directives upon health policy (although it has had a higher profile in policy-making in the area of early childhood development). Yet SUFA did represent more abstract victories for both levels of government. Despite some minor unilateral forays into provincial jurisdiction (such as the Millennium Scholarships program), Ottawa has since 1999 been more circumspect about its overall use of its spending power. What it gained from SUFA, at least at the time, was popular recognition of the very concept of a Canadian "social union": the widespread acceptance, however inchoate, that a collective responsibility for, and a shared purpose regarding, health care on a national level does exist and ought to be protected. This national pride in public health care had served the federal Liberal party very well politically at least from 1984, and in 1999 it again acted as an effective counterweight to demands for strict provincial authority over health care. Thus, SUFA symbolized, at the very least, both a resumption of federal-provincial relations as usual (however fractious these normal relations were) and an acknowledgment of the national character of health care. Interestingly, however, the attempt at pan-provincial collaboration put into motion from the Calgary Declaration to the Victoria Proposal did not simply end with SUFA. On the contrary, SUFA said little about the underlying problem of the vertical fiscal imbalance, an issue that provinces perceived would still require a solid front against Ottawa.

As many have pointed out, the idea of a formal institution representing provinces as a bloc vis-à-vis the federal government has a long history in Canada, and the Quebec Liberal Party has played a notable role in articulating this idea for over a century. Claude Ryan, for example, notes that "the idea of concerted action among the provinces dates back to the late 19th century," when Honoré Mercier, leader of Quebec's Liberal party (and premier of Quebec from 1887 to 1891) invited the other provinces to engage in collaborative meetings that could "safeguard the autonomy of every province in the federation" (Ryan 2003, 2). In 1953, the Quebec Liberal Party supported a recommendation of the Tremblay Commission to form a "Council of the Provinces," and when Jean Lesage was elected premier in 1960 the concept was implemented as an annual premiers' conference, a practice that has continued to the present (Ryan 2003, 4). At the federal level, the Task Force on Canadian Unity published its final report in 1977 (the Pépin-Robarts report) and included a recommendation to establish a "Council of the Federation," which was designed (using the German Bundesrat as a model) to replace the Senate (Meekison 2003, 6). The Quebec Liberal Party again proposed the idea of Council of the Federation under Daniel Johnson in 1995 but was preempted by the election of the Parti Québécois in 1995 (Rae 2003, 3). Thus, the antecedents for the Council of the Federation have been quite numerous: Meekison documents twenty-three separate proposals for interstate or intrastate mechanisms between 1973 and 2003 alone (2003, 13). Unsurprisingly, the new Liberal government of Quebec under Jean Charest became the main driver for the implementation of the present Council of the Federation. Building on the annual premiers' conference, the Council of the Federation established a permanent secretariat to provide a greater degree of continuity in interprovincial collaboration. This was especially important for Quebec, which hoped to build a pan-provincial base of support for the principle of asymmetrical federalism. It was, however, the continuing resentment over the vertical fiscal imbalance that compelled all provinces to formalize a common front against Ottawa.

This, in sum, was the interplay of political variables that resulted in the 2003 Accord on Health Care Renewal (appendix 1) and the 2004 10-Year Plan to Strengthen Health Care (appendix 2). The residual hostility of the provinces to Ottawa as a result of the 1995 CHST remained a slow-burning fire because of the provinces' resentment of a continuing vertical fiscal imbalance. The federal Liberal government, whose identity has traditionally embraced the need for a coherent pan-Canadian strategy of nation building, recognized both a potential political threat (the proposed interprovincial Council of the Federation undermining its nation-building role) and a potential political gain (the possibility of building on a public sentiment that still strongly favoured public health care). The hope that SUFA would be a major blueprint for the renewal of intergovernmental relations was dimming. At the same time, Quebec had just elected a new Liberal government that was ready to embrace federalism (albeit on its own terms). In fact, support in Quebec for public health care remained high as well and was a key issue that Premier Charest had used to his advantage during his election campaign. Finally, after several years of retrenchment in health care provision, a major and predictable infusion of funding was seen as essential to secure important structural changes in the Canadian health care system.

THE MOVE TO COMPETITIVE FEDERALISM

One of the most painful but valuable lessons of the 2003 and 2004 agreements has been that the attempt to "buy change" has not been particularly successful. Federal funding conditional upon provincial performance in health care was not a novel development in 2003: already in 1999 Ottawa had promised increases in federal cash transfers, along with a single-year supplement to the CHST, in exchange for provinces agreeing to develop their capacity to report on their progress in health care reform. The 2000 accord pushed further in this direction, referencing clear reporting, third-party verification, and more detailed indicators, and by 2002 a Performance Indicators Reporting Committee was established. But a more committed adherence to very specific activities on the part of the provinces (including a $16 billion Health Reform Fund targeting primary care, home care, and catastrophic drug coverage) was a key principle of the 2003 accord. This strategy was expanded still further in the 2004 10-year plan, which focused upon benchmarks, performance indicators, and the reduction of wait times in five targeted areas, along with a mandate for CIHI to monitor provinces' progress on wait times.

And yet, by 2007 it had become clear that neither dramatic structural change in Canadian health care nor a willingness to adopt a rigorous set of pan-Canadian performance indicators was forthcoming. Both CIHI and the Health Council of Canada have commented upon the difficulty of setting out clear indicators giving comparable information across provinces. Some have even argued that the attempt to ground intergovernmental health transfers upon conditional funding has been a clear failure (Fafard 2013). There are many reasons for this, including the refusal of several provinces to submit to the third-party oversight of their performance and a confusion about what was meant by "accountability" in provincial performance (Fafard 2013). While there has been a noticeable improvement in the amount of information regarding performance in the health care sector (usually in the form of provinces' reports to their own populations), the data are often selective, difficult to interpret, and impossible to compare with those produced by other jurisdictions. Regardless of whether one accepts the extent of Fafard's condemnation, it is clear that conditional funding is considerably more difficult to operationalize successfully than most people anticipated in 2003 (for a more technical discussion of why this is the case, see chapter 7 in this volume, by Levy and Sobolev).

Notwithstanding the difficulty of securing results, however, the principle of conditionality was widely considered to be the keystone of sound health care federalism, and if it was not effective enough as it was practised, the solution was seen to be *tighter* conditionality. Even the federal Conservative government had embraced the concept of conditionality in health care funding as a principal component of its election campaigns under Stephen Harper. Thus, the declaration by Ottawa in December 2011 that it would discontinue conditional funding in health care altogether was a bombshell.

This approach marked a clear shift in Ottawa's thinking from "open" federalism to "market-preserving" federalism. In 2006, the appeal of the new Conservative government was based partly on its ostensibly province-centric view of federalism. After the unilateralism of the Chrétien era and the bilateralism of the Martin administration, the Conservatives' emphasis upon open federalism seemed to augur a much more harmonious period of intergovernmental relations. Open federalism was a rather nebulous concept that consisted preeminently of clarifying the proper roles of each level of government while facilitating cooperation between them. Harper assured the provinces he would respect those areas under their jurisdiction, and he made tantalizing promises (which never materialized) formally to limit the federal spending power. This was more cynically seen as an attempt (partially successful in 2006) to secure the support of federal voters in Quebec. Early versions of open federalism also included references to the importance of the accountability of government, fiscal responsibility, and budget transparency (Harmes 2007), principles that seemed to have been all but forgotten by the time the minority Conservative government was found to be in contempt of Parliament in 2011 for refusing to disclose details of, and cost estimates for, spending proposals regarding federal prisons and fighter jets. Moreover, the principle of respecting provincial autonomy seemed less evident when considering potential externalities that could arise from new federal legislation (such as the costs of enforcing measures set out in Ottawa's omnibus crime bill, Bill C-10) or when Ottawa began attempting to build a stronger common market (including the undertaking to establish a national securities commission).

The key difference between open federalism and market-preserving federalism is that, in the latter, provincial economic sovereignty is upheld for a very specific purpose well beyond the simple sentiment of mutual respect. The point of market-preserving federalism is to use the institutional framework of federalism in a way that will "limit the degree to which a political system can encroach on markets" (Montinola et al. 1995, 55). For the dynamics of market-preserving federalism to be effective, subnational governments (such as provinces) must have clear autonomy over the raising of funds and the spending of public money. These subnational units must exist within an effective economic union that permits both capital and labour to cross borders with ease. Further, these governments cannot have easy access to money except through taxing their own populations (i.e., no transfers, no loans, no ability to print money). Finally, these structural changes to federalism must be permanent or self-enforcing so that businesses have confidence that their investments will be protected beyond the tenure of any particular government. Formally, the institutional conditions of market-preserving federalism are as follows:

- First, a hierarchy of governments with a *delineated scope of authority* (for example, between the national and subnational governments) exists so that each government is autonomous in its own sphere of authority.
- Second, the subnational governments have primary *authority over the economy* within their jurisdictions.
- Third, the national government has the authority to police the *common market* and to ensure the mobility of goods and factors across subnational jurisdictions.
- Fourth, revenue sharing among governments is limited and borrowing by governments is constrained so that all governments face *hard budget constraints*.
- Fifth, the allocation of authority and responsibility has an *institu-*

tionalized degree of durability so that it cannot be altered by the national government either unilaterally or under pressures from subnational governments (Montinola et al. 1995, 55; see also Weingast 1995, 4).

The essential condition here is that subnational governments compete against each other to attract private resources. The dynamics of democratic politics writ large tends to reward politicians for propping up inefficient industries or engaging in high levels of public spending. In a federal system that promotes the mobility of capital, however, the opportunity costs to governments of engaging in these activities become much more pronounced (Qian and Weingast 1997). Haardt provides a much more detailed account of market-preserving federalism in chapter 2.

In one sense, market-preserving federalism is similar to the position taken by Ottawa under earlier Liberal administrations: provinces have the capacity to raise taxes themselves, if they choose to do so, and therefore should not demand higher transfers from Ottawa. The distinct focus of the Conservative government, however, was in its apathy (and even hostility) toward the national vision of a Canadian social union that had been articulated under several previous Liberal governments. The Conservatives had a quite different conception of nation building, and this was one grounded upon the pre-eminence of the market. As Harmes (2007) notes, market-preserving federalism does not assume a weak or passive central government but rather a federal government willing to act strongly and decisively in areas that strengthen the role of the common market.

Thus, the dramatic statement by the federal government during a meeting of federal and provincial finance (and not health) ministers in December 2011 regarding the future of health care federalism was part of a much larger strategy with a clearly defined conceptualization of what federalism was for. In place of conditionality, Ottawa agreed to an unconditional transfer (from 2017 on) that would be based upon a three-year average of the economy's rate of growth (with a guaranteed minimum of 3%). Moreover, after 2017 funds would be transferred on an equal per capita basis, rather than a weighted basis. This "weighting" was a product of the shift in taxing authority from the federal to the provincial governments negotiated in 1977, which reduced cash transfers in exchange for a tax point transfer, and was made to recognize the fact that provinces with stronger economies could take greater advantage of these transferred tax points. The new funding regime exacerbated inequalities between provinces, with the unsurprising consequence that some provinces supported the changes, while others did not.

The strategy of market-preserving federalism achieves a number of objectives for Ottawa. First, it removes the federal government from any role in or responsibility for health reform and cost containment. Health care is a potential liability to any fiscally conservative government in Canada: either the government increases funding in an attempt to achieve significant reform (and gets labelled a big spender), or it becomes mired in a massive reorganization of systems that potentially achieves very little (and gets labelled incompetent), or it promotes privatization (which remains an anathema to the majority of Canadians). Strategically, eschewing responsibility for health care is a tactful move for a fiscally conservative government. Second, by presenting a funding formula that rewards provinces differentially, the federal government effectively undermines provincial solidarity and reduces the likelihood of provinces establishing a unified political force against Ottawa (as they were able to do with the issue of vertical financial imbalances). Third, by constructing a self-enforcing environment that is highly receptive to the requirements of private capital, it creates a dynamic that undermines public spending on social programs while permitting the federal government to retain the appearance of a passive and unbiased observer.

This dynamic has already become quite apparent in the European Union, another federal system that was explicitly designed to facilitate a common market. As Scharpf has explained in some detail, once the institutional structure of a federal system – including the decision rules that govern organizational protocol – is established, it is "bound to create strong asymmetries, favoring some actors and some policy goals, and impeding or obstructing others" (2009, 7). Given such a clear institutional impact, the ideologies, interests, and strategies of key political actors become less directly influential. Unpleasant effects and externalities can be attributed to the logic of the system, and not to the agency of any particular political actor. In the case of a federal system established to facilitate commercial activity (i.e., an economic union or common market), the functional organization principle is *negative* integration (that is to say, certain forms of political behaviour are not permitted), while the attempt to establish a social union across federal units requires *positive* integration (in other words, active agreement between units). Given that positive integration often requires a complicated set of co-determination rules (based, for example, upon vetos or supermajorities), there exists an institutional asymmetry in federal states toward negative integration (which favours economic union over social union). In the case of the European Union, as Scharpf notes, the emphasis upon negative integration (economic union) has meant that "national problem-solving capacities are reduced by the dual constraints of more intense economic competition and by the legal force of negative integration, while European [collaborative] action is constrained and often blocked by conflicts of interest under decision rules imposing very high consensus requirements" (1997, 2).

There is, then, a fascinating political dynamic underlying the attempt to construct a regime of competitive federalism in Canada. As both Weingast (who espouses competitive federalism) and Scharpf (who is critical of it) acknowledge, there is a self-reinforcing quality to competitive federalism that makes it increasingly difficult for subnational governments to pursue social objectives. These structural imperatives can be politically useful when a federal government wishes to distance itself from the charge that it is directly responsible for undermining popular social programs such as public health care. The strategy for the federal Conservative administration has clearly been to establish the conditions of market-preserving federalism. The fundamental conditions required to achieve this form of federalism are the establishment of a common market, the political autonomy of subnational units, the clear delegation of fiscal responsibility to the provinces, and the imposition of harder budgetary constraints upon them. All four trends are evident, and particularly so in the field of health care. After winning a majority government in 2011, the prime minister outlined a new approach to intergovernmental relations. A key point was having Ottawa play "a more active role in promoting the economic union," particularly through "tearing down the walls of provincial interest" that hampered the growth of the economy (Curry et al. 2012, A1, A4). The need for a clear division of authority also explains the current federal government's position that health care remains solely under provincial jurisdiction and that provinces must therefore take full responsibility for the implementation of health care within their borders. (This explains why Ottawa is refusing to take any leadership role in the discussion of health care reform.) The federal finance minister has been quite forthright about stating that he expects provinces to cut social spending and to keep corporate tax

rates low. When asked how the provinces could cope with cuts in federal funding even as they entered into a period of deep austerity, the
prime minister replied that provincial affairs were not his concern
(Curry et al. 2012, A1, A4). Whether provinces feel obliged to permit
greater privatization of health care to maintain their economic competitiveness, in this way, is seen to be the direct consequence of provincial, and not federal, policy-making.

THE MOVE TO SOFT FEDERALISM

One of the most pointed ironies of the federal government's shift
toward competitive federalism is that it seems to give the provinces
exactly what they had been demanding for over a decade: unconditional health care funding. Although global structural changes trig-
gered the recession of the 1990s, it was the fateful 1995 federal budget that ignited the stormy interprovincial debate over the vertical
fiscal gap. By 1997 provincial and territorial leaders had drafted a
common position against Ottawa, arguing that existing transfers had
to be renegotiated to facilitate the adequate provision of health and
social programs at the provincial level as the severe vertical fiscal
imbalance that existed between the two levels of government strained the capacity of the provinces and territories to sustain their social
programs. Of course, the concept of vertical fiscal imbalance is both
a fluctuating and a subjective phenomenon. It was Ottawa, for example, that experienced a diminished fiscal capacity vis-à-vis the
provinces throughout the 1980s (when its deficits deepened far more
dramatically than those of the provinces), but the 1990s had a much
more severe impact upon the provinces (Lazar et al. 2004). Nonetheless, even the definition of vertical fiscal imbalance (that the revenue
raised by one level of government is insufficient relative to its expenditure responsibilities, especially in relation to the fiscal capacity of
the other level of government) leaves much unsaid in the determination of what the spending duties of each government *ought* properly
to be.

   In the 2000 accord, the federal government increased its funding
levels significantly in exchange for agreement from the provinces that
they would pursue common policy goals in health care, but the
provincial and federal governments continued to spar for the next
two years over the gap in fiscal capacity between the two levels of government. The most notable document of this period was the report of

Quebec's Commission on Fiscal Imbalance (the Séguin report), which recommended abolishing the CHST and distributing federal GST tax points to the provinces (for a up-to-date discussion of this strategy see chapter 8, by Boessenkool, in this volume). In response, Ottawa released a document outlining its own financial liabilities, including diminished revenue owing to tax reductions, large federal debt payments, increased federal transfer payments to provinces, and a global economic slowdown. Moreover, it pointed out that not only did provinces have the ability to set whatever level of taxes they chose but also many provinces had decided to reduce their taxes (and thus their revenue base) of their own accord (Lazar et al. 2004, 141–4), implying that the provinces themselves were responsible for the existence of a vertical fiscal imbalance.

Notwithstanding the political rhetoric over the funding gap, the 2003 accord and the 2004 10-year plan did channel a considerable amount of funding to the provinces. Nonetheless, the provinces were determined to keep the issue of fiscal imbalance alive and used the new Council of the Federation to establish the Advisory Panel on Fiscal Imbalance in 2005. The following year, the first Harper government was elected federally. The Conservatives had campaigned on a promise to address the vertical imbalance and, over the next five years, that is exactly what they did, although not in a manner that the provinces had expected. The Conservatives recognized the relativity of the concept of vertical fiscal imbalance and understood that an equally sound strategy to make spending capacity more symmetrical was to increase federal spending in areas of undisputed federal jurisdiction and to reduce federal revenues. Thus, spending on national security (first with the war in Afghanistan and then with the promise to buy expensive new frigates and fighter jets) and public order (police and prisons) became much more pronounced as the Conservatives progressed from minority to majority government. Health care transfers under the 2003 accord and the 10-year plan as well as equalization payments (including the bilateral deals made by the federal Liberals to Newfoundland and Nova Scotia) further diminished the ready cash held by Ottawa that the provinces had in their sights. At the same time, Ottawa's capacity for collecting revenue had been reduced not only by the federal tax reductions made by the previous Liberal administration but also by the GST reductions upon which the Conservatives had campaigned. "If the government was daring the provinces to raise their sales taxes by a comparable amount, and thus help to redress the alleged vertical fiscal imbalance," observed Stevenson, "there were (predictably) no takers. Was this merely a lack of courage, or a tacit admission that the vertical fiscal imbalance was a myth?" (2006, 10). Federal revenues were reduced even further because of the collapse of the world economy late in 2008. By 2009, discussion of the vertical fiscal imbalance – the main impetus for the 2003 accord and the 10-year plan – had all but vanished.

Part of the reason for this was the peculiar way in which health care transfers in Canada are intertwined with calculations of equalization payments to the provinces. As Courchene (2006, 50) explains, sky-rocketing energy prices (favouring energy-producing provinces) "served to convert the 2004 consensus over VFI [vertical fiscal imbalance] into a zero-sum, fiscal free-for-all over HFI [horizontal fiscal imbalance]." This was especially pronounced in the case of Quebec, as it "would only receive its population share (about 24 cents) of every new VFI dollar, whereas its share (at the margin) of a new equalization dollar is 48 cents, and could jump to nearly 70 cents when Saskatchewan, British Columbia, and Newfoundland and Labrador join the ranks of the 'have' provinces" (Courchene 2006, 50). Thus, any discussions about health care transfers must also take into consideration any changes in which equalization payments are reconfigured (see also Courchene 2010). Ontario is particularly dissatisfied with the current allocation formulae, as its critical mass of population means that "it would be footing most of the bill for the equalization increases caused by the soaring revenues of the energy-rich provinces" (Courchene 2006, 50).

These political dynamics also underscore the weakness of a confederal body such as the Council of the Federation. Any decision-making institution that relies upon unanimity will always have difficulty executing policy decisions. As Brown (2003) notes, for a confederal decision-making body to be effective it must generally have specific voting procedures (e.g., a qualified majority), inter-governmental agreements must be enforced through embedded legislation, and a fair and effective dispute settlement process must exist (7). He adds that "Canadians and their governments may not be ready for European-style co-decision" and, lacking this, the Council of the Federation was destined to become "nothing more than a continuation of the annual Premiers' Conference by another name" (Brown 2003; this prediction was also accurately made by Marchildon 2003). Beyond the operational structure of the institution, the political dynamics that bedeviled any hope that it could have an enhanced function included the refusal of several provinces (most notably Quebec and Alberta, which had championed the idea most emphatically) to cede any provincial authority to third-party processes or parties. Yet effective codecision-making traditionally requires that the parties involved surrender a certain amount of sovereignty in exchange for achieving a wider shared purpose and, to the extent that provinces refused to acknowledge this, their political power was limited to a more exhortatory function. Another dynamic was the political interplay between smaller and larger provinces. Smaller provinces may have been as unhappy as the larger ones with the overall behaviour of the federal government, and particularly its refusal to address the vertical fiscal imbalance, but they were also aware that they had more to lose by snubbing federal transfers. This dynamic was exacerbated by the Martin administration's willingness to make bilateral deals with some provinces, a move that effectively undercut provincial solidarity. Indeed, the council's first major document, the Gagné-Stein report on fiscal imbalance, was openly repudiated by at least three of the provinces (Bakvis et al. 2009, 111). By 2011, the political importance of the council seemed to be mirroring the slow decline of its main raison-d'être: the vertical fiscal imbalance.

This changed dramatically and abruptly. Meeting in January 2012 to discuss Ottawa's decision to opt out of health care governance, the premiers issued a communiqué that they were "committed to the proposition that ongoing collaboration and cooperation is essential to providing Canadians with access to the best health care in the world." They also established a Health Care Innovation Working Group to examine issues associated with scope of practice, human resource management, and clinical practice guidelines. The provinces, noted the premier of Saskatchewan, "are ready and willing to fill the void left by the federal government in reforming Canada's health care system" (Scoffield 2012). Another foray by the provinces into horizontal policy-making followed soon after, with the province of Ontario calling for a united front on its attempt to roll back doctors' fees for services that had been made easier through technological advancements. What is quite remarkable here is that the premise of competitive federalism – that subnational governments are constrained in their attempts to place political limits on economic activity because of the mobility of labour and capital – has been called into doubt. The provinces have reacted to federal strategy by engaging not in competitive behaviour but in collaborative behaviour.

Why did the provinces perceive a need for collaborative activity at all? The common front presented by the premiers through the Council of the Federation in the 1990s was driven by the common interest all provinces had in closing the vertical fiscal gap. In 2012, funding was not a key issue for many of the provinces, as the wealthier provinces acknowledged that they would actually do quite well with the switch to a basic per capita funding formula. Nonetheless, the shock and consternation of the provinces in response to Ottawa's refusal to play a leadership role were quite palpable. The reason for this, as noted at the beginning of this chapter, is that the nature of health care provision has been changing quite substantially. It is no longer a matter of a "merely local and private nature"; rather, it has become a highly complex, interdependent, and expensive set of systems that require a high level of coordination, reorganization, and regulation. If more efficient, state-of-the art health care is to be provided in Canada, it is crucial that effective patterns of coordination and investment in technology and planning be applied across the nation. It is here that federal states in general remain at a disadvantage vis-à-vis more centralized systems. One example of this disadvantage is the way in which federal states have found it much more difficult to implement electronic health care systems. Patient safety, the effective treatment of chronic conditions, and the provision of efficient preventive care services now rely considerably upon sophisticated information technology systems; the failure to be able to implement these systems compromises the quality of care statewide.

A recent Commonwealth Fund survey of six states found that centralized states tended to outperform federal states on a number of health care indicators, particularly those that required effective coordination and monitoring. While Canada did rank very high in terms of "long, healthy, and productive lives," its overall ranking was quite low because of the Canadian health care providers' difficulties in tracking and coordinating care. In terms of chronic care treatment, for example, "U.K. physicians are most likely to report it is easy to print out a list of all their patients by diagnosis. This finding may reflect the major push made by the U.K. government to implement health information technology (IT). Alternatively, low levels of IT use pull down the U.S. and Canada's scores" (Davis et al. 2010, 5). Moreover, Australia, Canada, and the United States had the highest rates of medical and medication errors, while "Canada, Germany, and the U.S. lag in terms of using IT to receive computerized alerts or prompts about potential problems with drug doses or interactions, with scores markedly below international leaders. Only 20 percent of physicians in Canada reported receiving such alerts compared with 95 percent in the Netherlands" (Davis et al. 2010, 6).

In sum, it is increasingly possible that some manifestation of what Banting and Boadway (2004) term a "predominantly provincial sharing" community will replace the current dual-sharing model, notwithstanding Ottawa's attempt to structure Canadian federalism on a more competitive framework. This scenario raises a number of questions, both in terms of execution and consequence. The first issue, the extent to which Ottawa can unilaterally change the nature of health care funding, has effectively been settled. Certainly there have been other precedents: the move to block funding under Established Programs Financing in 1977, along with a tax point transfer, was clearly initiated by the federal government. The SUFA protocol of 1999 did call for a greater degree of forward planning and negotiation on such a major policy move, but the bottom line is that the provinces cannot block Ottawa from moving out of a field of taxation clearly under its jurisdiction, let alone prevent it from removing itself from a field of regulation that belongs to the provinces. The second issue is the larger fiscal context: establishing a tax-based transfer of any sort will require some renegotiation of the equalization formulae (especially if such a move focuses upon income rather than consumption taxes). The third issue is the political negotiation between the provinces. Any major withdrawal by the federal government as a key player in health care means that there is a potential for provinces to become net winners or net losers; such a zero-sum situation means that much is at stake in the negotiation of the terms of any tax transfer or change to equalization payments. Political friction between provinces may well increase accordingly. The paradox that arises here, however, is that as the political dynamics between provinces become more intense, the need for them to cooperate more seamlessly and harmoniously increases.

Serious governance problems underlie any potential provincial sharing model of health care. This is largely because of the dynamics of the "joint decision trap" (Scharpf 1988, 2006; Falkner 2011), in which the ability of any governmental actor to veto decisions unilaterally leads to decision-making by the lowest common denominator.

This is precisely the kind of deadlock that threatens to undermine the use of a body like the Council of the Federation in developing a "predominantly provincial sharing community." Before 2012, the only health-related policies presented by the council were fairly uncontroversial, or stated in very general terms, or rhetorical declarations that required no real concerted action (such as the premiers' exhortation that Canadians should reduce their daily intake of sodium). The achievements of the council were limited by its *de facto* mandate as a body constructed to provide a common political front against Ottawa, rather than as an institution that would actively design and execute substantial policy reform. Interestingly, initial discussions about the Council of the Federation involved the possibility of "European-style codecision processes" that would "subject the exercise of their sovereign powers to the common goals and minimum common standard necessary to maintain and strengthen the Canadian economic and social union" (Burelle 2003). As we have seen, provinces have simply not been willing to engage in this European-style codecision process. There is analysis to suggest that the possibility of achieving such collaborative engagement is both politically difficult (Cameron et al. 1997; Kennett 1998) and theoretically inappropriate (Marchildon 2003) in Canada. Another reason for skepticism regarding the administrative effectiveness of the council as a major decision-making body would be its current dependence upon corporate sponsorship by such bodies as Rx&D and Johnson and Johnson, especially in the already politicized area of pharmaceutical policy-making (see www.councilofthefederation.ca/meetings/summer_meeting2011.html).

The political conundrum for provinces is that, while a collaborative attempt at health care policy-making presents numerous difficulties, Ottawa's attempt to impose competitive federalism upon the provinces does not present attractive solutions to health care policy-making either. There have been concerns that competition between provinces leads increasingly to a dynamic of "racing to the bottom" (Harrison 2006), and especially so in social policy. This is why, despite the structural constraints, provinces have been willing to consider and to experiment with cooperative approaches to the challenges of health policy formation. What is new to the process is that provincial governments have been increasingly turning to soft governance as a means of avoiding the joint decision trap that arises when federal units attempt joint policy-making in the absence of hierarchical leadership.

To date, soft methods of governance in federal systems have, at a theoretical level, focused largely on international or supranational decision-making (most commonly within the European Union), as the starting assumption is that national governments wish to engage in collaborative decision-making without undermining their sovereignty. But this principle holds equally well in a federal system in which sub-national units have autonomy over specific policy areas that require coordination. The point of soft governance is that it is based upon voluntary action and entails no *hard* sanctions for failure to comply. The advantage of soft governance rests upon its capacity to encourage participation in circumstances where governments would otherwise refuse to engage, as legislative agreements entailing hard sanctions potentially involve a loss of autonomy (see chapter 4, by Lahey, in this volume). From a political perspective, the discipline and utility of soft governance rest upon three pillars: first, the assumption that it is in the interest of each party (in either the short or long term) to be part of collaborative ventures; second, the *soft* sanctions involved in failure to comply (such as "naming and shaming"); and third, the educative value of open, continuous, and thoroughgoing communication between parties. In many European states (particularly the Nordic ones), and within the European Union itself, "soft law constitutes a way of combining local autonomy with integration and coordination within a larger political community" (Fredriksson et al. 2011).

Obviously, the conditions under which soft governance can work as a form of federal governance are limited. Parties must believe that they have a common interest: zero-sum disputes can rarely be resolved through soft governance. The dependence upon public shaming can backfire on occasion, as taking responsibility for unpopular decisions can sometimes improve a government's appeal to its own electorate even when the wider political community disapproves. Open communication can sometimes make a party more aware of how its interests actually *differ* from those of other stakeholders. But if it is important not to overstate the political advantages of soft governance, so too is it useful not to diminish them.

In an important way, mechanisms of soft federalism have a clear advantage over uniform legislative approaches such as the Canada Health Act (which is not justiciable against the provinces, but which comes with hard sanctions nonetheless). In the first place, as noted above, soft governance encourages collaborative action by reducing the cost of participation. Simply agreeing to a process of communication does not entail that a government will be backed into corner and obliged to swallow mandates that it finds disadvantageous or unpopular. In the second place, soft governance acknowledges and accommodates diversity among units: the principle of one-size-fits-all approaches is eliminated. In the classic open method of coordination, for example, all governments identify particular policy targets as common concerns, with the understanding that the choice of policies used to address these concerns remains under the jurisdiction of each government. But each government also submits an individual action plan that addresses how the unit proposes to reach the policy target in question. A permanent representative committee evaluates these action plans and makes specific recommendations to individual governments. This process of coordination lowers the probability of governments pursuing negative-sum strategies that produce negative externalities for other governments, or for the federal unit as a whole. Although individual governments are free to pursue whatever action they choose, the likelihood of collaborative behaviour is enhanced because there exists a process that identifies potential problems (the communication function), suggests constructive alternatives (the learning-through-best-practices function), and obliges governments openly to defend potential beggar-thy-neighbour practices that would be self-defeating were all parties to adopt them (the accountability function). Governments' actions and progress are clearly benchmarked and analyzed relative to each other, with specific attention being given to the particular constraints, problems, and advantages each government faces. The point is that the institutional integrity and political autonomy of governments are respected where uniformity and centralization are neither necessary nor possible, and yet the same governments are "are required to focus on jointly defined problems and policy objectives, and to consider their own policy choices in relation to these 'common concerns'" (Scharpf 2002, 654; see also Scharpf 2001; Atkinson 2002; Sabel and Zeitlin 2010; Tömmel and Verdun 2009).

Although the process of soft federalism has not, in Canada, experienced this degree of institutionalization, the provinces have embarked on this same kind of general approach in health care following Ottawa's declaration of non-involvement. Using the Council of the Federation as a vehicle to facilitate communication and formulate policy, the premiers declared in January 2012 that they were "committed to the proposition that ongoing collaboration and cooperation is essential to providing Canadians with access to the best health care in the world." Under the aegis of the Council of the Federation, they established a Health Care Innovation Working Group to examine issues to do with scope of practice, human resource management, clinical practice guidelines and, later, the joint purchasing of generic drugs. The provinces, noted the premier of Saskatchewan, were "ready and willing to fill the void left by the federal government in reforming Canada's health care system" (Scoffield 2012). The hallmarks of soft federalism characterize this policy approach, as the practice remains based upon voluntary, non-binding participation in the absence of hard constraints. As in the European process, the first step has been to identify national concerns that could usefully be addressed through coordinated action. Next, the provinces have been discussing "best practices" in a number of areas, including rural health care, clinical practice, and home care. What does not (yet) exist is an institutionalized structure of iterative policy engagement in which governments' commitments and strategies are articulated, evaluated, and tracked over time. Interestingly, provinces have also begun to experiment with the possibility of coordinated health care policy at a more informal level outside of the Council of the Federation. As mentioned earlier, Ontario, for example, sought horizontal governmental support for its attempt to roll back doctors' fees for services made easier through technological advancements. This is a very interesting response to the institutionalization of market-preserving federalism, which depends upon the free movement of goods and services to oblige provinces to respond to the demands of the common market. In this case, competitive federalism actually increases health care costs (as physicians can demand higher remuneration or threaten to leave), while soft federalism reduces health care costs by constraining physicians' rent-seeking behaviour (by limiting the profitability of moving to other provinces). Haardt discusses this phenomenon from a theoretical perspective in chapter 5.

POLITICAL AND THEORETICAL JUNCTURES

In sum, then, the way in which federalism is conceptualized in Canadian health care is shifting dramatically. On the one hand is a federal government committed to the institutionalization of competitive federalism, and on the other hand are the provincial governments who are resisting the rigours of competitive federalism by engaging in a soft form of federalism. Although the potential of soft federalism is limited (it cannot overturn or substitute for competitive federalism), there is good evidence that it can either mitigate the worst excesses of competitive federalism (Scharpf 2002, 2009) or even work in tandem with competitive federalism to produce balanced and stable economic growth (Braun 2006). The pre-eminent weakness of soft federalism, of course, is compliance: why would autonomous governments ever choose to engage in processes set by someone else if they are not formally obliged to do so? The answer is that they freely engage in such processes because they can easily withdraw if they find their interests are threatened, and that the potential gains of coordinated activity are too enticing to ignore. Given the tremendous costs of provincial health care – almost half of provincial budgets – and the hope that rationalization, coordination, and the implementation of best practices can reduce these costs, there is good reason to believe that soft federalism may well become more institutionalized in Canada.

Finally, at a more theoretical level, the discussion of the emerging dialectic between competitive and soft federalism sheds an interesting light upon the debate between rationalist and constructivist explanations of political behaviour in federal systems. Especially since the publication of Scharpf's analysis of the joint decision trap in both German and European federalism in 1988, the focus on "the pathology of public policy" has tended to analyze the way in which state actors, operating within specific structural constraints, find difficulty in making significant collective decisions that veer too sharply from the status quo. In an ongoing joint-decision process, Sharpf explains, the worst outcome of non-agreement is simply the continuation of existing common practices. Therefore, where unanimity is required, policies "cannot be abolished or changed as long as they are still preferred by even a single member" (1988, 257). Discussions of federal policy-making, then, have in the past two decades generally used the theoretical framework of rational-choice decision-making (or, more specifically, rational-choice institutionalism), which looks at the incentive structures of federal decision-making processes. This has limited thinking about federalism both in substantive terms (the assumption is that change can only be achieved by manipulating the incentive structures themselves) and in explanatory terms (the structure of decision-making is what explains policy making; changes or "critical junctures" in federal policy-making can only arise because of exogenous variables or "shocks" to the system).

It is hardly coincidental that both rational-choice theory and market-preserving federalism have the same genesis in the Virginia school of economic theory. Market-preserving federalism, again, assumes that specific structural changes can oblige government actors to change their behaviour in accordance with their (economic) interests. Specifically, the imposition of hard constraints on subnational governments in a federal system with clear economic autonomy will oblige them to change their behaviour (to spend less and tax less) to secure their primary goals (economic growth and stability). Given these hard economic constraints and clear institutional boundaries, the softer values and aspirations of these subnational units become secondary, if not completely irrelevant.

But the emergence of soft federalism addresses weaknesses both in the explanatory and substantive force of rational-choice institutionalism. Like other forms of institutionalism (such as historical institutionalism), rational-choice institutionalism has been hobbled by a static quality that has made it difficult to explain change (or to suggest ways of achieving it). If the assumption is that institutions are in stable equilibria with fixed rationalist preferences, then the explanatory variables (self-interest and incentive structures) do a much better job of explaining why change does *not* occur, rather than why it does. This has led constructivists (or, more precisely, discursive institutionalists) to propose a theory of institutional change focusing on human agency and, more specifically, the dynamic interplay of ideas, debate, and discussion in effecting political change. For constructivist or discursive institutionalists such as Hay (2004), Schmidt (2008, 2010), and Blyth (2002), the solution to the determinism that underlies institutionalism "is to zero in on agency, but especially the subjective ideational and inter-subjective discursive realm, seemingly a more fluid and flexible environment in which to effect change, largely because this move ostensibly allows agents to 'construct' their realities and fields of action" (Bell 2011). According to Schmidt, for example, discursive institutionalism "simultaneously treats institutions as given (as the context within which agents think, speak, and act) and as contingent (as the results of agents' thoughts, words, and actions). These institutions are therefore internal to the actors, serving both as structures that constrain actors and as constructs created and changed by those actors" (2008, 314).

The literature on soft governance focuses precisely on aspects of human behaviour and action that are not simply reducible to the rational calculation of interests per se, and these observations are increasingly being applied to the politics of federal governance. In a recent study of the European Union's decision traps and their exits, for example, Falkner (2011, 15) argues that "our approach includes explanatory variables from both *rationalist* and *constructivist* paradigms. It is acknowledged in our concept not only that bargaining over pre-decided interests may take place, *but also that learning and socialization can play a role* … " [my emphasis]. Institutional constraints are real and cannot be ignored but, at the same time, "institutional design is not destiny" (Schmidt 2008, 317).

Conceptually, the way we understand reality has a direct impact upon our perception of what we can do to shape it. Thus, as we begin to challenge the dominance of explanatory models of federal policy-making, so too do the tools available to assist in policy-making themselves change. As we begin to move away from pure explanations of hard instrumental rationality, we must start more seriously to consider a wider range of reasons for acting, including, as Boudon (2003) argues, moral, prudential, and axiological bases of action. Soft federalism is an approach that takes these variables seriously. Again, the soft quality of this approach should warn us against imposing unrealistic expectations on what this methodology can achieve either in explanatory or in substantive terms. But it does focus our attention on the fact that neither citizens nor provinces are just passive vessels in the larger interplay of federal politics.

4

The Legal Framework for Intergovernmental Health Care Governance: Making the Most of Limited Options

WILLIAM LAHEY

There is an understandable tendency in discussions of health care policy in Canada to regard Canada's federalism as a significant barrier to good health care governance. Outside of Quebec and perhaps segments of opinion in the west, there is also a tendency to regard more assertive leadership by the federal government as the key to getting federalism out of the way of improved health care governance. The failure of successive federal governments to act on this imperative tends to be attributed to political circumstances, including the resistance of some provinces, particularly Quebec and Alberta, to national approaches, and more generally, the absence of federal political will.

In this context, it will be natural for many to attribute the mixed results achieved under the 2003 First Ministers' Accord on Health Care Renewal (appendix 1) and the 10-Year Plan to Strengthen Health Care of 2004 (appendix 2) to the weak accountability that each of these accords placed on provincial governments to show results in exchange for the increased federal funding that both agreements promised. An obvious aspect of this weak accountability is the character of both instruments as mere political agreements that were not in themselves enforceable and that were not reinforced by stronger federal legislation. In other words, the weakness of the accords would appear to fit with their inherent weakness as "soft law."

My argument in this chapter is divided into two parts. First, it is that this assessment may pay inadequate attention to the legal realities of

Canadian federalism and to the constitutional rationale for these realities. Independently of the question of political will or capacity, the
law of Canadian federalism makes it impossible for either the federal
or provincial level of government to unilaterally determine Canada's
approach to health care governance. It also makes it hard if not impossible for these two levels of government to implement a mutually
determined approach to health care system governance through binding agreements, assuming they both wish to do so. These legal realities are not the consequence of the application to health care governance of arbitrary rules. Instead, they are a consequence not only of
how legislative jurisdiction over health care is divided between the
two levels of government but of the fundamental status of federalism
as a core value of Canada's constitutional order and system of government. Arguments for particular approaches to health care governance, including those based on the fundamental values that underpin medicare, would undoubtedly be relevant to how these legal
realities are interpreted and applied to particular jurisdictional disputes. But in the end, such arguments and their supporting values
would be subordinate not simply to the division of legislative jurisdiction once interpreted but to Canada's constitutional commitment
to federalism.[1]

The second part of my argument is that the legal realities make
intergovernmental cooperation that is supported and guided by soft
law absolutely essential if Canada is to achieve a more comprehensive
and cohesive approach to health care system governance that com-
bines the governance assets that each level of government controls. In
this context, the argument here is that the 2003 accord and 2004 10-
year plan need to be evaluated for what they have accomplished as
well as for what they have failed to accomplish. These accomplish-
ments include the role that they played because they were merely soft
law in making possible any significant federal-provincial-territorial
agreement on health care reform. Both instruments were also significant for extending federal-provincial-territorial cooperation beyond
the realm of public health care insurance and into the highly provincial domain of health care system management. Finally, my argument
is that the accord and the 10-year plan have been important for the
contributions they have made to the development of a pan-Canadian
layer of health care governance that is potentially complementary to
the governance frameworks that exist in each of the provinces and
territories.

At the same time, I recognize that accountability has been the weak link under the 2003 accord and the 10-year plan of 2004. I argue that unless future soft law frameworks address the question of accountability more directly and aggressively, they are unlikely either to build on the successes that have been achieved under the 2003 accord and the 10-year plan or to address their failure to deliver promised reforms. That being said, I suggest that future soft law frameworks should strengthen accountability by building on the emphasis that the 2003 accord and the 10-year plan placed on the accountability of governments to their citizens rather than on intergovernmental accountability. This approach is likely to be the more politically feasible one. It is also the approach that is most likely to harness the space that Canadian federalism creates for governance that is not only collaborative but effective.

The point of departure for this chapter is the view that health care governance in Canada must include an effective national or intergovernmental (pan-Canadian) dimension if Canada is to have a health care system that meets the aspirations of Canadians in relation to health care. My concern here is not why this is so but how it can be achieved in the framework of our constitution. To provide context for that focus, I simply note that I believe that health care governance in Canada must be significantly national or pan-Canadian for three reasons: to ensure that access to health care based on relative need and not relative wealth continues to be a defining characteristic of Canadian health care policy; to ensure relative equality among regions (and especially among large and small provinces) in the benefits and burdens that are entailed in defining health care as a public good to be accessible on the basis of relative need; and the growing evidence (including as explored by David Haardt in chapter 2 and by Katherine Fierlbeck in chapter 3) that suggests that countries that take a centralized approach to health care governance outperform those that take a decentralized approach.

THE FLEXIBLE BUT HARD LAW OF HEALTH CARE FEDERALISM

The Rules of the Game

Everyone knows that jurisdiction over health and health care is divided between Parliament and the provincial legislatures (Jackman 1996, 2000; Braën 2004). The broad outlines of this division of jurisdiction are also well known, despite the characterization of health by the Supreme Court of Canada as an "amorphous" legislative field that is not distinctly federal or provincial (*Schneider v. The Queen*, 1982). Only the provinces can legislate directly on the health care insurance of most Canadians. For this reason, it can be said that jurisdiction over health care insurance is very provincial. Jurisdiction to legislate on the delivery of health care services (or on their organization, management, or regulation) is also highly provincial. In both jurisdictional domains, the exceptions to exclusive provincial jurisdiction consist largely of federal jurisdiction (and responsibility) for First Nations health and federal jurisdiction over health care for members of the armed forces and, until recently, the RCMP (Leblanc 2012). In relation to health care for members of First Nations, it is important to note that the members of First Nations communities – and Aboriginal citizens more broadly – are not excluded from provincial jurisdiction over (or responsibility for) the delivery of health care services to their residents.

Provincial jurisdiction in relation to the delivery of health care is also subject to federal laws validly enacted under various federal "heads of power," including the federal jurisdiction over criminal law. This is a broadly defined jurisdiction that encompasses prohibitory laws that provide for penal consequences to advance a public purpose that can be advanced by criminal law, such as public peace, order, security, health, and morality (*The Margarine Reference*, 1949 S.C.R. 1, 50 (per Rand J.); *Canadian Federation of Agriculture v. A.-G. Quebec*, 1951; *R. v. Hauser*, 1979; *Knox Contracting v. Canada*, 1990). This is the jurisdiction used by Parliament to adopt legislation, such as the Food and Drugs Act (R.S.C., 1985, c. F-27), which overlaps with provincial jurisdiction over the delivery of health care services.

The limits to this source of federal legislative jurisdiction in respect of health care and health care governance are significant. By its nature, the criminal law is a blunt instrument for achieving health policy objectives. In addition, in the *Assisted Human Reproduction Act Reference*, the Supreme Court of Canada ruled that the federal government had jurisdiction to prohibit injurious and unethical reproductive practices but not to regulate the provision of beneficial reproductive technologies and services (*Reference re Assisted Human Reproduction Act*, 2010; see also Newman 2011). In doing so, the court emphasized the exclusiveness of provincial jurisdiction over the provision of health care and the importance of maintaining a balanced federalism. It rejected the argument that a broader interpretation of federal jurisdiction was necessary because a consistent and comprehensive regulatory scheme for reproductive technologies and therapies was unlikely to be achieved by coordinated provincial efforts. Albeit decided by the narrowest of majorities, this decision casts doubt on the ambitious arguments that have been put forward for a broader interpretation of federal powers to deal with health care (or other social programs) based on arguments of provincial inability (Choudhry 2002). In broad terms, the outcome aligns with wider patterns in division of powers analysis. In the *Securities Reference (Reference Re Securities Act*, 2011), the court once again emphasized the importance to jurisdictional analysis of "the principle of federalism" – and more specifically, of a balanced federalism – in rejecting the argument that securities regulation had become a matter of national concern that required federal legislation. It also emphasized the distinction between "what is optimum as a matter of policy and what is constitutionally permissible."

The most significant federal jurisdiction in relation to health care is the federal spending power. Although its very existence can still be called into question, it is the power by which Parliament enacted both the Canada Health Act (R.S.C., 1985, c. C-6) in 1984 and the predecessor statutes that brought medicare as we currently know it into existence between the 1950s and the early 1970s.

Under the spending power, Parliament can authorize federal spending on matters in and outside of federal legislative jurisdiction. It can use this power to authorize conditional grants to the provinces, including for health care. Such legislation establishes the authority of the federal government to make or to withhold grants where the federal government decides that the conditions specified in the legislation have or have not been satisfied. Such decision-making is subject to judicial review in administrative law but in the case of the Canada Health Act, judicial intervention is a remote possibility given the breadth of the discretion given to the federal government by the legislation and the breadth of the policy considerations that are relevant to the exercise of that discretion (Lahey 2011; Choudhry 1996; *Canada (A.-G.) v. Inuit Tapirisat of Canada*, 1980).

Under the Canada Health Act, the conditions require the provinces to fund most hospital and physician services through a universal scheme of public health insurance.[2] Since Parliament could not directly implement such a scheme, the spending power allows the federal government to indirectly accomplish what the constitution prohibits it from doing directly. It is important to emphasize that federal decision-making to distribute or withhold payments under the act is the only means by which it can be enforced against the provinces. On the surface of things, this is because the act is written to apply only to the federal government. But the deeper reason is that legislation based on the spending power can only apply to the federal government, not to the provinces. The Canada Health Act is not written to be directly enforceable against the provinces because such legislation would be constitutionally incapable of applying to the provinces.

It is safe to say that this contributes to the apparent willingness of provinces to act in contravention of the act, sometimes persistently. The federal government is understandably blamed for not acting aggressively to deal with these contraventions (Choudhry 2000). Indeed, to the extent that the act gives the federal government the discretion to withhold funds for non-compliance with the conditions laid down by the act, it is striking that this discretion has never been exercised. But the other reality has to be that withholding health care dollars is a relatively blunt instrument for controlling provincial health care decision-making and governance. Moreover, given the extent of general provincial compliance with the basic and non-debatable requirements of the act, the truth may be that the threat of penalization has been enough to achieve provincial adherence, perhaps partly because the strength of that threat has never been tested. Even more so, the extent of compliance absent any penalization shows that compliance has as much to do with widespread voter identification with the values and purposes of the act as with the risk of financial penalization by Ottawa.

Another factor is the continuing debate about the constitutionality of the spending power.[3] Both sides in this legal debate agree that the spending power allows the federal level of government to do indirectly through the provinces what it cannot do directly by its own action. What they disagree on is whether this is consistent with federalism. The spending power is not a power expressly provided for in the text of the Constitution Act, 1867. It is said by some authorities to be inherently inconsistent with the nature of federalism because it undermines the autonomy of the provinces and creates confusion and uncertainty about lines of accountability between voters and the two orders of government. These are views held particularly strongly by many Quebec scholars.

The alternative view is that there is implied textual authority for the spending power and that the operation of the spending power is consistent enough with federalism because provinces are not compelled by spending power legislation to abide by the conditions it creates but instead choose to abide voluntarily (Hogg 2007, 6–17). The further argument that can be made is more pragmatic: the spending power has played a critical role in combining the fiscal capacity of the federal government with the jurisdiction of the provinces over the big three in social spending: health, education, and social welfare. If faced squarely with the question of constitutionality, it seems likely that the Supreme Court of Canada would draw on its constitutional pragmatism and frequently demonstrated support for collaborative federalism, including in the *Insite* and *Security Reference* cases, to find in favour of the power's constitutionality (*Canada (A.-G.) v. PHS Community Services Society*, 2011).

Nevertheless, the debate is still an open one despite the long-standing and widespread use that has been made of the spending power and the numerous instances of implicit judicial acceptance of a federal spending power that encompasses federal spending on provincial matters – see, for example, the decisions of the Supreme Court of Canada in *Eldridge v. British Columbia (A.-G.)* (1997) and *Auton v. British Columbia (Attorney General)* (2004). No authoritative judicial ruling depends on judicial determination of the arguments for and against the existence of the spending power. The point to be emphasized here is that whether or not arguments about the inconsistency of the spending power with the "federal principle" would lead to an adverse ruling for the spending power in the courts, they are relevant and potentially very influential in the decisions that different federal governments may make as to when and how they use the spending power in proposing legislation to Parliament and as to how they administer and enforce legislation based on the spending power. For example, the existence of room to argue that the spending power is a legal myth (Petter 1989) lends encouragement to those, like the Harper government, who seek to minimize the leadership role of the federal government in matters of provincial jurisdiction (Mendes 2008; Lazar 2008).

The (Somewhat) Dynamic Nature of the Rules

In various ways, the courts have sought to soften the rules I have outlined to facilitate the effective governance of the country. More particularly, the courts have tried to decide jurisdictional disputes in ways that accommodate collaborative federalism and the practical need for cooperation between the federal and provincial governments in how each uses their respective legislative powers.[4] In large measure, this reflects the understanding that what the constitution of 1867 describes as legally distinct and mutually exclusive legislative domains must of necessity in a complex world be used by each level of government to enact legislation that overlaps with and otherwise interacts in multiple ways with legislation adopted by the other level of government.

This concern for flexibility is core to how the courts resolve disputes about legislative jurisdiction (Hogg 2007, 15-1 to 15-23, and 15-38.4 to 15-56). Long ago, the courts rejected the watertight compartments understanding of sections 91 and 92 of the Constitution Act, 1867, the sections of the act that outline federal and provincial legislative powers ((U.K.), 30 & 31 Vict., c. 3, reprinted in R.S.C., 1985, App. II, No. 5). In determining the pith and substance of challenged legislation for the purpose of determining whether the matter of the legislation falls under a federal (section 91) or provincial (section 92) head of power, the courts eschew characterization of the legislation by reference to its incidental effects on matters within the jurisdiction of the other level of government. Instead, they uphold the constitutionality of legislation if its essence, determined both by its purpose and its effect, deals with matters within the jurisdiction of the enacting level of government. Similarly, the courts adjudicate on the basis that the matters on which governments legislate can have a double aspect, meaning that they may be governed both by a valid federal law that pursues an objective that is within federal jurisdiction and by a valid provincial law that pursues a different objective that is within provincial jurisdiction (*Reference re Securities Act*, para. 41).

The result is that federal and provincial jurisdiction over many areas of governmental activity is either overlapping or intermingled, such that federal and provincial laws in the same legislative and administrative field can both be valid even if the laws are very similar to each other. This is possible because of the restrictive approach taken to defining the paramountcy that federal legislation enjoys over provincial legislation: in general terms, it only applies where overlapping provincial and federal laws that are each otherwise validly enacted require those subject to both laws to do under one what they are prohibited from doing under the other (Hogg 2007, 16-1 to 16-19).

The result is a wider field for overlapping legislation than would otherwise be the case.

The concern for flexibility is also apparent in the permissive approach to inter-delegation. Long ago, it was decided that constitutional supremacy precluded both Parliament and the legislatures from enacting legislation that transferred legislative powers to the other (*A.-G. N.S. v. A.-G. Can. (Nova Scotia Inter-delegation)*, 1951). But it was then quickly decided that both levels of government could enact legislation that delegates administrative power to a subsidiary body created by the other level of government (as well as to subsidiary bodies that are simultaneously created by both levels of government) (*P.E.I. Marketing Board v. Willis*, 1952). Federal or provincial legislation that incorporated the law of the other jurisdiction by reference, including by anticipatory reference, was also upheld. On the basis of this flexibility, regulatory regimes that are simultaneously federal and provincial have been established to handle the marketing of various commodities and to oversee the oil and gas industry on Canada's east coast.

Federalism also does not prevent the federal and provincial governments from entering into agreements with each other, including agreements that purport to commit each level of government to introducing and securing passage of legislation (Waddams 2005, 461–8). Indeed, the functioning of Canadian federalism depends on a multitude of intergovernmental agreements, many reached at the ministerial or bureaucratic level between federal and provincial departments of government (or their agencies) that share responsibility in a field of governmental responsibility that is both federal and provincial. Health care, public health, the environment, immigration, highways, financial regulation, and the economy are among the leading examples of such fields of shared responsibility. Most of these agreements are framed as memoranda of agreement that do not give rise to legally enforceable rights and obligations. Although this accounts for the limited effect that many of these soft agreements have, it does not prevent many of them from being quite assiduously implemented as normatively if not legally binding.

Moreover, there is nothing in principle to preclude the federal and provincial governments from entering into legally binding contracts as the basis for collaborative efforts. Such contracts (as opposed to non-binding agreements) are unlikely, however, where the subject matter of the agreement is cooperation in a broad field of public policy. This is because governments can be expected to be wary of binding themselves to specific actions or outcomes in such fields through judicially enforceable contracts, rather than expressing their intentions through broad enabling legislation or generally worded memoranda of understanding. It is also because the broad terms of such agreements are not easily encompassed within the precise language and formal structure of binding contracts. Moreover, courts are likely to hesitate to conclude that such agreements were intended to be binding contracts to be enforced through the kinds of remedies, such as damages, given in the ordinary courts (*Canadian Environmental Law Assn. v. Canada (Minister of the Environment)*, 1999). Nevertheless, binding intergovernmental agreements are a legal tool available to governments who wish to give a legal foundation to their cooperative efforts across jurisdictional boundaries.

This overview of the flexibility of Canadian federalism law and of the opportunities it creates for intergovernmental collaboration – as well as the statements made in various cases suggesting judicial recognition of and support for collaborative federalism – shows the capacity of federalism to respond to change, to minimize its legalistic restrictiveness and to accommodate combined effort on problems and opportunities that cannot be addressed without combined effort. However, it is critical to recognize two essential points about these sources of flexibility. The first is that all are subject to constitutional limits that cannot be adjusted except by constitutional amendment. For practical purposes, this means they cannot be adjusted. In the case of the flexible interpretation of the division of powers, these limits are vividly demonstrated by the recent decision of the Supreme Court in the *Assisted Human Reproduction Reference*, mentioned above. When all is said and done about pith and substance, incidental effects, double aspects, and concurrency, there are certain legislative subjects that are exclusively under either federal or provincial jurisdiction.[5] In the case of inter-delegation and intergovernmental agreements, the limits lie in the reality that all such mechanisms for combined effort are established and operated subject to the constitutionally protected legislative authority of each government to bring the collaboration to an end. Even where governments reach an enforceable agreement, such an agreement remains vulnerable to lawful unilateral rescission by either level of government through the passage of clear legislation to that effect (*Reference re Canada Assistance Plan (B.C.)*, 1991).

The second point is that some of the available sources of flexibility may not have much applicability to the collaboration that governments might agree to in the context of health care governance. For example, it is fair to say that the two levels of government could be expected to use inter-delegation to delegate specific administrative functions to a shared intergovernmental agency in specific areas of health care governance, such as pharmaceuticals or technology assessment. But it is harder to imagine either a multilateral or bilateral agreement by which the federal and provincial governments would delegate their broader responsibilities in health care governance to a shared arm's-length agency. Similarly, it is hard to envisage the terms of an enforceable contract on general matters of health care policy, even if political agreement to a robust collaboration on health care governance was to be achieved.

These points lead to the following conclusion: if health care governance in Canada is to include an effective federal-provincial dimension, it requires mechanisms that are capable of facilitating combined or coordinated effort between the federal and provincial governments that are compatible with the coordinate and equal sovereignty of both levels of government within their distinct (if overlapping) legislative spheres. The distinct sovereignty of each of the provinces means that similar mechanisms are needed to facilitate pan-Canadian collaboration based on interprovincial collaboration. The need for such mechanisms is particularly salient in health care given that the equal and coordinate sovereignty of each level of government is combined in that policy sector with a jurisdictional allocation that assigns much of the authority over health care governance to the provinces. In such a constitutional framework, a national approach to health care governance must largely be an intergovernmental approach that depends on coordination of decision-making and implementation among the governments of subnational jurisdictions (Courchene 2004).

Across policy fields, the mechanism that performs this work on a wide scale is intergovernmental soft law agreements, often called memoranda of agreement or memoranda of understanding. The quality of these agreements as mere soft law emphasizes their consistency with the equal sovereignty of each level of government. Soft law does not create enforceable rights and obligations. It therefore does not purport to interfere with symmetrical jurisdictional autonomy but rather to express it. Soft law agreements are designed to inform how each level of government uses its powers and execute its laws but they are not capable of determining these matters. At the same time, such agreements work by creating mutual expectations that have a normative quality. Even though compliance with the agreement is voluntary in the sense that the agreements cannot be enforced through legal procedures, compliance is obligatory in the sense that it can be validly expected of each participating government by all other participating governments. In some cases, as with the 2003 health accord and the 10-year plan of 2004, the fact that the soft law agreement promises benefits to Canadians reinforces the normative weight of the non-enforceable agreement.

At this point, it is worth once again turning attention to the Canada Health Act. It is clearly "hard" law. It is a statute that has been through the parliamentary process and that has received royal assent. It does work that only hard law can do, namely authorizing the making of grants of federal monies to the provinces. Its meaning is justiciable, even if its interpretation is unlikely to come before the courts (Choudhry 1996). However, the act binds the provinces in ways that are indicative of soft law. It is not binding because it is legally binding but rather because of the administrative actions that the federal government may take if the provinces do not sufficiently adhere to the act. Even more to the point, it is binding from a provincial perspective because of the support it enjoys with voters and important interest groups who have influence with provincial politicians, legislatures, and governments.

This highlights the fact that the line between hard law and soft law is not a precise and definitive one (Sossin and Smith 2003; Sossin 2003, 2005; Trubek and Trubek 2007; Trubek et al. 2006). Much hard law relies on the mechanisms of soft law for its implementation and works in parallel with complementary soft law instruments. Conversely, soft law can sometimes acquire the normative force that is expected of hard law. When this happens, soft law sometimes functions as a precursor to the adoption of hard law. These are points long understood in the literature on law and regulation, especially by those who write on regulation from the responsive regulation, smart regulation, or new governance perspectives (Ayers and Braithwaite 1992; Gunningham et al. 1998; Parker 1999, 2002; Trubek 2006; Baldwin and Black 2008; Ford 2008). In the case of the Canada Health Act, the permeability of the boundary between soft and hard law suggests that it may be misleading to think of the act and non-enforceable intergovernmental agreements as two sharply distinct legal approaches to achieving a more integrated and optimal approach to health care federalism. Instead, the focus should be on how the two can be made to work together to achieve more optimal results than could be achieved by sole reliance on one or the other. In this connection, it is worth stressing that although the Canada Health Act operates as soft law in important respects, its success in doing so undoubtedly depends in significant ways on the fact that it is ultimately not soft law but an act of the Parliament of Canada.

SOFT LAW AND HEALTH CARE FEDERALISM

Between the turn of the century and the end of 2004, first ministers' conferences produced three intergovernmental health agreements, with the most significant ones being that of 2003 (which was called an accord) and that of 2004 (which was issued in the form of a communiqué and labelled, *sui generis*, as "a 10-year plan to strengthen health care").

These agreements are obviously soft law. They were political agreements, not legal contracts. They did not meet or purport to meet the criteria they would have had to meet to be enforceable on a contractual basis. The commitments they contained were mostly of a general rather than a specific nature. They called for objectives to be reached in areas such as the reduction of waiting times in five clinical services, the expansion of access to primary care through multidisciplinary teams, the wider availability of public insurance to cover catastrophic drug costs, and the availability of first dollar public coverage for access to certain home care services. The actions to be taken to accomplish these objectives were not specified. Moreover, in relation to these objectives, the provinces made commitments to their constituents rather than to the federal government or to each other. In areas such as a national pharmaceutical strategy, health human resource planning, and electronic health records, all of which contemplated action at the national level, the 2003 accord and the 10-year plan committed governments only to continue to work together to achieve vaguely defined objectives.

The softness of both of these agreements was starkly reflected in how they addressed their own implementation. In combination, the 2003 accord and the 10-year plan called upon the federal government to increase funding to the provinces by billions of dollars from the implementation of the 2003 accord to the expiry of the 10-year plan in 2014. These increases were to flow to the provinces through the Canada Health Transfer that is paid under the Canada Health Act. In that way, they became conditional on continuing provincial adherence, as determined by Health Canada, to the act's program criteria, all of which relate to public financing of hospital and physician services through the single-payer model. Provincial eligibility for the increases promised by the two agreements was not made conditional on whether or not the provinces met their commitments to (for example) cut waiting times, expand access to multidisciplinary teams, or enhance public insurance against catastrophic drug costs.

Instead, both agreements (and more specifically, the federal governments of Jean Chrétien and Paul Martin) placed faith in the political accountability of provincial governments to their own voters. They sought to strengthen this accountability by reinforcing it with arm's-length monitoring and reporting. The 2003 accord gave the Canadian Institute for Health Information (CIHI) the job of tracking and reporting, publicly and regularly, on the progress of provinces in reducing the specified waiting times. It also created the Health Council of Canada and gave it the task of monitoring and reporting on the accord's overall implementation. Both mandates were continued by the 10-year plan. The one on waiting times data was strengthened by the only element of conditionality attached by either agreement to promised increases in federal health care dollars: the increased funding was made conditional by the 10-year plan on provinces providing the data the CIHI needed to monitor waiting times.

For many, these characteristics of the 2003 and 2004 agreements do more than establish their status as merely soft law – they establish their weakness and one-sidedness. The accords effectively assured the provinces of increased and stable funding without doing enough to ensure it would be used to accomplish meaningful health care reform. It follows that they have produced the kinds of results that one should expect from such instruments. They have brought financial and intergovernmental stability but not change. Even in the field of their greatest relative success, the reduction of wait times in five clinical services (CIHI 2011b), the accords have achieved their modest ambitions more slowly and unevenly than was promised, with limited or uncertain impact on the wider problem of unacceptable waiting times (Health Council of Canada 2008). Even these modest successes have been put at risk (Barua et al. 2011; Wait Time Alliance 2012). On the commitments that were clearly intended to address the underlying enablers of improved health system performance, such as continuing health human resource planning on an intergovernmental level, a Canadian pharmaceuticals strategy, and universal deployment of comprehensive electronic health records, the 2003 accord and the 10-year plan have achieved even less. Indeed, as intergovernmental priorities, these commitments seem to have been largely abandoned (Health Council of Canada 2008, 2011).

This discouraging track record would have formed the backdrop for the negotiations for a new accord (or multi-year plan) that many expected as the expiry of the 10-year plan in 2014 approached. All indications are now that these negotiations have been pre-empted by the announcement by the federal government in December 2011 of the levels of health care funding it will provide to the provinces without any new agreement beyond the expiry of the 10-year plan (Bailey and Curry 2011). To say the least, this suggests federal disinterest in further experimentation with soft law options for influencing and guiding health care reform in broadly consistent pan-Canadian directions.

Many may think this is no great loss. This would no doubt be true for those who question or are opposed to federal government meddling in how provinces and territories manage their health care systems. But it may also be largely true for many who favour federal leadership or at least effective intergovernmental collaboration, given the disappointing results in health care reform under the agreements of 2003 and 2004. Indeed, the concerns expressed about the unilateral federal announcement of late 2011 have overwhelmingly been about the level of promised funding and the formula used to distribute it. Little attention has been addressed to the apparent decision to forego another accord on programmatic reform.

Undoubtedly, many who would like to see continuing federal leadership would want it to take a stronger shape than a new non-enforceable accord. My view is that despite the patent limitations of the intergovernmental agreements of 2003 and 2004, the disinterest of the federal government in a new agreement that links federal funding to shared pan-Canadian health policy objectives is regrettable. The primary reason is the limited alternatives that are available for all the reasons given above for establishing a common framework of national dimensions for accomplishing coordinated improvement in Canada's system of health care systems. The secondary and closely associated reason is the advantages that agreements such as those struck in 2003 and 2004 have over the hard law alternatives that might be imagined, precisely because of their core limitation, that is, their status as soft law.

The first of these advantages is the political and procedural achievability of soft law agreements precisely because of their non-enforceability, at least when governments want or are at least willing to do a deal. Since they are merely soft law, such agreements are incapable of impinging on jurisdictional boundaries or autonomy: obvious as the point is, it has to be recognized that this makes them achievable. The closely related advantage of soft law agreements is that they can be agreed to and implemented independently of the formal legislative process. This eliminates the perilous task of coordinating the passage of enabling legislation through Parliament and provincial legislatures that would be required for hard law agreements or the inter-delegation of administrative powers. Of course, it is difficult to imagine there would ever be the political will for such an aligned legislative process. But even if the initial will could be achieved, perhaps for some if not all provinces, it is doubtful if it would survive the vicissitudes of the political cycles and other complications that can upset plans for coordinated law-making among multiple jurisdictions and legislative bodies.

In a closely related vein, soft law agreements designed along the lines of the 2003 accord and the 10-year plan avoid the contentious issue of provincial accountability to the federal government that would arise if provincial commitments to health care reform were added to the Canada Health Act or to new federal legislation that separately addressed provincial commitments in the broad area of managing health care, as opposed to paying for it. This also explains the relative achievability of accords and other kinds of soft law agreements.

In short, the qualities that make accords non-enforceable as law are also what make them viable politically. To put it another way, the offset to their non-enforceability is their availability in a constitutional paradigm that does not provide many alternatives. In addition, the non-enforceability of soft intergovernmental agreements in the health care context has to be kept in perspective. As discussed above, the Canada Health Act is enforceable in the sense that it authorizes the federal government to withhold funding from provinces that fail to comply with its program criteria for public health insurance. The federal government has never exercised this option. Yet, the Canada Health Act is largely adhered to by the provinces, probably in significant measure because of the support of voters for the act and its objectives and values. To the extent that there has been enforcement of the Canada Health Act by the federal government, it has been through the soft law mechanisms of behind-the-scene communications between Health Canada and provincial ministries of health or through public comments by the federal minister of health on provincial plans that raise compliance concerns.

In other words, to the significant extent that the Canada Health Act successfully regulates the provinces, it does so more as soft law than as hard law. There is nothing in the nature of an accord or multi-year plan that would prevent it from being implemented in roughly the same way. In particular, there would be nothing to stop Health Canada and the federal minister of health from playing roles similar to the ones they play under the act to encourage the provinces to deliver on their soft law commitments. The fact the federal government has not played such a role under the 2003 accord or the 10-year plan reflects a choice by the federal government (Hébert and Stanbrook 2010). It was not an outcome that was dictated by the soft law nature of either framework.

The related point is that the non-enforceability of intergovernmental soft law probably makes it possible for the provinces to accept the recognition that such "law" necessarily gives to a federal role in shaping health care reform that goes beyond the question of how hospitals and doctors should be funded. In the 2003 accord and the 10-year plan, this recognition was largely implied and minimalist. But it was there nevertheless. For those who accept that Canada's health care system faces challenges that require national or at least coordinated intergovernmental action, one option is to regard the role given to the federal government under the accord and the 10-year plan as that of impotent paymaster. But this role could also be regarded as a beachhead that could have been developed through the process of implementation if the federal government had retained interest and insisted on continuing intergovernmental collaboration. It might also have been developed through the negotiation and implementation of subsequent accords.

In any event, the more important point is probably not the potential that soft law has to establish (or broaden) a hierarchical intergovernmental relationship. Rather, it is the role that it can play in shifting the focus from accountability between governments on behalf of citizens to accountability of governments to citizens, including through third-party monitoring and reporting. As discussed above, the 2003 accord and the 10-year plan gave a focused mandate to track and report on waiting time reductions to CIHI, a well-regarded institution that enjoys relatively strong independence. The agreements gave a more diffuse mandate to monitor and report on overall implementation to the Health Council of Canada, a now-discontinued body governed by a board of directors largely appointed by provincial governments and that therefore enjoyed much less independence. In both regards, the agreements of 2003 and 2004 instituted a minimalist version of what the regulatory literature calls information-based regulation (Gunningham 2009). Criticisms of the narrow mandate given to CIHI and of the Health Council of Canada's compromised independence are warranted. Nevertheless, under these soft law agreements, provincial governments became subject for the first time to evaluation, on a national scale, of their achievement of pre-defined policy objectives in health care management, at the hands of public institutions that were (to varying degrees) arm's-length from governments and that reported openly to the public.

It seems highly likely that the relative success of the 2003 accord and the 10-year plan in reducing some waiting times depended on the monitoring and reporting carried out by CIHI and on the publicity CIHI's reports received (CIHI 2011b). This suggests that soft law agreements can be effective in making change happen in Canadian health care governance, at least when they include measurable performance indicators and mechanisms of arm's-length accountability to publicly track progress against those indicators. The literature on soft law's effectiveness in other settings supports this conclusion. Indeed, in some of its applications, the concern is that soft law enjoys an effectiveness that is comparable to that associated with hard law without going through the open and transparent legislative processes that is typical with hard law (Mather 2010). To be sure, provincial governments' focus on waiting time reduction has been driven in the past decade by many factors apart from the 2003 accord and the 10-year plan, including the high levels of public concern about accessibility. But it is hard to believe that it did not matter that these push factors were reinforced by the pull factor of an accountability to report on a regular basis to Canadians through CIHI.

Of course, the independent monitoring and reporting instituted by the 2003 accord and the 10-year plan were very basic. Some have argued that the emphasis on waiting times, or conversely, on so few waiting times, was misplaced. Meanwhile, recent evaluations call earlier and encouraging evaluations of the success of the accord and the 10-year plan on waiting time reductions into doubt (Barua et al. 2011; Wait Time Alliance 2012). The weakness of the accountability for other commitments and the absence of attention to other and more revealing performance indicators have constituted a larger problem. Nevertheless, these points argue more strongly for a new accord that provides for more extensive, demanding, and sophisticated accountability through independent monitoring than they do either for an assertion of direct federal oversight of provincial health care governance under federal legislation based on the spending power or for abandonment of pan-Canadian monitoring and reporting. A new accord that instituted more demanding and more independent third-party monitoring and reporting would not be easy to achieve. But direct oversight by the federal government would be a non-starter, even if the federal government was not as hostile to such a notion as the Harper government would no doubt be.

Besides, federal oversight of the provinces under the Canada Health Act does not provide grounds for optimism as to what federal oversight would accomplish. As noted above, it has not resulted in discretionary penalization of any province despite numerous instances of provinces failing to abide by the act's program criteria. Observers have also criticized Health Canada for not actively seeking or rigorously analyzing the information that would allow proper evaluation of provincial compliance with the act. It seems clear that this approach to enforcement is supported by the weak transparency and accountability that applies to the highly discretionary executive decision-making that determines the administration of the act.

These criticisms reflect the extent to which broader policy or political considerations determine the act's administration. The same would likely to be true with federal legislation that links federal funding to outcomes that provinces were expected to achieve in the broader management of their health care systems. Intergovernmental accountability should therefore not be the issue. Rather, governmental accountability should be. The federal government could make a positive contribution to that kind of accountability by continuing to push for the role that independent institutions and processes can play in reinforcing the accountability of each government and of governments collectively to Canadians. Beyond pushing for provincial agreement for a stronger role for these kinds of institutions and processes, the federal government could use its spending power to ensure that arm's-length institutions and processes have the independence, resources, and tools they need to be effective. The federal government could also lead by example by agreeing to subject its administration of the Canada Health Act and the discharge of its health care governance responsibilities, including to First Nations health, to the same kind of independent oversight and scrutiny.

There is one other off-setting advantage of the formal weakness of non-enforceable intergovernmental agreements as mere soft law. It is that they allow intergovernmental agreement on shared policy objectives that will not and that possibly should not be made in hard law. For good reason, governments should probably be wary about giving the force of law to specific long-term policy objectives in a policy field as complex as health care. For example, to the extent that policy objectives such as those laid out in the 2003 accord and the 10-year plan could be carved into hard law, the intergovernmental process could be forced to choose between complying with the law and improving the health care system when changed conditions call for reappraisal of policy options.

Soft law agreements may represent a better balance between the force and clarity that law can bestow on the intergovernmental process and the flexibility and adaptability that is demanded by good health care governance. At the same time, they can serve to inform citizen expectations and government accountability to citizens. More specifically, they can inform the making and administration of hard law where hard law is appropriate and give others a stronger basis on which to evaluate and demand accountability from those who make or administer hard law.

In these ways, soft law intergovernmental agreements can contribute to the consistency and coherence of legislative and administrative decision-making. Similarly, to the limited extent that the courts are called upon to adjudicate on the legality of government's management of health care, as they were in the *Chaoulli* case (*Chaoulli v. Quebec (A.-G.)*, 2005), they may be able to take guidance from such agreements. For example, in *Chaoulli*, the courts were called on to adjudicate the reasonableness of the access that the health care system of Quebec provided to necessary medical services. Even though a soft law accord that defines the level of access that governments have committed to provide to their citizens would not be capable of binding the courts, it could inform such adjudication. It could thereby give judges a realistic understanding of the levels of access that have been promised by democratically elected governments that, unlike courts, have the difficult task of implementing those promises while reserving capacity in government and the health care system for other work that is probably more important to the health of Canadians.

THE FUTURE OF HEALTH CARE GOVERNANCE BY SOFT LAW

In the previous section, I have tried to show that evaluation of the merits of intergovernmental agreements based on soft law as instruments of national or pan-Canadian health care governance needs to recognize the absence, in the context of Canadian federalism, of clearly superior alternatives. Evaluation needs also to recognize that the formal weakness of non-enforceable instruments can contribute to their political achievability. Finally, evaluation needs to recognize that such agreements can, notwithstanding their formal weakness as soft law, acquire sufficient normative weight to be a meaningful lever for coordinated action among governments on health care governance.

In this section, I will offer some thoughts on how the potential effectiveness of soft law agreements in pushing health care reform can be maximized. I will, however, also raise a caution: as the effectiveness of such agreements in shaping government health care policy increases, it becomes important to recognize that they are not, as soft law, subject to the same transparency and openness that accompanies the making of hard law. This raises concerns about the transparency of the policy choices that get made in the formulation of soft law agreements and about the accountability of the governments that make those choices. This is especially important in light of the fact that the tendency of soft law to focus on outcomes, rather than on the mechanisms that will be used to achieve those outcomes, means that fundamental policy choices as to means are likely to be implied rather than explicit. Finally, I will comment briefly on the utter failure of the 2003 accord and the 10-year plan to address what should be Canada's foremost health care governance objective, improved health for Aboriginal Canadians and in First Nation communities.

Accountability and Effectiveness

As the discussion above indicates, the effectiveness of intergovernmental soft law agreements depends overwhelmingly on the accountability they bring to bear on governments and through governments on provincial health care systems. Specifically, the relative success of the 2003 accord and the 10-year plan of 2004 in reducing waiting times in targeted clinical areas toward agreed benchmarks suggests some room for optimism for what can be accomplished by a soft law accord that seeks to coordinate multi-jurisdictional effort on common objectives through arm's-length accountability that concentrates on monitoring and reporting on performance. But given that health care reform demands much more than limiting waiting times for some important clinical services, the limited success of the 2003 and 2004 agreements beyond wait times also suggests the need for a broader range of performance objectives and a more sophisticated set of performance indicators.

A broader performance framework of this nature could build on the analysis laid out in chapter 7 by Adrian Levy and Boris Sobolev. Implementation of such a framework would require a broader institutional framework than the one constructed by the agreements of 2003 and 2004. One aspect of this broader framework may be a wider and more explicit connection between the reporting commitments made in intergovernmental agreements and the arm's-length accountability frameworks and processes that now exist in most provinces and that arguably should exist in all provinces and territories (Lahey 2010). This might happen as a consequence of the creation of a more robust and expansive process of accountability at the national or pan-Canadian level. But it is even more likely to happen if an intergovernmental framework dealt directly and explicitly with the actions that were to be taken at the provincial level to enhance accountability through processes linked to pan-Canadian processes of accountability. The benefits would go beyond the contribution that improved accountability systems at the provincial level would make to the functioning of national accountability processes. The benefits would first and foremost consist of improved governance at the provincial level.

Particular note needs to be taken of the fact that the 2003 accord and the 10-year plan have been least successful in making change happen where change required the making and implementation of policy decisions that would direct system restructuring and force governments to confront strong stakeholder opposition. They also have largely failed to deliver on promises that would have required continuing collaboration among governments and their officials, such as in health human resource planning or on a national pharmaceutical strategy. This suggests pessimism as to the capability of soft law in such policy domains. It is in relation to the need for fundamental structural change that the discrepancy between the aspirations that get written into soft law and the inherent weakness of soft law is probably greatest.

One option is to simply accept that soft law is likely to have limited utility in addressing more systemic policy challenges. A more optimistic option is to think about how to make larger policy commitments more amendable to performance-based accountability by reframing them more directly in terms of the outcomes that structural changes in domains such as health human resource strategies are to produce. In other words, the solution may partly lie in focusing less on the means and mechanisms for change and more on the outcomes that provide the rationale for the means or mechanisms. Another part of the solution may be to strengthen the institutional component of a future accountability framework by, for example, instituting a Health Council of Canada that is more like the one recommended by Romanow (2002, 52–9). One of the key differences from the council that was created is that such a council would have a mandate to facilitate, support, and lead continuing intergovernmental collaboration (such as that proposed on health human resource planning by Gail Tomblin Murphy in chapter 6) in place of, or in addition to, the *post facto* evaluation mandate given by the agreements of 2003 and 2004 to the Health Council of Canada.

The apparent abandonment of a national pharmaceuticals strategy warrants particular attention (MacKinnon and Ip 2009). In part this is simply because of the importance of the issue of pharmaceuticals policy relative to the ability of the health care system to live up, on a continuing basis, to the values and objectives that underpin medicare. In part also it is because pharmaceuticals policy is where real benefits can be achieved by collaboration that goes beyond coordination. It is also an area that may either need or greatly benefit from a level of federal contribution that is different from that which may be envisaged in other areas of system improvement. Most importantly, given the dollar amounts involved, a national pharmaceuticals strategy may require dedicated use of the federal spending power. This raises the question of the appropriate legislative vehicle for that contribution. In addition, the fact that the federal government has jurisdiction over the regulation of pharmaceuticals may mean that intergovernmental collaboration on pharmaceuticals policy is not, as it tends to be in other areas, a matter of the federal government and the provinces talking about what the provinces can or should do. On pharmaceuticals strategy, the conversation may be partly about what the federal government can do under whatever plan is agreed upon. Perhaps this argues not only for deeper federal involvement on this file but also for decent prospects for a positive negotiation.

The centrality of accountability to the effectiveness of health care governance based on soft law argues for more than just stronger accountability mechanisms, as important as these may be. It argues, as Romanow recognized, for recognition and acceptance of accountability as a core value of Canadian health care governance. Ideally, this recognition would include, as Romanow advocated, an amendment to the Canada Health Act that would add accountability as a new program criterion for provincial eligibility for the Canada Health Transfer (Romanow 2002, 48–52 and 59–64). This would create a foundation in hard law for the reliance on accountability that is essential to making governance through soft law work. But at a minimum, a soft law commitment to accountability as an underlying principle of both the intergovernmental and the federal and provincial spheres of health care governance should be a priority.

Effectiveness and Policy Transparency

By their nature, soft law agreements focus on the outcomes or common objectives that participating governments agree to pursue. They leave the choice of means largely to governments. This is how jurisdictional conflict is avoided and agreement facilitated. It is also how managerial authority is left with the provinces, where it should be left to reflect both the constitutional accountability and the superior expertise that the provinces should have given their direct accountability for health care governance. In addition, the focus on outcomes and objectives can also help to maximize the effectiveness of soft law agreements. It makes such agreements more amendable to the kinds of accountability that are appropriate to soft law and upon which the effectiveness of soft law depends.

The focus on outcomes and objectives can, however, reinforce the idea, already prevalent, that Canadians care about the productivity and efficiency of their health care system, not the means deployed to achieve productivity or efficiency. It can in other words reinforce the commodification of health care, as styles of health care governance that rely on soft law have been said to do in Europe (Newdick 2008).

In addition, the focus on outcomes and objectives can by default and without debate validate policy choices on the means used to achieve these outcomes and objectives. It can either intentionally or unintentionally drive changes to the system that would not be accepted by Canadians if they were presented as explicit policy choices. All of these consequences are particularly problematic given that soft law agreements are designed and agreed to through the relatively inaccessible and opaque processes of executive federalism rather than the comparatively transparent processes that must be used to create hard legislative law. In this, intergovernmental agreements framed as soft law can give rise to one of the most frequently expressed concerns about the growing reliance of governance on soft law: its tendency to remove policy choices from the public scrutiny that would otherwise apply if the same choices were made through legislative processes.

These points can be illustrated by once again drawing attention to the relative success that the agreements of 2003 and 2004 have enjoyed in accomplishing objectives to reduce waiting times. Questions can be asked about the relationship of that success to the growing role of for-profit clinics in the delivery of diagnostic and surgical procedures. The issue is not the priority given to reducing waiting times but the priority given to that objective in the absence of any agreement on the methodologies that should (and should not) be used to accomplish it. One aspect of this issue is the consequences that the growing role of the clinics may have for the core policy objective of making care universally available on the basis of relative need while limiting the overall cost of doing so (Premont 2007). Another aspect of the issue is the concern that a potentially fundamental change in the structure of the system is taking place without public debate while possibly being aided and abetted by agreements that are finalized during closed bargaining sessions that focus attention on the reduction of waiting times.

The point is not that the management of waiting times should not be a priority. Instead, it is that no problem should be made a priority in isolation from the answer that we would give to the larger policy questions that may be implicated in our efforts to solve the problem. On the particular issue of waiting times, a national initiative to reduce waiting times should be accompanied by a clear decision on privatized care. Although I would want this done to prevent or halt privatization, I think everyone, including those who believe in the benefits of privatized delivery, should want it done to prevent or halt privatization by stealth.

The remedy is not to oppose more accords or soft law more generally. Instead, it is to require more transparency, openness, and public involvement in the broader process that informs the negotiation
of intergovernmental agreements and in the intergovernmental process in general. It is also to require that policy questions that are core
to the fundamental principles of the Canadian health care model
should be answered as policy questions. The former may require
institutional structures such as those recommended by Romanow to
lead the intergovernmental process and to enable citizen participation in it. The latter may require clear decisions on the innovation
that will and will not be regarded as consistent with Canada's version of public health care, including as defined by the Canada Health
Act.

These enhancements of process can also be said to be required by
the consideration that soft law agreements may influence legislative,
administrative, and judicial decision-making. This warrants transparency and openness in their negotiation independently of the interest of the public in the policy choices that underlay their terms. In
addition, greater transparency and openness promise to increase the
extent of public awareness of intergovernmental agreements and of
the commitments they contain. This in turn will nurture the element
of continuing accountability that is probably vital to their effectiveness as instruments of governance, much like the role apparently
played by public awareness in underwriting the soft law effectiveness
of the Canada Health Act.

Aboriginal Health

Both the 2003 accord and the 10-year plan of 2004 essentially left
responsibility for addressing the deplorable health status of Aboriginal Canadians and of First Nation communities to the federal government. Neither document set out specific actions that would be
taken to address Aboriginal health. This is unsurprising given that
First Nations were not part of the health accord process in 2003 or
2004. This reflects the consistent pattern of Canadian health care
reform, whereby the needs of First Nations are treated in a peripheral
way, if at all, usually through a process that is divorced from discussions of the reforms needed for the broader system (MacIntosh 2006).
This is almost certainly one of the reasons for the continuing failure
of Canada to improve Aboriginal health.

To change this, the needs of First Nations should in the future be at the forefront in intergovernmental health care negotiations, should such negotiations take place. This would require negotiation with First Nations of an accord on Aboriginal health before the negotiation of an accord on the remaining elements of health care reform. The idea would be to make an accord on Aboriginal health the foundation on which a broader accord would be negotiated. There is no guarantee that this would finally ensure vigorous action on Aboriginal health. But our history suggests that unless we give priority to Aboriginal health in this kind of tangible way, we will continue to deplore the state of Aboriginal health while doing little to fix it.

CONCLUSION

It is not unreasonable to evaluate the 2003 accord and the 2004 10-year plan with reference to the values and principles articulated within these documents. At the same time, however, it is unfair to declare the agreements to be failures simply because the ideal model implied in these values and principles still remains dismayingly distant. The strategic utility of softer governance mechanisms like accords rests precisely in their limitations: because sanctions related to noncompliance are not as clearly justiciable as ones established in harder legal formats, political actors otherwise inclined (or pushed) to intergovernmental collaboration may be more willing to engage in such agreements. Yet these agreements, despite their softness, can create meaningful processes of third-party accountability. They also are capable of producing public expectations (e.g., on waiting times, or responsiveness, or quality care) that can (although inchoate) act as a form of accountability more ephemeral yet more exacting than harder legal sanctions that must navigate the equal sovereignty of the provinces and the federal government that is core to Canadian federalism.

Canada's experience under the soft law agreements of 2003 and 2004 provides some evidence for these conclusions. But its experience over decades under the Canada Health Act (and its more prosaic legislative predecessors) provides even stronger evidence for these attributes of soft law governance in an intergovernmental frame. In the end, the reason that Alberta backed away from a series of privatization strategies, and more recently Quebec from user fees, is because their citizens made it quite clear they did not want such "reforms."

The key is to harness this form of accountability to the public for effective health care governance and to incorporate it into a flexible system of intergovernmental governance that has some of the attributes of formal third-party accountability that we associate with law. To accomplish this, we may begin by praising the soft law of intergovernmental health care governance, rather than burying it.

NOTES

1 *Reference re Secession of Quebec* (1998), at paragraphs 55–60, recognizing federalism as one of four underlying principles of the constitution, along with rule of law, democracy, and protection for minorities.

2 The program criteria are well known: public administration, universality, portability, comprehensiveness, and accessibility, all in relation to public health insurance (as opposed to governance of the broader system of delivering services) (see Lahey 2011, 1, 35–45).

3 See papers published in the *Queen' Law Journal* in 2008, including the following: Mendes (2008), Kong (2008), Lajoie (2008), and Adam (2008).

4 See, for example, the comments of Justice Abella in *NIL/TU,O Child and Family Services Society v. B.C. Government and Service Employees' Union* (2010).

5 In *Reference re Securities Act* (2011), the Supreme Court of Canada succinctly makes this point as follows, at para. 62: "In summary, notwithstanding the Court's promotion of cooperative and flexible federalism, the constitutional boundaries that underlie the division of powers must be respected. The 'dominant tide' of flexible federalism, however strong its pull may be, cannot sweep designated powers out to sea, nor erode the constitutional balance inherent in the Canadian federal state."

Challenges and Opportunities in
Health Care Federalism

5

Economic Trends and Challenges

DAVID HAARDT

In this chapter, I explain some of the economic trends and challenges in health care federalism in Canada. I argue that Canadian health care federalism exacerbates existing and creates new inequalities and inefficiencies. I want to start by giving a brief overview of the time trend of health care expenditure in Canada. In Canada, as in all industrial countries, health care expenditure as a percentage of GDP has been increasing for many decades. A useful approximation is that in Canada, the level of health care expenditure as a share of GDP increases by one percentage point each decade (see Table A.1 in CIHI 2010c, 111).

While it is clear that this rate of increase will have to level off eventually – few among us would want to live in a society that spends 50%, 60%, or 70% of its productivity to purchase health care services – the problem is that the levelling off will not happen any time soon, unless major reforms are implemented. This is demonstrated by the US example, where levelling off cannot be observed despite a markedly higher GDP share of health care expenditure than in any other country in the world.

Canada could therefore be described to have two problems in this regard. First, the level of health care expenditure as a share of GDP is high (especially as a share of provincial budgets, an important point to which I shall soon return) and second, the growth rate of health care expenditure as a share of GDP is high. What is driving these spending increases? According to my calculations from CIHI data (based on Table A.3.1.2 in CIHI 2010c, 120–1), the percentage of health care expenditure that is spent on hospitals decreased by 36% between 1975–77 and 2005–07. The percentage spent on prescription drugs, on the other hand, has increased by 116%. In this chapter I want to make the case that it is not by chance that prescription drugs have more than doubled their cost share: after all, Canada's health care federalism is particularly wasteful when it comes to prescription drugs, and the fact that more than 50% of the cost of prescription drugs is paid for by private health insurance and out of pocket makes cost containment particularly difficult (see Commission on the Future of Health Care in Canada 2002a).

Given the earlier observation that the percentage of GDP that we spend on health care is increasing by "only" one percentage point each decade, one may be tempted to say that the sustainability of the Canadian health care system is not endangered. However, such a view completely disregards the impact federalism has on the sustainability issue: even though health care spending remains a reasonable percentage of GDP, it has become a very high percentage of provincial budgets (ranging from 28% in Quebec to 39% in Ontario in 2009, see Statistics Canada 2009). This is even more so the case if one includes in the denominator only the provinces' own revenue, and only that part of it which does not have to be used for debt service, that is, to address past overspending. In the near future, health care expenditure will put a particular strain on provincial budgets in Atlantic Canada, which has unfavourable demographics (little immigration, a low fertility rate, and outmigration of young individuals to other provinces, exacerbating the impact of aging) and where health behaviours are poorer than in other regions of the country.

When analyzing the sustainability issue it is also important to take into account the effects of fiscal federalism in Canada. In 2004, Canada spent $131.6 billion on health care (Table A.1 in CIHI 2010c, 111). The 10-Year Plan to Strengthen Health Care of 2004 (appendix 2) provided a total of $41.3 billion of *new* federal health care money (CIHI 2010c, 10), which represented $4.1 billion per year. This implies an extra 3.1% in federal spending on the basis of the 2004 base level. Alternatively put, the total value of the accord over its 10-year duration is equal to 31% of 2004 health care expenditure. As CIHI (2010c, 10) notes, "[t]he increases in federal transfers were reflected primarily in increased expenditures by the provincial and territorial governments over the past several years." This is not surprising: if you put more money into the health care system it will be spent. (This is similar to the old adage that any additional hospital beds will be filled, regardless of medical necessity.) As predicted by the economic theory of federalism, provinces exercise less fiscal scrutiny if they spend federal transfers than if they spend money they had to raise themselves. This is also the result of a recent empirical study by Kneebone (2012, 19–20), who analyzed the effects of federal transfers on provincial health care spending during the last three decades.

The remainder of this chapter is structured as follows. In the following section I will give some insight into the causes of the worldwide trend toward health care regionalization. In the next one I will highlight some of the problems caused or reinforced by interprovincial competition in the Canadian health care system. The subsequent three sections will each focus on one of these problems: equity and efficiency, power and bargaining power, and economies of scale. The penultimate section analyzes what the Canadian constitution has to say about health care and the final one concludes the chapter.

EXPLAINING THE WORLDWIDE TREND
TOWARD REGIONALIZATION

Rico and Costa-Font (2005, 231) emphasize that government decentralization with respect to health care "rank[s] high on the political reform agenda ... worldwide." In a similar vein, Petretto (2000, 213) argues that there is "an international trend towards regionalisation" in health care policy, citing Canada, France, Italy, Spain, Sweden, and the United Kingdom (Petretto 2000, 216).

In my view, even though the economics literature has analyzed at length the possible consequences of such decentralization, too little attention has been paid to the causes of this phenomenon. Decentralization with respect to health care is, as far as I can tell, never a free and conscious choice taken because a decentralized health care system is seen as being better. It seems to me that wishes for decentralization always stem from problems with federal budgets – that is, federal governments want to give up responsibility for a subject matter with which they cannot come to grips. Health care could be seen, in a way, as a hot potato that nobody wants to finance because nobody can think of (or dares to implement) effective ways to battle ever-increasing health care costs. This is why federal governments worldwide try to shift health care costs to regional governments and patients, why regional governments try to shift health care costs to federal governments and patients, and why (but this is certainly the smallest of these three directions) patients try to shift health care costs to federal and regional governments. Patients are the least powerful in this triangle and hence will end up having to bear the majority of the cost increases. Moreover, because of the importance of the provincial and federal levels of government in financing Canadian health care, it is relatively easy for one of these levels of government to shift the blame to the other level of government, and voters end up not being able to determine which level of government is responsible for the cost increases. (The idea of determining responsibility here does not necessarily mean determining which level of government created the cost increases but rather determining which one could have avoided or mitigated them, but didn't.)

Donahue (1998, 403) argues that the "progressive cost-shifting [from the federal government to provincial governments has] ... transferred the incentive for cost-containment entirely to the provinces." I agree only in part, because federal transfers remain important for health care financing in Canada. The Fraser Institute, which is well known for its agenda to promote private health care, recently published yet another study asking for user fees to be introduced. As the authors of the study wrote in the *National Post*, "[u]nless provincial governments shift some of these costs onto medical consumers, they risk eventual bankruptcy" (Skinner and Rovere 2011). This is an important statement because it makes it clear that the purpose of the exercise is not to save money on health care – it is simply to shift costs to consumers. What the authors do not mention is that for the consumer it is irrelevant whether he or she will have to pay more money for health care in the form of higher taxes or in the form of user fees. Moreover, the authors ignore the fact that the bargaining power of the provinces will further decrease as their funding share falls, making it more and more difficult for the provinces to push for cost containment. Finally, the authors of course ignore the consequences of such a move for equality of access to health care. From the economic theory of federalism I discussed in chapter 2 it is clear that provinces are more limited than the federal government in their ability to raise taxes. Because of that, shifting more and more of the responsibility for health care to provinces increases the probability that out-of-pocket payments will be introduced. I suspect that this is the reason why some people push for a further regionalization of health care.

Despite the evidence for a worldwide trend toward health care regionalization, it is important to keep in mind that regionalization can take many forms and that it may be inappropriate to analyze all instances of health care regionalization as if they were identical. Before giving a few health care examples, I want to discuss briefly the findings of Buettner (2002), who shows that the degree of income smoothing in response to income shocks to states is approximately the same size in Germany as it is in the United States. This may at first seem surprising because most people would assume that federal transfers are less important in the United States than in Germany, and the reason for this phenomenon is actually very instructive: Buettner (2002, 200) shows that in Germany the effect of unemployment insurance and public pensions is larger than in the United States, whereas in the United States the effect of federal tax receipts and direct federal transfers is larger than in Germany. In other words, the two countries have a similar overall degree of federal income smoothing across states, but the mechanisms for doing so are very different. This shows that to be meaningful, a comparison of the degree of fiscal federalism across countries must examine as large a number of mechanisms as possible.

I would now like to return to differences with respect to health care regionalization across the globe. The OECD figures that Petretto (2000, 217) presents show that regionalization is highest in northern European and North American countries and lowest in central and southern European countries. However, I believe it is important to distinguish between northern European health care regionalization and North American regionalization: northern European health care regionalization is based on a unified national health care system and a unified national system of tax collection and redistribution that allows and indeed encourages local decision-making. North American health care regionalization, in contrast, emphasizes the role of regional tax collection and, in the case of Canada, regional health care systems, with a much lower uniformity across regions than in the northern European case. Interestingly, when Rico and Costa-Font (2005, 236) compare historical changes in North American and European (health care) federalism, they do not emphasize this important difference between the two continents (even though they do briefly mention that fiscal autonomy in Spain has been relatively limited until recently, see Rico and Costa-Font 2005, 237).

To wrap up this section I would like to remind the reader of what I have written in chapter 2, namely that fiscal pressures during the past ten years have led to health care re-centralization in many European countries (Saltman 2008, 105).[1]

PROBLEMS CAUSED OR REINFORCED
BY INTERPROVINCIAL COMPETITION

At first glance the solution to Canada's health care woes seems to be simple: raise provincial taxes to allow provinces to cover the rising share of the rising total cost of health care that they have to cover and implement effective cost-containment policies that limit abuse of the fee-for-service system. However, this simple solution is not being used because it would be dangerously ineffective. In this section I will cover the problems that are caused by and/or reinforced by competition between provinces. The first part of this section is devoted to competition for taxpayers (both individuals as well as firms) and the second part to competition for health professionals.

As explained in chapter 2, companies and high-income individuals would find it easy to relocate to a different province, and they might be motivated to do so if interprovincial disparities in taxation became sufficiently large. This is particularly dangerous because high-income and healthy individuals are much more mobile than unhealthy individuals. Those provinces that have the biggest need to raise more tax revenue for health care would therefore run the biggest risk of losing potential contributors and would be left with an even higher percentage of unhealthy individuals. Only provinces that have major competitive advantages, such as Ontario, which is Canada's financial and manufacturing centre and can offer the attractiveness of life in the Greater Toronto Area, would be able to raise provincial taxes without major repercussions. If provincial tax raises took place they would have to occur in slow rounds of small increases, which would take considerable time and might scare away investors and mobile high-income individuals. The alternative would be to raise federal transfers to provinces, but that would entail considerable inefficiencies because, as already mentioned, provincial governments exercise less fiscal caution if they spend somebody else's money than if they spend money they had to raise themselves.

Let me now move on to interprovincial competition for health professionals. Health economics is not only about who is paying how much and about who gets how much: it is, equally importantly, about the structure of payments and the corresponding incentive effects (compare, for example, a salary to a piece rate and think about the consequences of the two remuneration schemes on output and hence costs). We reward physicians (and many other health professionals) for providing as much care as possible rather than for providing the amount of care that fulfills what society thinks are acceptable cost-effectiveness criteria. (Perhaps even more importantly, we reward physicians for providing health care, not for improving the health of their patients.) Because of that, it is not surprising that the uptake of new procedures and drugs is high, even in areas where there is no evidence of clinical effectiveness, in areas where the evidence shows that there is no clinical marginal benefit, and in areas where the evidence shows that the marginal benefit is small compared with the marginal cost. This is important because new technologies, interpreted widely, are responsible for a large percentage of the increases in health care costs we experience – and the vast majority of new health technology is cost-increasing (see Rettig 1994). Similarly, because of these perverse incentives when rewarding physicians, it is not surprising that we see a lot of fee-code creep (see Chan et al. 1998 and Nassiri and Rochaix 2006).

All of these facts have been known for a long time and have been emphasized over and over again by most health care researchers. They have also been widely published in mass media (for a recent example, see Picard 2011). However, policy-makers do not act on this knowledge. Incentive effects are often underestimated and/or misunderstood, sometimes even denied. Kirby (2002, 77), for instance, in his report, recognizes the problems of the fee-for-service system for physicians but, bizarrely, asks for this system to be introduced for hospitals because it would "[reduce] cost escalation ... in the long run" (see Kirby 2002, 43). These incentive effects are important because of their link to health care federalism: because provinces compete for health professionals, isolated reforms in one or two provinces would always be inefficient since health professionals could easily sort into the payment system that is most profitable for them. Health professionals with high effort and/or high patient frequency would sort into a fee-for-service system whereas health professionals with low effort and/or low patient frequency would sort into a salary system. Therefore, a fundamental reform of the payment system that actually has the desired effects would have to be a coordinated national effort rather than something that a single province does on its own.

EQUITY AND EFFICIENCY
IN THE CANADIAN HEALTH CARE SYSTEM

It is quite clear that health care federalism is at odds with equity considerations. In a way the issue reminds me of the old question of whether health care is a consumption good or medical necessity. If health care is indeed a consumption good then regional customization is important; if, on the other hand, health care is a medical necessity then regional customization is not important, and equity across the country is important. When the Canada Health Act was adopted in 1984 its intent was to list health care services that should be available to every Canadian. In other words, it provided parameters within which provinces can operate their health care systems. The reality has been that provinces have made quite different health care decisions and have interpreted quite differently what "medically necessary" means. This is perhaps not surprising given that provinces vary not only by voter preferences and demographics but also by their fiscal environment. Nova Scotia, for example, can be characterized as a province with high income taxes, a high sales tax, high aging, and high health care expenditures. It is also characterized by high rates of adverse health behaviours, such as smoking, drinking, and inactivity. (Most of that is true of Atlantic Canada as a whole.) Because of that, Nova Scotia and Atlantic Canada as a whole are facing double pressure: health care demand pressure because of their adverse demographics and health behaviours *and* fiscal pressure because of their adverse economic development. As a result, Atlantic Canada will have to take much harsher steps in health care reform than much of the rest of Canada. This, in turn, will exacerbate existing health care inequalities across provinces, leading to further deviations from the Canada Health Act.

The point I want to make here is the following: health care federalism has the lowest economic costs in societies in which it is politically the least necessary, that is, in countries in which preferences are very homogeneous across their geographical units. Put more dramatically, health care federalism makes the most economic sense in situations in which people will not want it, and, conversely, it is very expensive to maintain health care federalism in situations in which people want it. Although this is true of federalism in general, it is particularly true of health care federalism, because health professionals are more mobile than the average person. In this context it is important to note that general federal transfers tend to reward bad fiscal decision-making by provinces, which gives them very poor incentives. It would be more efficient to establish interprovincial health transfers that adjust for differences in demographics and make sure that provinces have to pay for any remaining excess cost that has been caused by poor provincial decision-making.

Related to this topic, the revenue sharing literature within the fiscal interest literature is important for Canadian health care federalism (see Weingast 2005, 158). Not surprisingly, regional governments will oversupply public goods if they only have to bear part of the cost themselves. This is exactly the case with federal health care transfers in Canada: they foster excessive health care spending because they give provinces the wrong fiscal incentives. Rodden (2002) showed that governments are smaller in federal systems in which regional governments raise their own taxes. This effect is mitigating excessive health care spending in the Canadian example (see Weingast 2005, 159).

Which steps should be taken if one takes the federal health care system that exists in Canada as given and aims to increase its efficiency? The economic literature has two important suggestions: first, harden the provincial budget constraints, and second, earmark funds. When it comes to health care federalism in Canada, it is important to understand the importance of soft budget constraints. What economists mean by that is a situation in which subnational governments know that they do not have to be fiscally prudent because they will be bailed out by the federal government if they ever face a risk of default. In Canada such a risk may seem very remote but, given health care and aging-induced budget problems in provinces such as New Brunswick, we should at least consider them.

The theory of soft budget constraints can also be used in a much less dramatic context: provinces can use the "threat" of bankruptcy to extract higher federal transfers. It is in this form that understanding soft budget constraints is crucial for Canadian health care policymakers. I would argue that soft budget constraints, in the classic bankruptcy variant as well as in the milder transfer variant, are an inherent feature of federal countries: residents of a region will always expect the federal government to help with exploding health care costs whereas residents of a centralized country have no higher level of government from which to expect a bailout. (An exception to this is the European Union, which is currently struggling considerably with the role of soft budget constraints and their impact on fiscal policy, especially in southern Europe.) This effect will lead to excessive health care spending in a situation in which health care is a provincial subject matter compared with a scenario in which health care is a federal subject matter.

Petretto (2000, 217) argues that regionalization is "desirable" from an efficiency point of view if there is "an increase in financial responsibility, i.e. if a system of hard budget constraints prevails across the regions." However, this is somewhat misleading, since a system of hard budget constraints across regions would merely restore the same level of efficiency as under a centralized system. Therefore, I would argue that such a system of hard budget constraints is a *necessary* condition for efficiency but certainly not a *sufficient* condition for efficiency.

Qian and Roland (1998) use the case of China to investigate when regional governments will receive a bailout and when they will not. Their model has a three-level hierarchy with a federal government, regional governments that compete with each other for mobile factors (such as capital and taxpayers), and enterprises that compete for subsidies. Qian and Roland (1998, 1144) show an interesting "competition effect": "competition among local governments in attracting capital to their region ... increases the opportunity cost of subsidizing inefficient enterprises, which in turn reduces the incentives for bailouts." However, it is important to keep in mind that this result cannot be transferred to the health care context: regional governments can individually assess the productivity of companies and individually set subsidy levels, whereas with respect to health care consumers, that is, the population of the region, such individual health and premium assessments would be deemed unethical. This would be exactly what we want to avoid with public health care. They also show another result that is very important for the health care context: transfers from the federal government to regional governments will harden the budget constraint, as long as they are earmarked. However, they do not discuss the case in which these transfers are not earmarked, which would be particularly important in the Canadian context: the many requests by provincial governments in Canada to have less control by the federal government over how they spend their federal (health care) transfers could be dangerous because they might soften the budget constraint.

BARGAINING POWER
IN THE CANADIAN HEALTH CARE SYSTEM

I have just discussed some of the problems caused or reinforced by interprovincial competition. However, power and bargaining power are important for health care policy even beyond this mobility threat. In the health care debate, and the health care reform debate, professional associations have a very large impact whereas patients and taxpayers have little or no voice. Again, this is important because of its link to federalism: professional associations have understood very well the importance of speaking with a unified nationwide voice, to prevent provinces from enacting cost-containing policies (because even enacting such policies in a single province could trigger a domino effect). Health professionals have managed very well to speak with a unified voice and hence maintain or even strengthen their bargaining power whereas patient and taxpayer voices are fragmented and hence powerless.

Rico and Costa-Font (2005) examine the importance of path dependency in health care decentralization using the Spanish example, using a power and politics related conceptualization of path dependency rather than a traditional institutional conceptualization (Rico and Costa-Font 2005, 232). They argue that traditional path dependency theory neglects behavioural and causal mechanisms (Rico and Costa-Font 2005, 234; see 234–6 for a discussion of how power, and concentration of power, can create path dependency). They emphasize the power of physicians, unions (as they relate to health care providers), insurance companies, and pharmaceutical companies (Rico and Costa-Font 2005, 239). The authors argue that private health care providers have seen substantial cutbacks in Spain because of their much lower degree of organization than public health care providers and hence much lower political power (Rico and Costa-Font 2005, 248).

ECONOMIES OF SCALE
IN THE CANADIAN HEALTH CARE SYSTEM

The most recent CIHI (2010c: 33) forecast says that Canada spent 11.7% of its GDP on health care in 2010. However, it is important to recognize that this percentage varied dramatically across the country: it was only 8.2% in Alberta yet 17.4% in PEI, 16.1% in Nova Scotia, and 15.9% in New Brunswick. It is important to know that this is not an artifact of the currently very high GDP in Alberta; rather, it has been a longstanding phenomenon. I think it would be very difficult to find somebody who thinks that you get twice as much or twice as good health care in the Maritimes versus in Alberta. Clearly there is something we can learn from Alberta. More generally, the provinces with the highest health care spending are the ones with a low population (hence low economies of scale) and a high population density (hence most exposed to public pressures to expand coverage); see Haardt (2012) for an analysis of these two factors.

Economists have a very precise definition of what economies of scale are, and when they occur. Think about a scenario in which you multiply *all* inputs to a production process by x. For the following blood clinic example, assume that $x = 2$. Therefore, assume that we multiply the number of receptionists, the number of nurses, the number of desks, and the amount of space in a blood clinic by 2. By how much will output by multiplied? If output is multiplied by more than 2, we have economies of scale. If, on the other hand, output is multiplied by less than 2, we have what economists call economies of scope. In other words, the term *economies of scale* is used to describe a production process in which size allows you to be more efficient, that is, to increase production more than proportionately when increasing all inputs. (The term *economies of scope*, on the other hand, is used to describe a production process in which smallness allows you to be more efficient.)

International comparisons of industrial countries show that the lowest health care prices and the lowest health care expenditure can be observed in policy environments that are monolithic and that allow for only a small role of private health care (see Davis et al. 2010). (By private health care I here mean health care that is paid for using private health insurance or out of pocket – there is a lot of private health care in the Canadian and every other health care system in the world in the sense that physicians and many other health professionals are self-employed businessmen and businesswomen.)

This is important because of its link to federalism: both Canadians as well as observers elsewhere often talk about "Canadian medicare," about Canada's national health insurance system, or about Canada's single-payer system. There is, however, no such system – we have at least fourteen single-payer systems (one for each province, one for each territory, and a federal one for Aboriginal men and women, for federal inmates, and for members of the Canadian Armed Forces). Because of that, there are many advantages of single-payer systems from which we are not able to benefit. This is true because of factors such as interprovincial competition for health care professionals and a lack of coordination in negotiations with pharmaceutical companies.

Corporations carry out mergers and acquisitions all the time, because economies of scale are so pervasive in most of today's production processes. They also carry out mergers and acquisitions because of the ensuing market power that allows them to procure less expensively and to sell more expensively. Contrary to the situation for corporations, public entities are exposed to the forces of competition and fiscal pressures only very remotely, if at all. Because of that, mergers and acquisitions, which have been contributing so much to the success of corporations, have been virtually absent from public entities. There are many opportunities for economies of scale in the Canadian health care system that we do not make use of – we waste resources because we do not coordinate policy.

I would like to note two things here: first, this is of course not limited to health care. The same phenomenon can be observed in public administration overall. Second, private health care is not the solution. Private health care would lead to mergers and acquisitions, but to the disadvantage of patients. It is well documented that, because of regional markets, the importance of expertise and licensure, and the very low price elasticity of demand for health care goods and services, health care does not lend itself to a competitive market (for a detailed exposition, see Rice 2009).

I will give a few examples. First, most health districts across Canada have their own drugs and therapeutics committees. After reviewing the same literature, each of these committees makes (somewhat) different decisions on which drugs and therapeutics to cover under which circumstances. Is there really a reason why such decisions on drugs and therapeutics should be different in each health district? Or would not a single such committee for all of Canada be sufficient? Second, Ontario has put a lot of thought and effort into the Ontario Health Technology Advisory Committee. There is also the Canadian Agency for Drugs and Technologies in Health. Many small-scale initiatives also serve the same function. Again, using the same literature, all of these agencies and committees make (somewhat) different decisions about which health technologies to cover under which circumstances. Is there really a reason why these decisions should be different in every province? Third, each province has its own drug formulary. Again, each of these drug formularies is (somewhat) different but has been developed on the basis of the same literature. Is there a reason why different drugs should be covered in province A than in province B? Furthermore, do these differences not violate the spirit of the Canada Health Act?

I would like to argue that all of these committees and administrative bodies use the same evidence to make their decisions and tend to arrive at similar (but slightly different) decisions. Their existence is extremely important, but their multiplicity is extremely wasteful.

Despite all this, there have been some (modest) attempts to reduce bureaucratic overhead. Alberta and New Brunswick recently reduced the number of health regions. It is important to recognize that, despite the problems that occurred when doing so, this is a step in the right direction. These problems should be seen as a reason to make refinements to these reforms rather than questioning them altogether.

HEALTH CARE IN THE CANADIAN CONSTITUTION

Interestingly, the Canadian constitution does not mention "health" with a single word. The only mentions directly related to health care are the following: "Quarantine and the Establishment and Maintenance of Marine Hospitals" (Powers of the Parliament; see Department of Justice no date, 22) and "The Establishment, Maintenance, and Management of Hospitals, Asylums, Charities, and Eleemosynary Institutions in and for the Province, other than Marine Hospitals" (Exclusive Powers of Provincial Legislatures; see Department of Justice no date, 25). This, together with the fact that provinces started public health care plans, together with the interpretation that health care is a matter "of a merely local or private Nature in the Province" (see Department of Justice no date, 25; an interpretation that would be extremely difficult to maintain in today's interconnected world), has led to the fact that today's courts agree that health care is under a provincial jurisdiction. In principle, it would be hence possible, even though unfortunately very unlikely, that the courts might one day realize that the past assumption that health care is "merely local or private" is no longer appropriate in modern Canada.

In light of this it is particularly fascinating that the preamble to the Canada Health Act states "that it is not the intention of the Government of Canada that any of the powers, rights, privileges or authorities vested in Canada or the provinces under the provisions of the Constitution Act, 1867, or any amendments thereto, or otherwise, be by reason of this Act abrogated or derogated from or in any way impaired" (Department of Justice 2011, 1) – in other words, the federal government emphasized that it did not want to take away any powers from the provinces that they only had because they had assumed them over time.

So what has caused the remarkable stability of an interpretation of the constitution that is certainly debatable? From an economist's point of view (as Lindner and Rittberger [2003] argue), switching costs may be so high that suboptimal constitutional arrangements prevail even though their shortcomings are well known. Weingast (2005, 149), in his survey in the *Handbook of New Institutional Economics*, posits that economists have usually focused on the economic performance (or efficiency) of federalism, and he attempts to add to this an analysis of the political performance and stability of federal systems. He argues that the stability of federal systems is endangered from both sides of the arrangement, from federal governments wanting to expand their power and from regional governments wanting to free ride (Weingast 2005, 149). Weingast's (2005, 150) goal is to bring the three literatures together and hence to contribute to the development of "a more complete theory of federal performance." The final part of Weingast's (2005) survey focuses on endogenous federalism. What is meant by that expression is that federalism cannot be taken as given; rather, there have to be mechanisms in place that make federalism emerge, and then make it live on (see Weingast 2005, 160). As Weingast (2005, 161) explains, the federal government "must have sufficient power to prevent the states from free-riding; yet not be so powerful as to be able to overawe the states." It is questionable whether, in the case of Canada, the federal government has sufficient power to mitigate the negative effects of federalism and whether it has exerted its existing powers sufficiently.

CONCLUSION

Continuing with the constitutional train of thought, it has always struck me as interesting that in the US health care reform literature a national health care system is often seen as an almost mythical unattainable ideal – something that would be optimal but that cannot be reached because of political and legal obstacles. Bobinski (1990, 340), for instance, concludes her article by saying that a national system with universal coverage would be "[t]he most obvious solution" but argues that it is politically unlikely (Bobinski 1990, 257, 274, 340). Similarly, Donahue (1998, 385) begins his article by arguing that any health care reform will have to be incremental in the United States because of the federal structure of the country. This is a point that many researchers make, although the consequences of this are only rarely discussed explicitly: federalism leads to substantial slowdowns in policy-making and, more specifically, in health care reform.

I think it is important to keep in mind that Canadian federalism came into being under very different circumstances: there was much less communication between provinces at the time, economic and social links were much weaker than they are today, and lifestyles varied much more across the country than they do today. In other words, Canadian federalism was a nineteenth-century answer to a nineteenth-century problem, but it may not be appropriate in a twenty-first-century situation unless major reforms are carried out. So what is the rationale for health care federalism? Is it really nothing more than a political artifact that we inherited from how Canada came into being? One argument that appears repeatedly is that the provinces are different from each other and that people in, say, Ontario have different health care needs than people in, say, Saskatchewan, for instance when it comes to service delivery. This is then used as a justification for health care federalism, as a justification to leave the status quo untouched.

But is that really true? Continuing with the example of service delivery, I would argue that people living in urban Ontario and urban Saskatchewan have quite similar needs, and likewise people living in rural Ontario and rural Saskatchewan have quite similar needs. I would argue that the real divide is urban/rural, not provincial. This urban/rural divide can only be addressed very indirectly by provincial governments, each of which has a given urban/rural split of its population. Another argument that is sometimes brought forward is that federalism has the advantage that it brings decisions closer to people. With a sensitive subject such as health care, this can actually cause problems: decision-making will be more emotional and less rational, and it is more difficult to focus on the facts, such as on clinical effectiveness and cost-effectiveness.

It would be possible to transfer the entire responsibility of health care, including raising funds, to the provinces. This would encourage efficiency because provinces would face the full extra cost of cost increases in health care, hardening their budget constraint. However, this would also be very costly in terms of the loss of even more of the potential economies of scale and would probably overburden provincial budgets because of provinces' reluctance to raise provincial taxes. Provinces would probably start to shift costs to patients. Because of these considerations, the only logical solution is to increase the proportion of federal funding *and* the proportion of federal decision-making (which is currently miniscule, except in areas such as public health). This would solve the incentive problem by ensuring that the decision-maker is fully responsible for raising funds, and it would enable Canada to capitalize on the huge potential for economies of scale in health care policy.

NOTE

1 Interestingly, northern Europe seems to be different again from the rest of the (sub-)continent: in Denmark, Finland, Norway, Sweden, and the United Kingdom, the focus has been on consolidation, that is, on reducing the number of regional players, whereas in Germany, Ireland, the Netherlands, and Poland, there have been instances of actual (re-)centralization (see Saltman 2008, 104–5).

6

Governance Challenges
in Implementing Needs-Based
Health Human Resources Planning

GAIL TOMBLIN MURPHY

INTRODUCTION

The primary objective of this chapter is to analyze the various challenges associated with the planning for health services and the health workforce in Canada's federal-provincial-territorial system using a needs-based model. The models that will be introduced are different from previous demand-based models in that they do not view environmental factors as constant, separate, and independent forces. The needs-based models are thus possibly better suited than the status quo models for addressing both current and future challenges facing the Canadian health system.

THE ROLES OF THE FEDERAL AND JURISDICTIONAL GOVERNMENTS IN CANADIAN HEALTH HUMAN RESOURCES PLANNING

It is clear that planning for health systems and the health workforce is a challenge in Canada because of the structure of the federal government and the provincial and territorial governments. As indicated in earlier chapters, according to the Canadian constitution and its interpretation by the courts, health care falls primarily under provincial jurisdiction and governance. Governance is the process whereby societies or organizations (including governments) interact to achieve and be accountable for common goals while operating in a complex world. Planning appropriately for health human resources (HHR) involves many key stakeholders, including governments, employers, academia, research organizations, non-governmental agencies, citizens, and policy-makers. The process of governance applies to multiple contexts – national, local, societal, institutional, and global.

The Canada Health Act is the key federal mechanism for governance and specifies the conditions and criteria to which provinces and territories must conform to receive federal transfer payments under the Canada Health Transfer (CHT). Although the Canada Health Act deals only with how the system is financed, it acts as a lever to ensure relative consistency of coverage across the country. Overall, ministries responsible for health set the infrastructure in which the health workforce will practise as well as the legislation and regulations that govern how health care providers can practise within a jurisdiction.

Across Canada, the provincial and territorial ministries responsible for health often delegate the management and delivery of health care services to local/regional health delivery systems. The legal parameters that define the responsibilities of the local/regional health delivery systems are set by the province or territory and are narrower in scope than those of the provincial and territorial ministries of health. The primary responsibilities of such local/regional health delivery systems are to manage health services and use available resources to address population health needs. This includes identifying specific population health needs, planning appropriate programs and services, ensuring that programs and services are properly funded and managed, and meeting performance objectives (Elson 2006; Tomblin Murphy and O'Brien-Pallas 2006).

The ministries responsible for health in the provinces and territories have general authority for ensuring the provision of essential and appropriate health services and establishing strategic directions and priorities through developing legislation, regulations, standards, policies, and directives to support strategic directions. Ministries do this through planning for and establishing funding models and levels of funding for the health system to support regional/local health delivery systems. They are also responsible for monitoring and reporting on the performance of the health system and the health of provincial or territorial residents.

Although the priorities of the various ministries of health change over time, there are recurring commonalities. Overall, the ministries aim to support their residents to achieve their best possible health and well-being, ensure residents have access to high-quality care services where and when needed, and support improved productivity and efficiency in the delivery of health services to ensure the sustainability of the publicly funded health care system.

The 1990s was a time of significant crisis and pressure for "big bang" health reforms. Despite this, a number of problems were not solved nor was there a clear consensus across countries or knowledge networks on the merits of new public management, and there were calls for new types of partnerships, privatization, and devolution of power. Many factors resulted in pressure to find new ways to work together, cooperate, define problems, and improve outcomes. In an era of a service-based, global economy, when nurses, physicians, and other health professionals are essential human resources, there is much pressure to not work at cross purposes and to find ways to collaborate rather than compete.

Governments have recognized that the risks associated with the status quo approach to health system and health workforce planning have the potential to perpetrate both political risk and financial costs. This limits each jurisdiction's ability to develop effective sustainable health delivery systems and to engage the workforce to support those systems and to meet the needs of Canadians. There is a growing awareness that health service planning, and HHR planning, should be more responsive to the changing needs of the population. It is encouraging that as part of the 10-Year Plan to Strengthen Health Care (appendix 2), signed by the first ministers in September 2004, provinces and territories have been working collaboratively on planning for health services and the health workforce required to deliver those services.

Subsequently, in 2005 the Federal/Provincial/Territorial Advisory Committee on Health Delivery and Human Resources (ACHDHR), in consultation with all jurisdictions and other stakeholders, developed *A Framework for Pan-Canadian Health Human Resources Planning* (ACHDHR 2007) to set out a vision, goals, and an action plan for collaborative planning. The effort has enhanced the evidence and the planning tools used to inform planning, has led to more meaningful partnerships across jurisdictions and ministries, has influenced changes in workplace initiatives, and has garnered political and policy support. This pan-Canadian framework will be discussed in greater detail later, as will the changing role of federalism in health care.

PLANNING FOR HEALTH SYSTEMS AND THE HEALTH WORKFORCE IN CANADA

Health systems have been organized on the basis of historical levels of service provision and have not emphasized systematic responses to the health needs of populations. There is a growing awareness, however, that health service planning, and therefore HHR planning, should be responsive to the changing needs of the population. People are any health care system's greatest asset and greatest cost (ACHDHR 2007). The health care industry accounts for more than $200 billion worth of spending nationally (CIHI 2012a) and 60–80 cents of every dollar of this sum goes toward health professionals: the fraction of every dollar spent on health professionals varies by jurisdiction (ACHDHR 2007). Given the immense complexity and scope of health care systems and the incompleteness of the available information relating not only to current delivery but also to future estimating, gaps in HHR are inevitable in every jurisdiction.

The difficulty is that governments, academic institutions, organizational and professional policies, labour market mobility, and public institutions are not flexible enough to adapt to the changing needs of people and the constantly changing health care system. Moreover, the consequences of misallocations will only be further amplified in the future as financial challenges increase, the workload of the health care system increases because of demographic changes and changes in levels of health, the health care workforce is diminished and further strained because of the wave of expected retirements and the lack of new workers to replace the retirees, and risks of health crises such as pandemics become greater. Given that the challenges posed by these needs are well established and that it is in the provinces' best interests to collectively address these challenges, why don't we have mature, effective policy universally in place to meet said challenges?

Challenges

Within each Canadian jurisdiction, HHR planning is shared to varying degrees between the province or territory and a number of other stakeholders, including health sector organizations, unions, professional associations, regulatory bodies, research institutes, Aboriginal groups, and federal health partners. The level of participation by the various stakeholders in such efforts is largely at the discretion of the province or territory in question. The difficulty is that although there are benefits to collaboration, obstacles and costs can also stem from such an effort.

Historically, planning approaches have been hampered as each province and territory in Canada has worked independently to design its own service system, develop service delivery models, and plan its own HHR plan. This has often resulted in competition between jurisdictions for limited HHR. This is understandable given that decisions made by one jurisdiction can have unintended impacts on other jurisdictions. For example, a change in the design of one jurisdiction's health care system could have a negative impact on the availability of certain health care providers for other jurisdictions. The risks are greater in the current reform environment where unilateral action by any one jurisdiction with a more attractive labour strategy could undermine system stability and affect other jurisdictions' ability to deliver on health commitments (e.g., reducing waiting times).

This is illustrated wherein an ACHDHR policy to attract foreign-credentialed medical professionals detracts from the ability of other nations to meet their health care goals and needs. Domestically and in a provincial scope, the availability of better health information to provinces that are more able to attract external talent on the basis of shifting economic strength will countervail against the best efforts by the same partners being collaborated with. Simply stated, then, challenges result from needs-based pan-Canadian planning as jurisdictions will have competing demands, and that collaboration can sometimes operate as a zero-sum game. While many stakeholders agree that there are advantages to taking a more collaborative approach to some aspects of planning, questions regarding provincial and pan-Canadian challenges to implementation arise:

- How can Canada enhance its capacity for collaborative HHR planning while still ensuring that each jurisdiction has the flexibility to make its own system planning decisions?
- How will jurisdictions determine which activities and responsibilities are shared and which are more appropriately pursued at the provincial, territorial, regional, or federal level?

- How can the system avoid creating unnecessary structure that might limit rather than enhance HHR planning capacity?
- How will collaborative HHR planning link with other provincial, territorial, regional, and federal HHR initiatives currently underway?
- How will collaborative pan-Canadian efforts involve other key players?

As mentioned earlier, the need for collaboration and coordination around HHR planning is not limited only to governments. Closer links among all players could ensure that the number, skills, and mix of providers reflect the health needs of the population and the needs of the health system. Allocating meaningful roles for stakeholders, however, usually requires some diffusion of decision-making power, and this is a difficult step to take for officials and institutions that are nonetheless held accountable for whatever decisions are made. Conversely, although each jurisdiction will continue to be responsible to plan for both health and education, greater exposure to inefficiency and risk will persist if planning is carried out in isolation. However, as the economy has faced a downturn, it appears that Canadian jurisdictions are defaulting to the status quo to continue planning in silos.

Aside from crises, collaboration can be stalled for reasons that include the following: a lack of high-quality, consistent data on all major health disciplines; a lack of national data standards, including common definitions and a common approach to collecting data; inconsistent information on HHR productivity, workload, utilization, demand, and efficacy; inadequate information about educational facilities and their capacity; inadequate capacity to assess health needs, model delivery systems, and forecast the demand for HHR; inadequate capacity to analyze HHR data and translate it into useful knowledge; and inadequate funding for ongoing data and modelling initiatives.

Paradigm Shifts and Excursions in Modelling

Planning for services to meet the health care needs of the public cannot be based solely on historical levels of workforce supply. Instead, planning systems must be employed that explicitly incorporate dynamic changes in the prevalence of risks and health conditions, the best practice evidence-based responses to these risks and conditions, and flexible intersectoral approaches for the production and delivery of these responses. To date, this sort of planning as a paradigm shift has not been common in Canada; for instance, little consideration has traditionally been given to changes in population health (Birch et al. 2003; Tomblin Murphy et al. 2007c), although this has been shown to change over time (see, for example, Birch et al. 1994; Tomblin Murphy et al. 2009c).

Recent advances in health workforce planning have included the development of an analytical model in which requirements for human resources are derived from the service mixes and configurations that decision-makers plan to provide based directly on health conditions within populations independent of current levels of service use. This needs-based approach to human resources planning has been employed to inform health workforce planning at a variety of levels, including the national, provincial, and regional levels. Such an approach has not been limited to a particular jurisdiction; it has been applied in Nova Scotia (Tomblin Murphy et al. 2007a, 2007b, 2008), Ontario (Tomblin Murphy et al. 2009a), the four Atlantic provinces (Birch et al. 2005), Jamaica, and Brazil (Tomblin Murphy et al. 2010b). In addition, a similar approach was used in the recent report on physician planning in Ontario (Singh et al. 2010) and by researchers in Australia (e.g., Segal et al. 2008) who have also begun implementing needs-based approaches to HHR planning. By basing human resource planning on the mix of services to be delivered to meet population needs, the approach can be generalized to intersectoral planning that extends beyond health care to incorporate contributions from the education, justice, workplace, and social services sectors to the prevention of illness and the production and restoration of well-being.

A number of HHR model frameworks and tools have been made available by decision-makers. Such models are not direct substitutes for this type of analysis but are rather mutually supportive in nature and to be used in different circumstances for different purposes. The two models that I discuss here are what are commonly called the pan-Canadian framework and the simulation model (Tomblin Murphy et al. 2009d). The pan-Canadian framework is a systems-based framework for analyzing the inputs and outputs of health and human resources and the factors that influence planning, whereas the analytical framework (Birch et al. 2007) and simulation model are to be

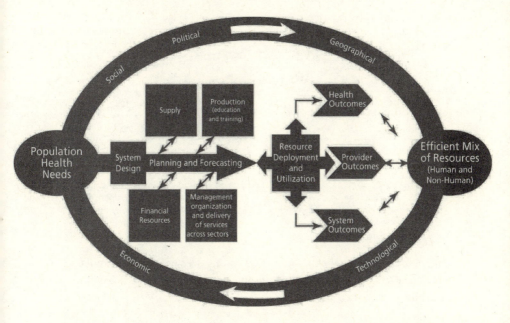

Figure 6.1   The Health System and Health Human Resources Conceptual
Framework. Adapted from O'Brien-Pallas et al. (2001a, 2001b, 2005) and
O'Brien-Pallas and Baumann (2000).

used to determine a quantitative gap and outline the policy options
that can be used to mitigate the gap in the future.

The application of the framework and the simulation model uses
an interdisciplinary, comparative jurisdictional, and policy-fields perspective. Case study examination and allusions to work domestically
and internationally will be used as a backdrop to discuss the governance challenges associated in planning for health systems and the
health workforce.

The Health System and Health Human Resources Conceptual Framework (O'Brien-Pallas et al. 2005) was originally developed to guide HHR
planning (figure 6.1). Colloquially known as the pan-Canadian framework, it demonstrates that HHR planning takes place within the context
of social, political, geographical, technological, and economic factors.
The model differentiates itself from alternative models in its recognition that such factors cannot be understood as constant, separate, and
independent forces, and thus it has appropriately been adopted as the

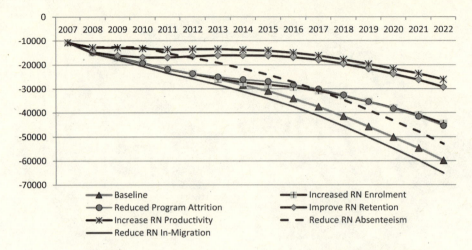

Figure 6.2   Individual effects of various policy scenarios on the simulated gap in the supply of registered nurses in Canada. Adapted from Tomblin Murphy et al. (2012).

guiding framework for HHR planning by Canada's Advisory Committee on Health Delivery and Human Resources (2005). The framework is circuitous in that these factors are to be considered to be in a state of flux, affecting the input factors as well as the output factors.

Applying the Needs-Based Approach

It is one thing to have a model; it is another thing to apply it. A nationwide 2011 analysis by Tomblin Murphy et al. (2012) hypothesized varying degrees of registered nurse shortages in future on the basis of a number of factors (figure 6.2). The policy options or solutions were described as being multifaceted, and this is appropriate given that the approaches prescribed included registered nurse retention, in-migration, enrolment, productivity, program attrition, and absenteeism. Each of these factors was compared against a baseline. The end result is an effective communication tool for stakeholders that will aid in assessing a government's or an organization's circumstances so that it can make better policy decisions in serving its populations.

Such an analysis is at the heart of the earlier proposed thinking shift that must occur within health and human resource planning. It is the movement toward a broader perspective to enact system changes that do not simply account for the sheer number of employees but instead consider the factors that are influencing the health needs of people and the system, and the supply of providers and the requirements for health care. In this way the important statement that is made in health system and HHR planning is as follows: what providers are required to deliver services depends on the changing health needs of people, the context in which care is being delivered, and the team delivering care.

Similarly, an earlier analysis was undertaken in 2009 by the same authors when examining shortages of registered nurses in Nova Scotia. This demonstrates that such efforts are successfully replicable under different circumstances ranging from ones involving a national scope and resources down to ones involving smaller jurisdictions. Poignantly, effective needs-based HHR planning can be conducted in resource-poor areas as minimal technological barriers exist to conducting such modelling, as will be discussed below.

The conceptual framework provides the foundation for an analytical model (Birch et al. 2007) upon which simulations are based and recommendations generated. It consists of two broad elements: provider supply and provider requirements. Provider supply relates to the number of providers available to deliver services to the population whereas provider requirements relates to the number of providers required to meet the health care needs of the population. These issues, addressed through this model, provide the foundation for the simulations to be undertaken. The subsequent model addresses these issues particularly well.

The Simulation Model

The second framework for analysis, the simulation model (figure 6.3), is intended as a communication tool to enable the participating parties to find common solutions to address their workforce gaps. Building on the analytical model, the simulation modelling approach (Kephart et al. 2005; Tomblin Murphy et al. 2009d) has been used to operationalize the analytical model in estimating both future human resources requirements for individual provider groups and future human resources supply from these groups. In the Canadian context, this would be between federal, provincial, and territorial bodies; this will be discussed in greater detail later. From such an analysis, evidence can be used and inputted to assess the gap between the requirements for and the supply of workers and assemble a range of policy options as before with the registered nurse gap analyses.

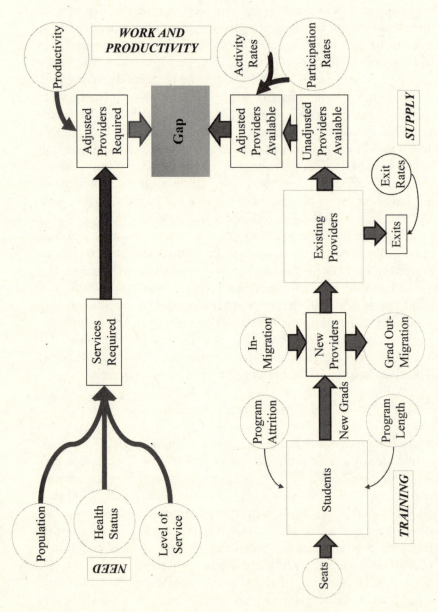

Figure 6.3   The simulation model (Tomblin Murphy et al. 2012).

Functionally, the model can be broken down into its two halves, one of which concerns the supply side and the other half the requirement side. The requirement side of the equation begins with examining the population, health status, and the number and type of services to serve the various health profiles to arrive at an estimate of the specific services required. The number of qualified providers currently employed, the average time taken for a given task, and the services that providers are able to deliver in a given unit of time are assessed to determine the overall number of full-time equivalents required to fulfill the health care need. The supply side is much the same. It takes account not only of the rates at which workforces become available in light of factors such as program length, attrition rates, number of seats, and net-migration rates but also of overall activity and participation rates.

Such gap analyses for health care professionals as a resource are not limited to the present but can also be applied retroactively or as an estimation tool in forward-looking studies.[1] Although originally designed to guide planning for professions within the health sector, like the conceptual and analytical frameworks, this simulation modelling approach can be adapted to identify gaps in other sectors such as education and justice. The crossover is acceptable and logical in such circumstances given that these are other provider groups delivering human services that arise from needs of the population as opposed to wants of individuals. This perhaps comes as no surprise given that the tools to perform such modelling are remarkably accessible on their own and offer no barriers to such use, as they run on any Windows-based personal computer and require only Microsoft Excel and free software.[2]

As mentioned, the simulation model can be applied to a variety of short-, medium-, and long-term planning horizons (e.g., Kephart et al. 2005; Tomblin Murphy et al. 2009a, 2009b) by using either external benchmarks for need indicators or fitting appropriate biostatistical models to existing data and identifying potential scenarios for projections into the future. Models have been applied at a variety of jurisdictional levels, including nationally, provincially, and regionally. This work has been performed both within Canada and in other countries. The simulation model incorporates interdependencies of various providers within and across sectors. For example, hospital discharge could be delayed as a result of a shortage of health workers, thus reducing the productivity of physicians, whereas a shortage of psychiatrists could ultimately result in an increased requirement for corrections officers.

Applications of the Framework and Models: Ongoing Progress

Two prominent case studies exhibiting innovative service delivery and planning are discussed below. One highlights a provincial undertaking and the other efforts by a regional health authority. The former is that of the Model of Care Initiative in Nova Scotia (MOCINS) and the latter that of the Care Delivery Model Redesign (CDMR) as undertaken by the Vancouver Island Health Authority (VIHA). MOCINS, launched in 2008, is a partnership between the Nova Scotia Department of Health and Wellness, the nine district health authorities, and the Izaak Walton Killam Health Centre. MOCINS uses a collaborative care model developed by a provincial interprofessional design team to address the growing HHR challenge in Nova Scotia and to achieve health system sustainability. MOCINS' mandate was "to design, implement and evaluate a viable provincial model of care for acute care inpatient services that was patient centered, high quality, safe, and cost effective" (Tomblin Murphy et al. 2010a, 12).

Facing similar challenges to the ones in Nova Scotia, VIHA undertook the CDMR initiative as a necessary effort to combat the trends they faced. More specifically, the challenges outlined within VIHA included "an aging workforce and scarcity of health professionals, coupled with an increasing demand for health services" (VIHA 2009). The CDMR approach at VIHA, developed in 2007, focuses on changing the way health care providers work together to deliver care so that they become more responsive to patient needs. This approach was developed largely in response to an observational study undertaken at VIHA that revealed the need to address the way care was delivered as well as the number of providers.

Both models have been evaluated by their respective entities and deemed to be successes and they continue to be used: MOCINS has been expanded in scope and depth within Nova Scotia, and the CDMR has moved into its sixth year within VIHA. The evaluation of MOCINS has found that the implementation of this model has resulted in shorter lengths of stay, fewer repeat admissions, fewer shifts missed owing to provider injury, and increased job satisfaction.

In addition to the improvements outlined earlier, such team-delivered care models were associated with fewer medical errors, fewer patient deaths per acuity-adjusted hospital cases, fewer workplace safety incidents, and better health status at discharge. Although these improvements cannot be solely attributed to the initiative, improved outcomes were associated with greater involvement of unit staff. In the VIHA, a region with only three major hospitals and five smaller hospitals, the initiative undertook an effort of continuous 24-hour observation of 930 staff across 15 different units, 24 hours a day, to attain baseline data on staff activities. A data gatherer was assigned for each staff person to ensure accuracy, and approximately 40,000 person hours were recorded. By comprehensively understanding how patient care was being delivered by VIHA staff, teams consisting of frontline personnel were not only able to participate in learning sessions to better operate in their interprofessional environment but were also evaluated to have undertaken a more systematic approach to testing and implementing changes to their method of practice. This was done under the banner of a structured learning collaborative wherein each unit tried at least six changes during their year as part of the effort to improve their quality of care and efficiency. This healthy, collaborative growth and experimentation through active, controlled attempts at approaches to change occurred in 2009 and 2010, and the effort was again launched in 2011 following positive evaluation. Such exercises continue to be of great value: they not only serve as models of successes for needs-based planning but they also act as living examples to foster greater knowledge and foster expertise in an alternative mindset.

These successful attempts, among others, to apply the model of needs-based HHR planning are instructive in thinking about how to *operationalize* a needs-based planning model in HHR. They tell us a number of things that might usefully be considered when discussing the possibility of applying such a model to Canadian jurisdictions. In the subsequent section I outline similarly broad lessons before delving into a solely Canadian scope with uniquely Canadian challenges.

What Can These Comparative Cases Tell Us about Health Human Resources Planning?

Needs-based planning requires careful consideration of the best ways to truly engage stakeholders with different interests and perspectives and mechanisms to engage citizens in meaningful dialogue and debate about the best ways to allocate resources, including health workforce resources, to those with the highest levels of need. Innovative communication strategies that consider language, levels of literacy, and culture are required with domestic as well as international efforts. Furthermore, resources and the necessary infrastructure for health information systems and commitment to ongoing monitoring and evaluation need to be a priority.

The importance of open, regular communication between partners when attempting collaborative work cannot be overstated. Appropriate resources must be dedicated to this area to ensure that linguistic and cultural differences are acknowledged and respected and, ultimately, that projects undertaken within such contexts are successful. Although the integration of current communication technologies is an invaluable support for collaborative ventures, there is no substitute for face-to-face dialogue in building and maintaining an effective, mutually beneficial partnership.

The complexities of highly decentralized governments and the influence these may have on research and policy initiatives are unpredictable; therefore, the organizers of such initiatives must be conservative in estimating timelines when working within such contexts. Knowledge to inform health policy will be greatly enhanced through collaborations and networks of policy-makers and researchers guided by mutual approaches reached by consensus and by optimal shared learning opportunities.

When collaborating to develop new products through original research, it is important for all partners to explain their respective contexts so that the framework within which the partnership is to function can be well designed from the outset. This includes clear protocols for acknowledgment of intellectual contributions to the shared work.

Most poignantly, perhaps, it is essential that key stakeholders, both within and outside government, be involved in the process from the outset if uptake of policy-relevant research is to be achieved. Failure to include these players early on may engender suspicion and resistance even to well-designed initiatives. Strong local leadership, demonstrated by shared goals and values, is necessary to build sustainable capacity to enhance research and policy-making. More specifically, needs-based HHR planning projects must be led by local mechanisms (such as steering committees) with both technical aptitude and political savvy. This involvement of key stakeholders, strong leadership, and participation by local contingents through early inclusion are paramount in efforts to foster collaboration in a country with fourteen separate health care systems.

TOWARD A PAN-CANADIAN FRAMEWORK

The vision for the ACHDHR pan-Canadian framework, as earlier mentioned, has been defined as "improved access to appropriate, effective, efficient, sustainable, responsive, needs-based health care services for Canadians, and a more supportive satisfying work environment for health care providers through collaborative strategic provincial/ territorial/ federal health human resources planning" (ACHDHR 2007). The goals of the framework are to enhance planning capacity, to align education and the workforce, to arrive at an effective mix and use of provider skills, and to achieve a sustainable health workforce and health work environments. It was determined that the critical success factors for the pan-Canadian framework would include appropriate stakeholder engagement, strong leadership, a clear understanding of roles and responsibilities, and a focus on issues that were cross-jurisdictional in nature.

The ACHDHR has developed an action plan designed to support collaborative pan-Canadian HHR planning. It sets out the principles for collaboration and identifies key actions jurisdictions can take together to achieve the following aims: overcome barriers to implementing system design, using population needs-based planning; avoid the risks and duplication associated with the current jurisdiction-by-jurisdiction planning approach; and increase their HHR planning capacity while respecting jurisdictional authority and regional planning initiatives. Even though a formal evaluation has not been carried out to date, this collaborative approach to planning has been both useful and timely. Some stakeholders indicate that pan-Canadian HHR planning offers benefits such as the following:

- greater capacity to implement policies and priorities to improve both access to and quality of health care services at a cost Canadians can afford;
- greater capacity to influence the factors that drive the health care system, determine HHR needs, share best practices, and affect health status and system outcomes;

- less costly duplication in planning activities, and better estimating/simulation models;
- improved information sharing to support compensation and related collective bargaining processes;
- better understanding of the interjurisdictional and national picture of the workforce (through a common minimum data set) and greater capacity to address common HHR issues;
- greater workforce stability in all Canadian jurisdictions, and more appropriate labour mobility; and
- health systems that are less vulnerable to global pressures and better able to retain providers (ACHDHR 2007).

IMPLEMENTING NEEDS-BASED HHR PLANNING ACROSS CANADA

Given that the Canadian health care system is faced with limited resources and emerging health conditions, it is in the interest of policy-makers in all jurisdictions, as well as the populations they serve, to align the capacities of health care workforces with the needs of these populations. This challenging task is made easier when information on the health workforce and the population's health needs is readily available to policy-makers. However, our comparative experiences with HHR planning suggest that HHR policy change is not inevitable and that context matters a great deal; history is littered with policy visions that never came to pass. It has been much more difficult to put theory into practice than generally thought by champions of new policy visions.

Experience to date has reinforced the view that some Canadian jurisdictions, even with an agreement to take a pan-Canadian needs-based approach to planning, seem to be more interested in and invested in developing needs-based models and estimation tools (like the one described earlier in the chapter) than in employing qualitative techniques to ensure that the perceptions and needs of communities (and those not reflected in more empirical methods) became part of the mix. Overall, during the development of the pan-Canadian framework there were many more resources available for investing in the needs-based framework and model, and much less interest in finding ways to effectively engage the community in the process of implementation. In some provinces and territories there seems to be much more interest in building capacity and teaching skills essential for needs-based decision-making and governance, but much less interest in creating new forms of engagement along the policy continuum.

In some Canadian jurisdictions – and in other countries – incremental, unilateral approaches to policy change are often considered to be very conservative. Although it is generally true that defenders of the status quo are naturally reluctant to facilitate new movements that may threaten the status quo, some stakeholders are much less keen to probe possible weaknesses of policies and programs and then create opportunities for building alternative knowledge networks. In Canadian initiatives, as well in our international experience, it would appear that size and power seem to matter (compare, for example, planning in New Brunswick or Nova Scotia with planning in Ontario or Alberta).

In conclusion, the investigation that my collaborators and I conducted into HHR restructuring suggests that context matters and that there is much we can learn from one another by focusing on the dissimilar games that have shaped patterns of policy discourse and action, or lack thereof. There is much to be gained by better understanding the drivers and constraints that shape policy reforms and what might be done to facilitate a more democratic and learning-based approach to organizing and governing ourselves. It is an approach that calls for a combination of empirical data and subjective perceptions of problems and appropriate solutions.

IMPLEMENTATION LESSONS: LOOKING FORWARD

As illustrated by Canada's competitive federal system, where professions are regulated on a provincial basis and the provinces enjoy much power and autonomy over both agenda setting and implementation, voluntary systems of intergovernmental systems have tended to operate behind closed doors with limited transparency or public engagement. The change in federal transfer payments is a critical consideration in planning for health systems and the health workforce. Because the allocation of the CHT payments on a population basis will be changed only in 2016–17, Alberta's CHT payments over the 2012–13 to 2022–23 period will go up 8.2% yearly on average. Newfoundland and Labrador, on the other hand, will see average annual CHT growth of just 2.9%. This change is not aligned with a needs-based resource allocation approach. One wonders whether the pan-Canadian framework actually influenced the thinking of the federal government when such a formula will be implemented in 2016. Funding based on demographics only is not consistent with the vision of the pan-Canadian framework. The needs of people and the health systems required to deliver services to meet the changing needs of people are not even considered in this narrow formula. Evidence-informed policy-making and decision-making is crucial, but this has not been the course of action taken recently with the announced changes for CHTS.

VANGUARD ORGANIZATIONS

For evidence-informed policy- and decision-making to become second nature, the challenges posed by acting on the evidence and the opportunities such actions present need to be considered carefully, and strategies to support evidence-based actions need to be supported by many stakeholders. No organization is more at the forefront of such an effort than the Pan-Canadian Health Human Resources Network (known by the acronym CHHRN[3]) funded by the Canadian Institutes of Health Research and Health Canada.[4] It is "comprised of national expert researchers and policy makers involved/interested in HHR research, policy and/or planning" (CHHRN 2012). The objectives of CHHRN are as follows: "The goal of this project is to establish a pan-Canadian HHR knowledge exchange portal and virtual network. This network and portal would be a national resource providing access to the latest HHR information and evidence on innovative approaches to HHR development, training, financing, regulation, recruitment, and retention, as well as up-to-date information on ongoing research and model-development at pan-Canadian, provincial/territorial and local/regional service delivery levels" (CHHRN 2012).

Understanding that such an organization cannot be a "preaching-from-armchair silo entity," CHHRN is anchored through three regional hubs (western, central, and eastern) and draws upon a wealth of domestic and international experience. Each hub has a regional head (I am the head of the eastern hub). The organization is further strengthened by an advisory committee drawing from provincial, territorial, federal, international, and non-governmental bodies. By its nature, such an organization must practise the principles of stakeholder involvement, effective communication, and effective leadership and must move toward regular and comparable reporting standards. The organization's key functions, as a facilitator of discourse and as a knowledge portal, are exhibited through the network's library, which has approximately 1,000 articles available (as of July 2012).

FINAL THOUGHTS

The needs-based HHR planning conceptual framework and analytical model described in this chapter demonstrate that, despite the competitive nature of our health system governance, it is possible to base our health workforce planning on the needs of the population. The flexibility of the needs-based approach allows for consideration of the changing realities in the geographical, political, technological, social, and environmental factors that can affect health systems and health workforce planning. The inherent governance challenges of the Canadian system need not impede the advancement of needs-based HHR planning.

Needs-based HHR planning across Canada is strengthened through the existence of a pan-Canadian network, CHHRN, that facilitates national discourse and sharing of the body of knowledge available. Such cross-national dialogue will serve to improve the ability of federal, provincial, territorial, and regional jurisdictions to respond to the challenges facing their health systems. The case studies presented in this chapter demonstrate how new and innovative collaborative models for health care delivery are beginning to address the challenges of meeting the needs of the populations and building sustainability into the system. They also highlight the importance of evaluation. Continuous monitoring and evaluation are essential if we are to successfully address current and future challenges in the Canadian health care system.

NOTES

1 Extending to the medium and long range.
2 The models based on this approach are designed using a system dynamics approach (see, for example, Sternman 2000) and implemented using Vensim (2002) simulation software.
3 Pronounced "churn."

4 The principal investigators of the Pan-Canadian Health Human Resources Knowledge Exchange Network are I. Bourgeault, G. Tomblin Murphy, and M. Barer. The principal knowledge users are K. Connell, T. Goertzen, and J. Tepper, and the knowledge user is I. St-Pierre. The co-investigators include P. Armstrong and A. Baumann.

7

The Challenges of Measuring the Performance of Health Systems in Canada

ADRIAN R. LEVY AND BORIS G. SOBOLEV

Improving the measurement of the performance of health systems is a wise policy option for federal, provincial, and territorial governments because it provides essential information for understanding the inevitable trade-offs involved in trying to reduce costs while striving to improve quality of care, access, and the health of the population. Performance measurement – monitoring, evaluating, and communicating the degree to which health care systems address priorities and meet specific objectives – is also garnering increased attention from many stakeholders at other levels of the system.

The intent of the 1984 Canada Health Act was to ensure that all residents of Canada have access to medically necessary health care on a prepaid basis. However, the act has not been uniformly applied across provinces and territories, leading to variability in available services and treatment in different jurisdictions. The federal government's determination to adhere to national standards while reducing funding to the provinces has recently produced additional challenges.[1]

The system currently used to measure the performance of the health system in Canada lags behind that of other countries such as the United States and the United Kingdom, both in terms of standardized indicators and research in the area. As a result, there is evidence indicating that the values of Canadians are misaligned with the funding and performance of the health care system (Snowdon et al. 2012).

In this chapter, we review the current state of knowledge about performance measurement in health care and examine current efforts in

Canada. We describe the structural, political, conceptual, and method-ological challenges of performance measurement in the field of health technology assessment. We argue that without more clarity around ethics and perspectives and a more systematic approach to performance measurement, it will not be possible to develop a coher-ent strategy for informing policy-making and decision-making throughout the entire health care system.

BACKGROUND

At a fundamental level, "the primary aim of evaluation is to aid stake-holders in their decision making on policies and programs" (Alkin 2004). It is intended to provide evidence on the degree to which gov-ernment policies and spending are effectively addressing specific issues identified by bureaucrats and elected officials.

Performance management in the public sector became a focus of interest in the late 1980s, starting with the re-inventing government movement (Osbourne and Gaebler 1992). In the United States, the 1993 Government Performance and Results Act obligated all federal departments and agencies to present five-year teaching plans linked to performance measures; annual performance plans were required after 1998. In the United Kingdom, the financial management initiative was introduced in the early 1980s.

In Canada, the federal government introduced a centralized evalu-ation policy in 1977. Using evidence from peer-reviewed sources and from reports of the auditor general, Shepherd argued that, between 1977 and 2009, Canada's evaluation policy was focused on opera-tional issues directed primarily toward program managers (Shepherd 2012). In 2009, federal evaluation policy was refocused on fiscal pru-dence and accountability.

PERFORMANCE MEASUREMENT
IN THE CANADIAN HEALTH CARE SYSTEM

Over the past 25 years, there has been an increase in measuring and reporting on the performance of the Canadian health care system at the federal, provincial, and territorial levels. On the demand side, provincial and territorial governments and health authorities have been subjected to intense pressure to contain costs; patients have greater expectations to be involved in decisions about their treatment;

and health care professionals and health authorities expect more oversight and accountability to be built into the health care system. On the supply side, the information revolution and progress in information technology have made it less expensive and more straightforward to collect, process, and disseminate data.

There have been several attempts to define the problem of how to measure health care performance in Canada, the necessary first step toward aligning goals and objectives. In 2000, the First Ministers' Meeting Communiqué on Health directed Canada's health ministers to meet to collaborate on the development of a comprehensive framework to report on health status, health outcomes, and quality of service using jointly agreed-upon comparable indicators. The intent was that such reporting would meet several objectives by providing information to Canadians on government performance, as well as assisting individuals, governments, and health care providers to make more informed health choices. In September 2002, all fourteen federal, provincial, and territorial governments released comparable indicator reports on a set of sixty-seven indicators. The 2003 First Ministers' Accord on Health Care Renewal (appendix 1) directed health ministers to develop more indicators to supplement work undertaken in response to the September 2000 communiqué and identified the following priority areas for reform: healthy Canadians, primary health care, home care, catastrophic drug coverage and pharmaceutical management, diagnostic and medical equipment, and health human resources. Federal, provincial, and territorial jurisdictions agreed on seventy indicators with eighty-one sub-indicators and established the Health Indicators Project to have them collated and made publicly available.

Priorities and directions for the Health Indicators Project were broadly revisited at a second consensus conference in March 2004. The resulting consensus statement established that health indicators must be:

- relevant to established health goals;
- based on standard (comparable) definitions and methods; and
- broadly available and able to be disseminated electronically across Canada at the regional, provincial, and national levels.

The primary goal of the Health Indicators Project was to support health regions in monitoring progress in improving and maintaining the health of the population and the functioning of the health system for which they are responsible through the provision of good-quality comparative information on:

- the overall health of the population served, how it compares with other regions in the province and country, and how it is changing over time;
- the major non-medical determinants of health in the region;
- the health services received by the region's residents; and
- the characteristics of the community or the health system.

No mention was made of other potential uses for performance indicators, including establishing the competence of organizations and identifying the effectiveness of programs to meet specific objectives.

The communiqué from the 2004 First Ministers' Meeting on the Future of Health Care, called A 10-Year Plan to Strengthen Health Care (appendix 2), included an explicit commitment to "accountability and reporting to citizens" that read: "all governments agree to report to their residents on health system performance including the elements set out in this communiqué." In so doing, the first ministers agreed that performance indicators would be required and would be used for reporting purposes. The intent of the effort was to hold health ministries accountable for stewardship of the health care system using performance indicators. The communiqué did not specify whether such reporting would be used in a formative (to improve specific health systems) or in a summative (to implement corrective measures or impose penalties) fashion.

Consultations continued with provincial and regional health authorities to ensure that relevant data were collected and consistent methods were used for performance measurement. In 2010, the eleventh in a series of annual reports presented health indicator data from the Canadian Institute for Health Information and Statistics Canada on a broad range of performance measures (CIHI 2010d). The data were grouped into four dimensions of health: (1) health status, which provides insight on the health of Canadians, including well-being, human function, and selected health conditions; (2) non-medical determinants of health, which reflect factors outside of the health system that affect health; (3) health system performance, which provides insight on the quality of health services, including accessibility, appropriateness, effectiveness, and patient safety; and (4) community and health system characteristics, which provide useful contextual information rather than direct measures of health status or quality of care.

That report used the following principles to categorize disparities in the health system:

- same access to available care for the same need
- same utilization for the same need
- same quality of care for all

Data Requirements

Those considering performance measurement are faced with many competing needs when designing information systems to serve a range of stakeholders (table 7.1). A set of consensus performance measures needs to be developed iteratively, and those involved in the process must have a deep understanding of existing and potential data sources that can be used to create the measures. The specific circumstances of health care in Canada – such as Canada's single-payer financing and several provincial and federal initiatives – have led to the development of key elements needed to produce some routine performance measures, including population registries, vital statistics, administrative health databases containing records of patients' interactions with various elements of the health care system, and patient and treatment registries. As a result of the large amount of data collected in Canada, this country has been characterized as a data-rich environment (Roos et al. 2005). This is reflected by the activities of provincial data centres, which both serve as data custodians and collate and use administrative health and other databases for research and evaluation (Suissa et al. 2012).

Existing performance measures reported by the Canadian Institute for Health Information depend on information from provincial and territorial population registries, vital statistics, hospital discharge abstracts, and physician claims. Even though performance measures have been reported annually since 2003, there are concerns about the provinces' ability to produce unbiased performance measures because of data quality; in Manitoba, the auditor was "unable to form an opinion on the accuracy of the data or on the adequacy of disclosure" for twenty-one of fifty-six health indicators used in the provincial report (Manitoba Minister of Health and Healthy Living 2004).

A CASE STUDY ON PERFORMANCE MEASUREMENT:
HEALTH TECHNOLOGY ASSESSMENT

In general, three types of outcomes are studied in health care evalua-tions: those related to patients, those related to treatments, and those related to the system (Levy 2005). Patient-related outcomes represent the effects of delivering care in a particular system on the patient's ability to care for himself or herself, physical function and mobility, emotional and intellectual performance, and self-perception of health. Treatment-related outcomes represent the biological and phys-iological changes in the patient's condition that occur as a result of administering therapy within the health care system. System-related outcomes represent the effect on the health care system produced by the provision of medical services to a patient population.

Examples of the outcomes include performance benchmarks, requirements for pain medication, length of hospital stay, waiting times, frequency of readmission, and frequency and severity of sec-ondary health complications. In health care evaluation, a performance measure summarizes the distribution of a health care outcome in the patient population. In most studies, the performance measure com-bines the observed responses for all patients or hospitals into a single number. For example, a performance study might record the timing and occurrence of a clinic appointment for each patient, with the dis-tribution of time to clinic appointment (the health care outcome) being summarized by the weekly rate of appointments (the perfor-mance measure).

There have been large investments in health technology assessment over the past decades, and use of new health care technology is an important driver of ongoing increases in health care expenditures. Before an expensive new technology is implemented and reimbursed in a jurisdiction, the expected impacts are assessed at the provincial level and the technology's incremental cost-effectiveness is often assessed by the Canadian Agency for Drugs and Technology in Health, by several provinces, such as Ontario and Quebec, or by some Canadian hospitals (Levin et al. 2007; McGregor and Brophy 2005).

At the time a new health technology comes to market, there is typ-ically little information on its benefits, safety, and cost implications for the population among whom the technology will be used. As such, health technology assessment provides an incomplete picture. It examines short-term safety, with a focus on the most common, seri-ous (potentially life threatening), and severe (potentially debilitating) unintended consequences; efficacy, often using data from the restricted conditions in randomized trials; the acquisition costs; and, sometimes, estimated cost-effectiveness on the basis of long-term project models drawing on the limited information available at market launch.

Once the technology is marketed, some information becomes available on the geographic distribution of the technology and sometimes its utilization. However, this descriptive information alone is not adequate for assessing the performance of the technology. Decision-makers need to understand how new technologies affect patients once they have been adopted for use in the real world, and they need to understand how they affect the health system in terms of who is actually treated, the long-term clinical benefits, severe unintended consequences, health-related quality of life, and productivity. Even less is known about the impact of less severe unintended consequences, downstream medical and health consequences (for the population to whom the technology is actually applied), population effectiveness, or incremental cost-effectiveness in actual use.

Many innovations have led to less invasive technologies being introduced to treat conditions previously managed surgically, such as percutaneous transluminal coronary angiography, which is now being undertaken in patients who were previously managed with coronary artery bypass grafting (Weintraub et al. 2012), and extracorporeal shock-wave lithotripsy, which has displaced surgical removal of kidney stones. Noninvasive technologies typically reduce patient morbidity and the length of hospital stay, often resulting in lower unit costs of treatment, and should therefore result in potential cost savings to the health care system. However, understanding the long-term consequences of such technologies requires formal assessment because those savings are often not realized. Angioplasty leads to a greater need for repeat revascularization over time, which reduces the cost differential, and, perhaps because of reduced morbidity, the number of patients and treatments may increase after a new technology becomes established (Levy and McGregor 1995).

Although measuring the performance of new health care technologies once they have been introduced into practice is crucial, it is done only rarely. The work of the Ontario Health Technology Advisory Committee is an exception (Levin et al. 2007). One reason is that there is a lack of indicators on a new health technology and a time lag of at least several years before administrative data become available for analysis in Canada. This knowledge gap is becoming increasingly problematic as governments, health authorities, and hospitals struggle to work within fixed budgets, with the federal government planning on indexing its spending to inflation. Decision-makers in these organizations have said clearly that they suffer from a lack of straightforward information about which technologies work, on whom, and under what circumstances (Health Technology Assessment Task Group on behalf of the Federal/Provincial/Territorial Advisory Committee on Information and Emerging Technologies 2004). There is no consensus on, or even an understanding of, what should be measured or how performance should be measured.

EXISTING RESEARCH ON PERFORMANCE MEASUREMENT IN HEALTH TECHNOLOGY ASSESSMENT

At least four groups of investigators have proposed methods to measure performance in health technology assessment. A group of investigators from the United Kingdom proposed a framework for describing decision-making systems that use health technology assessment to determine reimbursement of health technologies (Hutton et al. 2006). The framework groups systems under four main headings (constitution and governance, objectives, use of evidence and decision processes, and accountability) and identifies three processes (assessment, decision, and outputs and implementation). Hutton et al. assessed the feasibility of implementing the framework using published information on constitution and governance, methods and processes, use of evidence, and transparency and accountability, at the stages of assessment, decision-making, and implementation. They found that most of the information needed for their framework was not publicly available.

A group of researchers from l'Université de Montréal proposed a framework for performance assessment in health technology assessment organizations (Lafortune et al. 2008). Their conceptual model includes four functions and organizational needs that must be balanced for a health technology agency to perform well: goal attainment, production, adaptation to the environment and culture, and values maintenance. Although this model has a strong conceptual grounding, it has yet to be applied in practice. It requires analysts to make qualitative judgments, which may make it more useful for improving performance within an organization than for comparing performance between organizations.

More recently, a group of European investigators proposed an input-throughput-outcome model of the health care system in relation to the different types of health care technologies (Velasco et al. 2010). The thrust of their argument is that "health technology assessment should develop to increase its focus on the 'technologies applied to health care' (i.e., the regulatory and policy measures for managing and organizing health care systems)." They recommend that health technology assessment should have an increased focus on regulatory, financial, and policy measures for managing and organizing health care systems. They recommend that "countries embarking on health technology assessment should not consider establishing completely separate agencies for health technology assessment, quality development, performance measurement, and health services development, but should rather combine these agencies into a common knowledge strategy for evidence informed decision-making in the health services and the health system." Although ambitious, there would be much to be gained from such a strategy.

The framework closest to assessing some of the performance measures listed in table 7.1 was developed in Quebec (Jacob and McGregor 1993). These authors outlined a new methodology for evaluating the impact of health technology assessments on policy and expenditures and applied it to twenty-one assessments produced by the Quebec Council for Health Technology Assessment between 1990 and 1995. Using published documents, interviews, questionnaires, and administrative health data, the authors sought to evaluate the impact of health technology assessments by addressing three fundamental questions: (1) What impact was intended? (2) To whom was the message directed? and (3) To what extent was the hoped-for impact achieved, first in terms of policy and second in terms of actual distribution and use of the technology? The authors determined that eighteen of the twenty-one assessments had an influence on policy and that there were substantial savings to the health care system. They concluded that it will rarely be possible to precisely estimate impact, but systematic documentation of effects can be achieved. The self-stated limitations of their methodology included the identification of what they called critical incidents, systematic categorization of policies about health technology, and the use of documentation, which led to a degree of objectivity but also led to limitations relating to the reliance on analysts' judgment. The interpretations were improved by consulting with important stakeholders. They also acknowledged that the impact of any health technology assessment is influenced by many other factors, substantially complicating interpretations.[2]

None of the existing frameworks for performance measurement of health technology assessment have gained widespread acceptance or have been used widely to help guide allocation decisions. One reason for this lack of uptake may be that these frameworks are too complicated to be easily applied or understood. Part of the reason the frameworks are complex is that the variables that comprise the frameworks are not clearly defined. Without proper definition it is difficult to access the appropriate indicators, which in turn makes it difficult to examine the outcomes.

Other than the efforts of Jacob and McGregor (1993), existing publications on performance measurement in health technology assessment have focused on processes and not on outcomes. One reason for this is that outcomes are harder to measure in an unbiased fashion. Instead, existing performance measurement systems for health technology assessment are scattered and generated in a non-systematic fashion. Additionally, health technology assessments must presently rely on data that are made available because it is relatively convenient to do so, such as information generated using routinely collected administrative health data (Roos et al. 2005) and registries (Tu et al. 2007); only rarely is a performance assessment done using a primary data collection procedure (Goeree et al. 2009).

DATA SOURCES FOR PERFORMANCE MEASUREMENT IN HEALTH TECHNOLOGY ASSESSMENT

In terms of using existing data sources for performance measurement, investigators in the United Kingdom have proposed a typology of databases according to their potential uses in the following elements of health technology assessment (Raftery et al. 2005):

- Group I databases can be used to identify both health technologies and health states; these, in turn, can be disaggregated into clinical registries, clinical administrative databases, and population-oriented databases. These databases can be used to assess effectiveness, equity, and diffusion.
- Group II databases can be used to identify health technologies but not health states. These databases can be used to assess diffusion only.

• Group III databases can be used to identify health states but not health technologies; these, in turn, can be disaggregated into adverse event reporting, disease-only registries, and health surveys. These databases have restricted scope; they are focused mainly on unintended adverse consequences of treatment or disease.

In the environmental scan that Raftery et al. conducted in England and Wales, 270 databases were identified, of which an estimated six had some potential for health technology assessment, approximately one-half of which could be assigned to group I. These investigators made important recommendations for policy that are applicable in Canada: responsibility for the strategic development of databases should be clarified (in Canada, this might be refocused on the rationalization of data collection efforts with and across health authorities); more resources should be made available; and issues associated with coding, confidentiality, custodianship and access, maintenance of clinical support, optimal use of information technology, filling gaps, and remedying deficiencies should be clarified.

DISCUSSION

Efforts to measure and assess the performance of the Canadian health system in Canada are in the early stages, and the research agenda is enormous. Policy questions about what data to collect, and at what cost, now have equally important parallels in terms of how and when to most usefully summarize and report such information, how to integrate the information into governance and efforts to improve performance, and, ultimately, how to make wise decisions to optimize the health of the population.

Developing performance indicators can be seen as a four-step process consisting of policy, development, implementation, and evaluation phases (Ibrahim 2001). The process must address the conceptual, methodological, practical, and political considerations for developing performance measures for the Canadian health system. The lack of a conceptual framework for performance measurement in health means that research in the area is in its infancy. Methodological challenges are created by the nature of funding mechanisms in the Canadian health system and the potentially long time lags between cause and effect. Practical considerations include the daunting volume of work that would be required for greater performance measurement, including the cost and timing of such work. To date, many unresolved questions remain, such as the following: Who will decide the performance indicators? Who will measure them? How will the results of such measurements be presented? To whom and how often? Performance assessment should not be seen as a one-time effort: regular, ongoing follow-up is required. Political challenges include the different levels of governmental jurisdictions in Canada, with standards for care being laid out by the Canada Health Act; the federal government is responsible for protecting the health of the population by ensuring safety through the regulation of medical products and for setting and enforcing maximum reimbursement amounts for medications, whereas provision of health care is mostly a provincial and territorial responsibility. This complicated legislative and regulatory environment means that political and health reform cycles must be considered at an early stage in the development of performance measures (Roberts et al. 2008). Performance indicators would be developed and implemented much more effectively if there was cooperation between the federal, provincial, and territorial governments as well as health authorities and individual hospitals.

It is not possible for any subset of performance measures to capture all of the facets of health care that are needed by different stakeholders. What is required is a process of systematically identifying and prioritizing performance measures that will meet at least some of the needs of each stakeholder. Determining what performance measures should be used is, at the most fundamental level, an ethical question because the output must represent the different values and needs of multiple stakeholders.[3] Examples from the literature include performance measurement in the delivery of health care services (Roski and Gregory 2001), health systems (Evans et al. 2001), and the health of the community (Klazinga et al. 2001).

The inherent complexities of health care, such as the diverse expertise of health care professionals, the variety of organizational arrangements, the array of treatment protocols, and the myriad interactions between managerial and clinical activities, may necessitate that multiple outcomes be integrated in evaluating the effects of an intervention at the level of the patient, treatment, or health care system (Sobolev et al. 2012). Table 7.1 provides examples of health care performance indicators and information needs according to type of stakeholder. This list is not intended to be exhaustive, and the categories and information needs overlap between stakeholders.

Table 7.1
Examples of health care performance indicators and information needs according to type of stakeholder

Stakeholder	Goals	Types of needed information
CITIZENS	• to see evidence that resources on health are being spent efficiently and align with stated priorities • to have the information they need to hold policy- and decision-makers accountable for health policies and health care delivery that align with societal values • to be reassured that necessary care will be forthcoming in time of need	• transparent descriptions of stated priorities • comparative information on the health of the population versus that in other countries • comparative information on the performance of the health care system versus that in other countries • transparent access to indicators of access, quality of care, and resource use in the health care system
PATIENTS	• to be reassured that they will have access to specific health care when they need it, within a safe timeframe and at adequate proximity • to obtain information on the intended and unintended consequences of alternative health care options and on the out-of-pocket expenses associated with these options	• information on available health care services and modalities • information on trade-offs between services in terms of potential intended and unintended health outcomes and out-of-pocket costs
HEALTH CARE PROFESSIONALS	• to provide high-quality and appropriate health care to patients • to maintain and improve their knowledge and skills in health care delivery	• data on individual performance against benchmarks • up-to-date information on best practices, guidelines
HOSPITALS	• to monitor and improve use of health care resources • to manage local budgets • to identify and prioritize health technology acquisition and disinvestment • to ensure patient safety • to conduct continuous quality improvement	• collective data on health care quality, including patient safety indicators measured against benchmarks • information on distributions of access (utilization, waiting lists, and waiting times) measured against benchmarks

Table 7.1   (*continued*)

Stakeholder	Goals	Types of needed information
HOSPITALS (*continued*)		• a transparent health technology assessment process • information on patient experience and satisfaction • hospital-level costing information
HEALTH AUTHORITIES	• to ensure that hospitals and health care professionals provide appropriate and cost-effective health care • to ensure that patients have access to the specific health care they need, within a safe timeframe and at adequate proximity • to manage regional budgets • to assess the impact of health care on the regional health needs of the population • to ensure equitable distribution of resources	• information on the comparative health of their population versus that of populations served by other health authorities • information on the health needs of their region • information on the equity of health care resource distribution • information on distributions of access (utilization, waiting lists, and waiting times) across health authority • health authority level costing information
GOVERNMENTS	• to assess the impact of health care on patients and on population health • to establish current and future health policy goals and priorities • to set and manage governmental budgets • to plan for the viability and sustainability of the health care system • to demonstrate the adequacy and proper functioning of regulatory procedures for health care • to provide appropriate assessment and research infrastructure • to promote investment and innovation in health care	• comparative data on the health of their population versus that of populations in other provinces and territories and in other countries • information on the societal value of health care, elicited using transparent citizen engagement processes • information on the health needs of the region • information on the equity of health care resource distribution • information on distributions of access (utilization, waiting lists, and waiting times) across the jurisdiction • aggregate and decomposed expenditure data at the provincial, territorial, and national level

Table 7.1   (*continued*)

Stakeholder	Goals	Types of needed information
GOVERNMENTS (*continued*)		• information on societal productivity attributable to health and health care
REGULATORS	• to protect patient safety • to ensure protection of health care professionals and other consumers beyond patients • to uphold their fiduciary responsibility • to promote efficiency in health care markets	• safety signals from health care • integrity in reporting financial performance • information on innovation in health care

Once a performance measure comes into practice, it permeates the thinking of decision-makers and becomes normative (Murray and Lopez 1996). In so doing, it has the possibility of influencing policy decisions, spending, and even patterns of thinking about the health system. There is a risk of overreliance on existing performance measures to the detriment of other aspects of care. For instance, in 2004, Canada's first ministers agreed to reduce waiting times in five priority areas – radiation therapy for cancer, cardiac care, diagnostic imaging, joint (hip and knee) replacement, and cataract surgery for sight restoration – by providing hospitals with cash incentives from a $5.5-billion funding envelope. The Canadian Institute for Health Information has begun reporting on performance measures for waiting times (CIHI 2012b). The current emphasis on these five priority areas means that other necessary procedures not considered a priority are disincentivized. In orthopedics, for example, operations such as surgery to repair feet and ankles are paid for out of a hospital's global budget and are not eligible for the incentive payments, which creates a financial incentive for hospitals to prioritize hip and knee replacements.

RECOMMENDATIONS

A useful performance measure should always begin with detailed documentation of the indicators that constitute the measure, once defin-

itions have been agreed upon. Given the seemingly widespread acceptance in Canada of the four dimensions discussed earlier, indicators
should fall into one of these dimensions: health status, non-medical
determinants of health, health system performance, and community
and health system characteristics. There should also be a clarification
of responsibility for the strategic development of databases; more
resources for database activities; and clarification of issues associated
with coding, confidentiality, custodianship and access, maintenance
of clinical support, optimal use of information technology, filling
gaps, and remedying deficiencies.

The focus of measurement must be on outcomes as well as processes, and health performance measurement should have an increased
focus on regulatory, financial, and policy measures for managing and
organizing health care systems. There should not be separate agencies
for quality development, performance measurement, and service development, but rather these should be combined in a common strategy
that will inform decision-making throughout the entire health care
system.

There has been, to date, a lack of focus on strategic evaluations of
policy and program coherence, that is, whether policies and programs
are addressing the issues and values that are most important to Canadians, such as understanding and improving determinants of health
by reducing poverty and aligning health care spending with the principles embodied in the Canada Health Act.

NOTES

1 For more detail about federalism and health care in Canada, see Wilson
(2000).
2 Assessing causality when measuring performance of health technology is
among the most pernicious challenges facing the careful analyst. This is
made particularly challenging because of the impossibility of
randomization in most studies. The thoughtful study by Jacob and
McGregor (1993) is notable for its rigour and critical thinking in this area.
3 Depending on the perspective, performance measures could be developed
to represent the following three different perspectives. First, the *utilitarian
perspective* emphasizes the importance of achieving the greatest good for the
greatest number. Bureaucrats require performance indicators to provide
wise stewardship of the health care system and to balance equity of access

with efficient distribution. For example, some Canadian mid-sized cities may seek to establish catheterization laboratories to increase the speed of access to angioplasty for treating acute myocardial infarction, and provincial bureaucrats require access to information on both distributive and allocative efficiencies to balance the merit of these claims (Levy et al. 2010). Health care professionals and hospital administrators use performance indicators to identify the functional competence of individual practitioners and organizations and to decide which technologies to adopt. Surgeons must maintain their skills to minimize operative complications and health authority decision-makers may seek detailed information on post-operative infection rates when considering a technology for stapling versus sewing colorectal anastomoses (when closing the opening left after removal of a colostomy bag). This information is needed when making policy decisions about purchasing and planning skills training. Second, the *libertarian perspective* emphasizes the rights of individuals to access and choose between levels of health care. For example, patients choosing between different treatments may seek detailed comparative information on the intended and unintended consequences of different treatment modalities: for example, when patients are considering angioplasty and stenting or bypass surgery for coronary artery disease, their risk preferences may be elicited if information on benefits and risks is available and synthesized in an understandable fashion. Third, the *communitarian perspective* emphasizes the need to balance the rights of individuals against the rights of the community as a whole. Organ donation (e.g., with a presumption that all persons are organ donors unless donation is actively opposed by the family), abortion and family planning services, and issues associated with the use of tobacco and intravenous drugs are all health care matters in which communitarian values may be invoked.

Health Care Federalism and the Debate over Decentralization

8

The Future of the Provincial Role in Canadian Health Care Federalism

KEN BOESSENKOOL

THE ISSUE OF JURISDICTION[1]

In a remarkable interview with the prolific economist William Watson for the Institute for Research on Public Policy in the late 1990s, then Deputy Minister of Finance Scott Clark suggested that he missed the days of deficits now that they were gone (Watson 1999). It was a powerful way of pointing out the stultifying inertia that replaced the refreshing force of reform once Canadian governments got their fiscal houses in order. Nowhere is inertia more stultifying than in health care. In the decade since the implementation of the 2003 health accord (appendix 1), if not longer, the only thing that has happened in health care has been a drive to shove more money into the health care envelope. That money has not been directed toward improving health care delivery or toward reforming our single-payer system. Instead, cash infusions have done little other than drive up health care inflation via increases in wages to health care providers. Across the country we have seen large infusions of cash into the health care system translate into equally large increases in the pay of health care providers. With health care taking up ever larger shares of provincial budgets, the renewal of the health accord just around the corner, and the reality of deficits at all levels of government in Canada, the force of reform may be returning. The first order of business will be to establish who will drive the debate: Ottawa or the provinces.

During the last serious bout with deficits, Ottawa accelerated its three-decades-long retreat from the health care field when in its 1995 budget it proposed to reduce cash contributions to health by 40%. This made sense at just about every level, for there is no real reason for Ottawa to be involved in the evolution of health care in Canada. The provinces, not Ottawa, administer health care programs. Ottawa, generally, does not run hospitals, pay nurses, or bargain with doctors. It does not design payment mechanisms or decide which services should be funded. And although Ottawa has a public health agency, all provinces have a public health capacity that, arguably, could take over nearly all the functions of the federal agency (the exception might be health research, but that is not really health care; it is research).

All Ottawa really has is a bully pulpit based on the Canada Health Act and the stick of financial penalties under cash transfers to the provinces. Ottawa makes political use of its pulpit and penalties, which results in confusion about which level of government is responsible for health care. This confusion is not costless: it allows the provinces to shift the blame to Ottawa when they make mistakes and allows Ottawa to claim credit for reforms it had nothing to do with. Ottawa's cash transfers also mean that provinces do not have to bear the full tax cost of health care spending – particularly in recent years, as the provinces have allowed (nay, begged) the federal government to play a bigger financing role.

From an economic point of view, there are no interprovincial issues that warrant national oversight. User fees in Alberta will not affect the health of people in Saskatchewan. Agreements between provinces already address the issue of border crossers – a person carrying an Alberta health care card into a Saskatchewan hospital will trigger payments between the two governments. There are real advantages to allowing provinces to design health care systems that differ across provincial boundaries. Just as competition in the private markets results in greater innovation, so does competition between provinces allow for experimentation and a better alignment of health care to the desires of electorates. Contrary to Canadian health care mythology, there is no single Canadian health care system. Services covered in some provinces are subject to user fees in others (abortions, for example). Some Canadians pay health care premiums, while others do not. Private hospitals have been allowed to operate in some provinces (Ontario, Quebec, and British Columbia) but not in others.

The problem with Ottawa's pulpit and penalties is that they stand in the way of new experiments. If the people of Ontario wish to allow higher income individuals to take the strain off the system by purchasing health care without travelling to the United States, they should be allowed to do so. If Saskatchewan wishes to implement co-payments for certain services through a medical savings account funded by health care premiums, it should be allowed to do so. If the people of Alberta wish to have every possible service, including home care and pharmaceuticals, paid for by the government and are willing to pay the required taxes, they should be allowed to do so. The remaining provinces could then observe these experiments and decide which model they like. In the longer term, provinces should rally around the idea that Ottawa should replace its distorting cash transfers with additional tax room for the provinces to fund health. This tax room will enter the equalization formula, so all provinces would get similar amounts to fund health care demands. I argue below that this tax room should take the form of giving the goods and services tax (GST) over to the provinces.

·Canada's last bout with deficits produced some refreshing health care reforms: Ottawa reduced its role, most provinces restructured or regionalized their delivery systems, and a debate over the sustainability of our single-payer system began. The reform initiative receded when money became plentiful. The prospect of reform is now returning, because governments are facing the prospects of fiscal deficits coupled with the reality of a renewal of the health accord. The barrier to reform is transfers because, as Smart and Bird (2006, 4) point out, federal transfers result in a "federal government that is unable to commit credibly to a stable transfer system with clear and consistent incentives. Provincial governments have little incentive today to set their own fiscal houses in order, since spending restraint weakens the case for future increases in federal transfers."[2] In what follows, I flesh out the case for transferring the GST to the provinces to give them greater authority and autonomy over the future development of health care.

A final point to cap this introduction: if you were to ask me what the federal government should do about health care, my answer would be that it should do what the provinces are asking it to do. That is consistent with the view that the provinces, not the federal government, ought to be responsible for health care. So with that out of the way, I will begin with a detour into the world of federal-provincial transfers and the concept of the fiscal imbalance.

THE PROBLEM OF FISCAL IMBALANCE[3]

Essentially, defining the fiscal imbalance is straightforward: at current tax rates, the federal government has more revenue than it needs for its expenditures, and the provinces (as a group) have less revenue at their current tax rates than they need for their expenditures. Canada has closed the resulting gap by converting large amounts of federal revenues to provincial revenues through intergovernmental transfers. These transfers are large enough that some – including the current government in Ottawa – argue that the fiscal imbalance no longer exists. Yet I would argue that federal transfers are merely a treatment of symptoms – they are not a cure.

Our current fiscal arrangements mean that Ottawa raises the money and the provinces spend it. As a result of this fiscal churning, no government has clear responsibility for delivering key programs and both sides readily blame the other when something goes wrong. In economic terms, federal tax revenues have become a common pool of resources that are available to whichever province is the first to exploit them. As with all poorly managed common property resources, the result is an inevitable tendency to exploitation. We end up with a race among provincial governments to exploit taxpayers who reside in other provinces through federal transfer negotiations (Smart and Bird 2006).

Yet this economic argument cannot explain the tendency for even the rich provinces to push for greater federal transfers. That can only be explained by the fact that federal transfers allow rich provinces to deliver services for much less than the actual "tax cost" of delivering those services. Current transfer arrangements, then, create "fiscal illusion" on the part of voters and their elected leaders. In both cases, the critical point is that Canada is stuck in a sort of low-level intergovernmental fiscal game where poor provinces try to suck revenues from rich provinces, rich provinces try to suck revenues from Ottawa, and the taxpayer sees no accountability for the tax dollars that get sucked into either level of government.

Let's make this clear by talking for a moment about health care. One of the most important long-term issues facing Canada is whether further increases in public health care spending are warranted or whether more fundamental reforms to the health system are desired. Provincial governments have little incentive to frame the question this way for voters when instead they can try to suck money from other provinces or from Ottawa. The federal government also faces an implicit incentive to accommodate provincial demands, as long as voters reward federal governments that do little more than write larger and larger cheques while professing some sort of religious adherence to the Canada Health Act.

We could improve accountability and responsibility by giving provinces additional revenue-raising capacity and offsetting this by reducing federal transfers: in short, a transfer of tax points to the provinces. But which tax points should be transferred? In the section that follows, I make the case for a GST tax point transfer to provinces. Specifically, I argue that Ottawa ought to hand over the GST to the provinces while reducing transfers by an equal amount.

WHY A GST TRANSFER?

The 1997 final report of the Technical Committee on Business Taxation provides a useful set of principles for coordinating taxing authority (Mintz et al. 1997; see also Ip and Mintz 1992: see especially 123ff., where Ip and Mintz, too, recommend a GST transfer to the provinces).[4] It is worth testing the transfer of GST revenues in light of five principles proposed by the technical committee. This will also allow us to address reasons why transferring the GST is superior to transferring additional personal income tax room (as argued, for example, in Boothe and Hermanutz 1999). Those principles include the following principles.

Principle 1:
Encouraging the Free Flow of Goods, Services, Capital, and Labour
in the Economic Union

Under this principle, "all levels of government would refrain from levying taxes that would impair the flow of goods and services, capital and labour across provincial boundaries or that would discriminate against businesses owned by residents of other provinces" (Mintz et al. 1997, 11.3). A possible objection against transferring GST revenues to provinces is that the GST is an important part of the federal government's tool kit for fiscal stabilization. The GST can be used both as an automatic as well as a discretionary stabilizer. In terms of automatic stabilization, so long as all provinces continue to levy some level of GST, GST revenues will continue to function as a national tool for economic stabilization. In addition, as noted below, the

GST is less volatile than other revenue sources. Whether this budget (as opposed to economic) stabilization is better suited to provincial rather than federal determination is arguably a matter of taste. The federal government used the GST as a discretionary stabilizer in the recent downturn (Boessenkool 2008). Clearly, if Ottawa transferred GST revenues to the provinces, the federal government would cease to have this discretionary tool in its tool kit. Yet there is no reason why provinces could not do this in a coordinated fashion. Even if not coordinated, the GST in provincial hands could potentially be a powerful tool to address differences in regional economic swings (see Kneebone 2008).

Transferring GST revenues to the provinces may enhance our national economic union by providing a strong incentive for the remaining provinces to move to a system of provincial value-added taxes. This would clearly increase provincial (and hence Canada's) competitiveness (Mintz 2009). Finally, transferring the entire GST to provinces, as opposed to a portion of the personal or corporate income tax, would make it much more difficult for the federal government to reoccupy this tax room in the future, as Ottawa has arguably done with the personal income tax points it transferred in 1977 (see the Commission on Fiscal Imbalance 2002, 142–3, especially chart 41), which has arguably resulted in a higher total tax burden than would otherwise be the case. Consumption taxes distort trade flows less than a transfer of income taxes as they are destination-based taxes (with exports exempt and imports taxed). The only impact would be individuals going across the border to buy goods and services, but they have to do this as tourists, as mail-order and internet purchases are taxed at destination. From a more macro perspective, income tax differentials would have a much larger impact on labour flows and production decisions, making them potentially more distorting.

Principle 2:
Minimizing the Fiscal Spillover Effects
of Federal and Provincial Government Tax Policies

Under this principle, "there are instances where the tax policies of one government may directly affect the economic well-being of the residents of another jurisdiction. Such interactions, or fiscal spillovers, occur among governments at the same level of jurisdiction (provinces) as well as between federal and provincial governments, and should be minimized" (Mintz et al. 1997, 11.3–11.5). These spillovers can include tax exportation (when taxes in one jurisdiction fall on residents or governments in another jurisdiction), tax base flight (when taxes on a mobile factor cause it to flee), and joint occupancy (when raising taxes in one jurisdiction causes the revenues of that tax source to fall in another). As a destination-based tax, the GST will have little impact on tax base flight or tax exportation paid by residents. In addition, and unlike income taxes, the GST would not have any impact on capital income. This is particularly relevant for the personal income tax treatment of capital gains and dividends where the relief on the personal side in one province is helping to pay for the corporate tax in another province.

Principle 3:
Minimizing the Cost of Administration and Compliance

Perhaps the most serious criticism of giving provinces control over the GST is that it would result in ten separate administrations, with various provinces making changes to the tax base in ways that would result in spillover effects. There is the very serious challenge of "carousel trading" across provincial boundaries that would result from having multiple administrations and bases for the GST. The issue here is that provinces exempt exports and do not allow imports to be deducted from the base. Currently, the federal administration and auditing ensure that these issues are addressed between Canada and its trading partners, but there is no need to do so between provinces with a single administration and tax base.

The solution is that the federal government should continue to administer, collect, and audit the GST, even though all revenues would be turned over to the provinces. There are three arguments for doing so. First, our constitution clearly assigns responsibility for trade and commerce to the federal government. Even in a world where Ottawa transferred full responsibility for GST administration and collection over to the provinces, it could arguably use its trade and commerce powers to enforce a common base and resolution of these issues as part of these powers (these are the same powers many commentators argue that Ottawa should use to unilaterally eliminate interprovincial trade barriers).

Second, there is a strong precedent for a "tax on base" approach in Canada. Our current personal income tax works this way. With some exceptions and subject to tax collection agreements, Ottawa determines the base for personal income taxes in Canada and provinces determine the rate (the exception is Quebec, which has its own tax base, administration, and collection). There is no reason why Ottawa and the provinces could not come to a similar arrangement on the GST: in fact, the recent moves to harmonize the GST have demonstrated that the provinces can do exactly that. Some may argue that these tax collection agreements only work when tax bases are shared and that the provinces would never accept a federally determined base on a solely provincial revenue source. This objection can be dealt with as follows:

A CARROT The harmonizing provinces gave up control over their sales taxes when they converted to a harmonized sales tax. They simply realized that the economic benefits of harmonizing outweighed the lost autonomy they had with a retail sales tax. This was buttressed by the savings they could realize on collection and administration. The federal government should be willing to continue to bear the costs of collection and administration of the GST even if it will not receive revenues. Of course, Ottawa could charge the provinces for this service, since it would be cheaper for virtually all provinces to agree to a single collection agency (again, Quebec is the current exception here, as its harmonized GST is collected and administered provincially). In short, federal administration and collection would save the provinces money.

A STICK The federal government will, even after it transfers GST revenues and reduces transfers, still have a federal transfer to the provinces. Ottawa could make that transfer partly conditional on the provinces not stepping outside of a federally administered, collected, and enforced GST. Indeed, the federal government has a much stronger constitutional argument for making these kinds of conditions, which are related to trade and commerce, than it does for making conditions under the Canada Health Act. Ottawa could threaten to withhold transfers for any province that violates the GST tax collection agreement.

AN EXAMPLE Although the parallels are not complete, this GST collection system is precisely what Australia uses. (The key difference is that Australia uses its GST revenues to achieve horizontal equity between its states, something we do with our equalization program.

What is proposed here is to use GST revenues to achieve [greater] vertical equity.) Australia's national government collects the GST and then distributes the revenues to its state governments. Although Canada doesn't have to emulate the way in which Australia distributes its GST revenues, that country's national government does not receive revenues from its GST but still oversees its administration, collection, and harmonization across Australian states (for a criticism of the Australian approach of incorporating needs into their equalization program see Boessenkool 1997, 8–9). As Bird (2005, 803–9) shows, a system with differentiated provincial rates on a similar base can be administered with no technical or administrative problems.

As will be discussed more fully below, provinces – particularly as we enter a period of restraint – have strong incentives to prefer a GST transfer to federal cash transfers. In such an environment, they would likely be willing to allow Ottawa to collect and administer the GST if they were given full control over the rate and revenues.

Principle 4:
Facilitating Autonomy and Flexibility for Governments

Under this principle, "each level of government requires access to sources of revenue to fund its activities … adequate revenues sources play an important role in facilitating autonomous and flexible decision-making by governments" (Mintz et al. 1997). This ground has been well tilled in the discussion above, although additional points are worth noting with respect to whether a transfer of income tax room would be superior to a transfer of GST revenues.

First, the GST is a much more stable revenue source than income taxes and thus a better match with provincial expenditures on social programs. The GST is less volatile over time than income taxes, as consumption is less variable than income, whether it be personal or corporate. Figure 8.1 shows federal personal and corporate income tax revenues as well as GST collections (assuming a constant GST rate of 5%), alongside a profile of total federal cash transfers. Given the choice, most provinces would be hard pressed not to prefer the trajectory of GST collections to income taxes or actual transfers to fund health and other social programs. Tying the funding of social programs to GST revenue would provide more stability over time

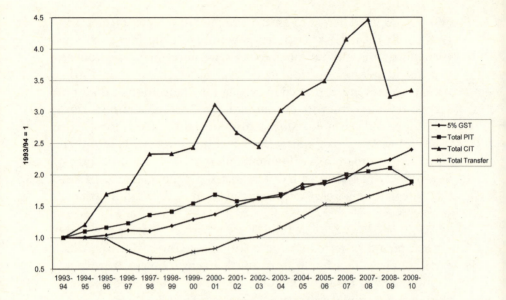

Figure 8.1 The volatility of revenue sources: transfers versus 5 per cent GST versus personal income tax versus corporate income tax. Current dollars are expressed as an index where 1993–94 = 1.

to provincial budgets. In addition, the variation of the GST across provinces is less than the variability of income taxes. The fiscal capacity for the GST ranged from around 81% of the national average for New-foundland to 132% for Alberta in 2007 (the latest year for which these data are available). In that year the Department of Finance estimates that personal income tax fiscal capacities ranged from 57% for Prince Edward Island to a high of 142% for Alberta. The lower variability for the GST means that Ottawa would have to pay less to equalize any trans-fer of GST points than it would for personal income tax points.

Second, the current federal GST program collects less money than is currently transferred to provinces. This means that the entire GST can be given to provinces with a corresponding decrease in federal trans-fers. This would give provinces exclusive access to this critical tax base. The exclusive responsibilities of the provinces should be matched with exclusive tax bases. This is, of course, an argument *in practice* rather than *in theory*, as clearly the federal government would retain the ability to introduce a new broad-based sales tax. However, it is probably safe to assume that until the memory of the introduction of the GST becomes very faint, the likelihood of this happening is, in practice, very low. This ties in well to arguments made above regarding improving accountability by tying spending responsibilities more closely to revenue responsibilities: that is, closing the fiscal gap.

Principle 5:
Improving the Accountability of Governments

In the words of the technical committee, "requiring that governments fund their programs through taxation, rather than relying on transfers from another level of government, can improve accountability" (Mintz et al. 1997, sec. 11.4). This is the central argument of this chapter and has been discussed extensively above. One area that requires special consideration, however, is the GST credit paid out by Ottawa to low-income families through the personal income tax system. Some have argued that the GST credit is just another federal spending program that has little to do with the GST. Bill Robson first made this case in 1997 and delights in repeating it often in his frequent analyses of federal budgets (see Robson 1997, as well as his annual publications before and after federal budgets, at www.cdhowe.org). Nonetheless, the GST credit would not exist today without the GST. If provinces took over the GST, they would almost certainly want to take over the GST credit as well. From an economic perspective, the GST can be made more progressive through a GST credit type of mechanism, which is more efficient and preferable than exempting certain goods (such as food, clothing, and some services) from the GST.

At least three options are available to address the GST credit:

- It could be rolled into and integrated into the existing child tax credit system by the federal government. This would detach the GST credit from the GST, which may cause provinces some political challenges on the progressivity front.
- It could simply be maintained by the federal government as it stands today. The federal government could continue to provide a GST credit to all Canadians. Under this option, Ottawa could even vary the size of the credit by province to reflect differential provincial GST rates.
- Provinces could take it over (whether administered federally or provincially) as a provincial program delivered through their provincial income tax system. Doing so would be fairly simple, as

the federal government collects provincial taxes on the basis of a
federally determined base for all provinces except Quebec.

Whichever option is chosen, Ottawa and the provinces could net any
cost against the remaining federal transfer to ensure fiscal neutrality.

THE PROVINCIAL PERSPECTIVE:
AUTONOMY AND INNOVATION

With federal transfers growing at double digit rates before the recession, the motivation for Ottawa to consider a tax point transfer is
rather obvious: it limits future ad hoc growth in federal transfers. But
why would the provinces want this? In fact, a number of provinces are
already supportive. Within Quebec, there is consensus among all
political parties for a tax point transfer. Indeed, the Quebec Commission on Fiscal Imbalance recommended precisely the swap proposed
in this chapter, and this recommendation received strong support
within the province. The Commission on the Fiscal Imbalance was
announced on March 22, 2001, by then Quebec premier Bernard
Landry. It was appointed two months later, and the final report was
delivered in March 2002. The Quebec Liberal party, in fact, has a long-
standing policy of support for a transfer of tax points (see Jerome-
Forget 2002, 29–32).
    Alberta, too, has pushed for the idea of replacing federal transfers
with tax point transfers. While an Alberta sales tax may cause some
heartache for provincial politicians, the reality is that this transfer will
mean no change for Alberta consumers who already pay the GST
(International and Intergovernmental Relations 2004). Although
Ontario has not explicitly called for such a tax point transfer, it has
been moving steadily in that direction. It is a very small step from
rejecting associated equalization and calling for all transfers outside
of equalization to be equal per capita, to a call for a transfer of tax
points. Manitoba is among other provinces that have explicitly
endorsed a tax point transfer, albeit under its former government
(Manitoba Department of Finance 1999). Saskatchewan, which is
quickly adjusting to life as a "have province," is likely to be supportive
as well. So as a starting point, Alberta and Quebec, the wealthiest have
and the wealthiest have-not provinces, respectively, would be on side,
and there is a reasonable prospect that Ontario and Saskatchewan
could be brought into the picture.

As for the other provinces, figure 8.1 suggests a good part of the answer. Given the choice between any of the lines in that figure to fund social programs, any province – whether Newfoundland and Labrador or British Columbia – would be hard pressed to prefer transfer payments to a transfer of income tax or GST tax points. Provinces may well argue that they have done well by relying on federal transfers in recent years, and they would be right. As noted already, federal transfers rose by double-digit rates before the recession. But the real question for provinces is whether they are at the top of this cycle. With Ottawa's rhetoric about resolving the fiscal imbalance, it seems unlikely that budgets in the coming years will increase transfers at anything like the current rate. Further, fiscal pressures on Ottawa only serve to put downward, not upward, pressure on transfers. Provinces should, from a purely self-interested point of view, take this opportunity to lock in their gains. Indeed, if past experience is any guide, the provinces should be very nervous about how the federal government will approach reducing its deficit. As Kneebone and McKenzie (1999) show, almost a third of federal deficit reduction was due to cutbacks in provincial transfers in the last large federal retrenchment.

If federal transfers have indeed peaked, the GST may in fact be more generous over time than what is provided by recent budgets. The Canada Social Transfer and the Canada Health Transfer have been growing automatically by an annual average rate of 5.1% over the last twenty years. By comparison, revenues from the GST have grown at an average annual rate of 5.4% since its introduction. Further, a transfer of GST revenues to the provinces would make it all but impossible for Ottawa to repeat the experience of transfers outlined in figure 8.1. Indeed, had the provinces received only tax point transfers in 1977 instead of a combination of cash and tax points, they would have substantially higher, not to mention more consistent, revenues today (Provincial and Territorial Finance Ministers 2001, see chart on page 9).

TAXPAYERS' PERSPECTIVES
AND THE DEBATE OVER NATIONAL STANDARDS

A final and perhaps most critical argument for provinces to receive more sources of revenue to meet their responsibilities is that it will enhance provincial accountability (McKenzie 2005; see also Mintz and Smart 2002). Today, it is simply too easy for provinces to off-load their responsibility for health care and other social programs on

Ottawa, blaming the federal government on the one hand for restraining their ability to act and on the other for failing to provide proper funding. The transfer of GST revenues to provinces and the elimination of health transfers will transfer accountability for health care to provincial governments and their voters, who will have a much better connection between taxes paid and services received. As Mintz and Smart state, under the current system, "Ottawa raises the money, and the provinces spend it. The result of this fiscal churning is the 'co-dependent' constitutional relations we have today. No government has clear responsibility for delivering key programs and both sides blame the other when something goes wrong ... A tax point transfer would put an end to this fiscal illusion" (2002, 1; see also Smart 2005).

Some critics will see these proposals as undermining the role of the federal government in health and other social policies, leading to a long-run decline in services throughout the nation. Under successive governments, Ottawa has long positioned itself to be the champion of pan-Canadian standards in health care, and cash transfers are the carrot and stick believed to keep the provinces in line. Perhaps it is high time to acknowledge that provincial voters are every bit as trustworthy as national voters in holding provincial governments accountable for the type of health and social programs that they want (Emery 2010). National standards could be stifling needed reforms in the health care system, and they have little economic rationale, since, as noted, health care policies do not create spillover effects for other provinces.

Although these tax changes have no direct implications for the level of consolidated (federal-provincial) spending on health care, hardening government budget constraints and forcing politicians to confront fiscal and demographic realities is likely to lead to long-run, fundamental changes to the system (see McKenzie [2005] on the importance of this constraint in the context of fiscal federalism). This is a good thing: the system needs such change. It is not enough to pour public money into the existing system. In the present system, the demand for funds is virtually unlimited, with no ceiling in sight. The only alternative is to limit the growth of health care spending, and this will surely involve equality-access rationing, catastrophe insurance, and price rationing in a sensible way. We must recognize that the fiscal flow supporting the current equilibrium is not unlimited. It hinges on expanded productivity, and dumping more and more money into health is not the way to expand productivity (see, e.g., Falkner 2011). It seems unavoidable that a greater proportion of public resources must be devoted to education and infrastructure in the future, and less to health – or we run the risk of having less to spend on anything. Until people stop pretending that more public money is the solution, we will never be able to reach a solution, and we might do a lot of damage to the health of our economy in the process.

An important benefit of placing more of the explicit fiscal burden on the more fiscally challenged level of government – the provinces – is that it should make us face up to these fundamental problems sooner. Moreover, and on past evidence with good reason, we might expect that ten minds are better than one: that is, give the provinces a freer hand, and a stronger stimulus, to find solutions and some of them will indeed try different things. One of the conventional arguments for the superiority of the federal system is that provinces are laboratories in which we can work out different ways of dealing with public policy problems. Saskatchewan led the way to our current health system in the 1950s. Perhaps it, or some other province, may lead the way to a sustainable health system for the 2010s. We should let federalism do its job.

CONCLUSION

In this chapter I have made the case for transferring GST revenues from the federal government to the provinces, with the cost of doing so offset by reducing federal transfers for social programs. The strongest argument for doing so is that this will help to eliminate the fiscal imbalance and produce a better alignment between provincial own-source revenues and provincial programs. I argue that GST revenues should be transferred to the provinces because it would push the final provinces to harmonize their sales tax with the GST, because the GST is a more stable revenue source for social programs, because the entire tax can be transferred, and because the dollars that Ottawa would still transfer to the provinces could be used as leverage to ensure the federal government would still maintain a consistent GST base across Canada. Governments should have to raise enough revenues to pay for the expenditures they make. Turning GST revenues over to the provinces will bring our provinces much closer to this very basic and important imperative.

Before World War II, Canada and the provinces each levied a bewildering array of taxes that was commonly referred to as a tax jungle. In 1937, the federal government created the Rowell-Sirois Commission to examine these fiscal arrangements and provide recommendations. In 1940, the commission recommended that the federal government exclusively occupy personal, corporate, and inheritance tax fields and in return assume all provincial debt and pay national adjustment grants to poorer provinces. Although the recommendations of the commission were rejected, a federal-provincial conference in 1941 resulted in the provinces relinquishing their access to personal, corporate, and inheritance taxes in recognition of the burdens the federal government faced to fund the war effort – in effect, a large tax point transfer from the provinces to the federal government. In return, the provinces received grants from Ottawa.

In the years following World War II, Ottawa established various shared cost programs with the provinces as provincial expenditures grew with the expansion of the welfare state. At the same time, provinces increased pressure on Ottawa to give them back some of the tax room they had transferred to the federal government to fund the war effort. This culminated in the creation of established programs financing (EPF) in 1977. EPF was a combination cash and tax point transfer to fund hospital insurance, medicare, and post-secondary education. EPF was to fund half of these provincial expenditures via a cash transfer plus 13.5 points of personal income tax and one point of corporate income tax. The federal government lowered its share in return for provinces increasing their take of these taxes: a tax point transfer. In effect, EPF resulted in the federal government providing a cash contribution to provinces that covered one quarter of the costs of these programs, with the tax point transfer covering another quarter.[5] These tax points were worth more in richer provinces than in poorer provinces. The equalization program captured a portion of the differences in the value of these tax points. In addition, the federal government reduced the cash portion paid out to wealthier provinces so that the tax points were fully equalized. This latter adjustment became known as associated equalization to distinguish it from actual payments made in the equalization program.

This associated equalization has become the source of much controversy (Boessenkool 1996). On the one hand, it has been referred to as back-door equalization that should be eliminated (Expert Panel on

Equalization and Territorial Formula Financing 2006, 47; Courchene 1995). On the other hand, the lack of transparency of associated equalization has led to calls that the federal government should establish a tax point adjustment program explicitly to pay this associated equalization as a distinct federal expenditure program (Advisory Panel on Fiscal Imbalance 2006, 71–3; note that the Government of Ontario explicitly rejected the creation of this Tax Point Adjustment Program: see http://news.ontario.ca/opo/en/2006/04/statement-by-premier-dalton-mcguinty-on-report-of-the-council-of-the-federation-panel.html). Recent federal budgets are starting to move in the direction of eliminating associated equalization. This would remove associated equalization from the Canada Social Transfer by turning it into an equal per capita cash transfer, and commit to moving the Canada Health Transfer to equal per capita cash payments when the 10-Year Plan to Strengthen Health Care (appendix 2) expires in 2014. This was principally done in the 2007 Budget Plan (Canada Department of Finance 2007, Annex, 359–61).

Clearly, a realignment of consumption tax rates would be worth more to the rich provinces than to the poor ones. The existing equalization system would deal with that automatically to some extent, ensuring that the additional provincial tax room had the same value to all equalization-receiving provinces. But that still leaves Alberta and (to some extent) Ontario and British Columbia getting more. To be absolutely clear: the do-nothing reform proposed by some, in which the federal government decreases the GST unilaterally and leaves provinces to raise their tax rates if they choose, would result in an implicit transfer of resources from have-not to have provinces that a majority of provinces would probably oppose.

NOTES

1 Much of this section comes from Boessenkool (2001). This chapter was written before the federal government announced its current position on renewing the health accords. As a result, some of the comments in this chapter, although not the basic argument, are slightly out of date.

2 This paper and numerous conversations with Smart and Bird made a significant contribution to my thinking on these matters.

3 The remainder of this chapter draws very heavily from Boessenkool (2010).

4 I borrow liberally from the report of the Technical Committee on Business
   Taxation in this section.
5 This historical summary of transfers draws heavily from the 2006 report of
   the Advisory Panel on Fiscal Imbalance (pages 21–5).

9

The Future of the Federal Role
in Canadian Health Care

GREG MARCHILDON

Today we sit on the cusp. Left unchecked, this situation will inevitably produce 13 clearly separate health care systems, each with differing methods of
payment, delivery and outcomes, coupled by an ever increasing volatile and
debilitating debate surrounding our nation, its principles and values. This is
no way to renew a program of such immense personal and national importance and, for sure, it is no way to strengthen those foundations that unify
us as a nation ... The reality is that Canadians embrace medicare as a public
good, a national symbol and a defining aspect of their citizenship.

> Roy Romanow (2002, xviii)

Under successive governments, Ottawa has long positioned itself to be the
champion of pan-Canadian standards in health care – and cash transfers are
the carrot and stick believed to keep the provinces in line. Perhaps it is high
time to acknowledge that provincial voters are every bit as trustworthy as
national voters in holding provincial governments accountable for the type
of health and social programs that they want. National standards could be
stifling needed reforms in the health-care system, and they have little economic rationale ...

> Ken Boessenkool (2010, 17)

In the foreword to the Commission on the Future of Health Care in
Canada's report, entitled A Message to Canadians, Roy Romanow
made the case for a continuing federal role in public health care

(Romanow 2002). What is interesting is that he felt compelled to do so because powerful voices in Canada were already beginning to call for a major retreat in the federal role. A decade after his report, the voices in favour of further decentralizing health care are even louder for three principal reasons. The first reason follows on from Mr. Romanow's argument. Instead of renewing medicare,[1] in particular by avoiding the question of how best to refurbish the federal role in publicly financed health care overall, those defending a federal role are doing so on the basis of the past, while the future seems to belong to those arguing in favour of a more vigorous role for the provinces. The second reason is that since the late 1980s, the federal government has done very little to live up to its existing role; it has been unwilling to protect the five principles enunciated in the Canada Health Act, much less suggest innovative ideas on how to reshape its involvement since the act was passed in 1984. Finally, the federal Conservative government under Stephen Harper has made it clear that it rejects the historic role of the federal government as one of the key stewards of medicare in Canada and wants to leave the policy entirely in the hands of the provinces.

Harper's own views on federalism and health care, both in opposition before 2006 and as prime minister since 2006, have been clear. In his view, health care is within provincial jurisdiction, and the federal government should not be using the Canada Health Transfer (CHT) or other transfers to set direction even at a very high level of policy. This perspective aligns with the long-standing views of his former policy and strategic advisor, Ken Boessenkool, who, in 2010, suggested a radical way in which the federal government could ensure provincial responsibility for health care: that is, replacing the CHT with a permanent tax transfer to the provinces, an idea that has a long pedigree (Boessenkool 2010; Rode and Rushton 2004). In fact, the proposal involved the transfer of the entire tax field of the GST to the provinces. Boessenkool's idea was already in circulation in the Conservative caucus weeks before the proposal was published, when Maxime Bernier, minister of state for small business and tourism, spoke of the possibility of the federal government replacing the CHT with a one-time tax transfer and leaving health care as an exclusive provincial responsibility (Fitzpatrick 2010). Both Boessenkool and Bernier concluded that the tax transfer would remove Ottawa from medicare, and the paternalism of federal standards represented by the five criteria of the Canada Health Act: public administration, portability, comprehensiveness, accessibility, and universality.

Although sympathetic to the objective, Harper chose a far more subtle approach to achieve a similar result, albeit over a much longer time frame. In December 2011, in a strategic coup that took provincial governments, the media, and knowledgeable observers by surprise, the federal minister of finance announced major changes to the CHT, including the way in which the quantum and annual increases would be calculated. Potential criticism was dulled by the slow phasing in of the changes – the new escalator formula, for example, was not scheduled to kick in until well after the 2015 federal election.

The details of these changes, including the implications of moving from an equalized to a pure per capita formula, a move that will produce a windfall for the richest province in the country, have been discussed elsewhere in this book so I will focus on one aspect of the new arrangement. Shortly after the reformulated CHT was introduced, the Harper government also announced that, while the CHT would continue in its modified form, the federal government would no longer use the federal spending power in general or this transfer in particular to play a decision-making role in health care reform, a role that, in its view, always belonged to the provinces. In effect, the Harper government distanced itself from previous federal administrations throughout the post-war period, including Progressive Conservative governments under John G. Diefenbaker, who implemented cost sharing for the introduction of universal hospital insurance on a national basis, and Brian Mulroney, who, however reluctantly, enforced the Canada Health Act in its infancy.

I can only presume that the Harper government chose a more gradual and subtle approach because it feared the public and political backlash from implementing the more direct and immediate tax transfer that Boessenkool recommended. At the same time, however, the Harper government has always been transparent about its vision for a more decentralized federation (whether it is in the form of the open federalism or market-preserving federalism), a position based on the assumption that health care had become far too centralized because of the actions of activist federal governments since the late 1940s, and the result has been to create an inflexible system that resists reform and improvement. This vision is fortified by the Harper administration's insistence that health care is firmly within provincial jurisdiction and that the post-war activism of successive federal administrations contravened the letter and spirit of the Canadian constitution. In other words, health care must be further decentralized to facilitate real innovation and reform, a development that is, in any event, more consistent with the distribution of powers under the constitution. Although I vigorously contest this interpretation on the basis of the evidence and history I present, I do not use the same evidence and history to uphold the traditional federal role in health care. On the contrary, I argue that a major shift in the federal role is required, one that elevates the federal role in one respect, but one that also gets back to the basics in terms of the Canada Health Act and the funding transfers to the provinces that support that law's five key principles.

FEDERALISM AND DECENTRALIZATION IN SOCIAL POLICY

In its most basic construction, a federation involves two orders of government that combine elements of shared rule through a common government and regional self-rule through substates, each with constitutionally recognized authorities and responsibilities. All federations, including Canada's, face the same struggle: to balance the diversity that is the real advantage of a federal structure with the necessary unity required to remain a country with a common citizenship. It is this inescapable and permanent conundrum of federations that lies at the heart of the issue of the appropriate federal role – past, present, and future – in social policy in general, and Canadian health care in particular.

Depending on the measure used, Canada is either the most, or the second-most, decentralized federation among the nine federations in the Organisation of Economic Co-operation and Development (OECD). As shown in table 9.1, on the basis of a twenty-point benchmark scale developed by a comparative federalism scholar measuring the degree of constitutional, political, and fiscal decentralization as well as asymmetry, Canada ends up with the highest decentralization score among the nine OECD federations (Requejo 2010).

Using a narrower measure of the central government's control over fiscal resources relative to the control wielded by substate and local governments, the Government of Canada has the smallest share of total fiscal resources of any central government in the OECD with the sole exception of Switzerland (Watts 2008). Moreover, federal control over resources has actually declined steadily relative to the control by provincial governments since the 1960s (Marchildon 1995). However,

Table 9.1
Degree of constitutional, political, and fiscal decentralization (from most
to least)

OECD *federation*	*Degree of decentralization (20-point scale)*
Canada	16.5
United States	14.5
Switzerland	14.0
Belgium	14.0
Australia	12.0
Germany	12.0
Spain	10.5
Austria	8.3
Mexico	5.0

Source: Derived from Requejo (2010, 287).

these facts offer little consolation to those who argue that the federal
government is using its "excess revenues" as conditional transfers to
alter the more "legitimate" and "well-grounded" priorities and preferences of provincial governments. Indeed, without this "imbalance" in
fiscal resources between the two orders of government, there could be
no spending power.

The use of the word "imbalance" itself conveys the impression that
a more ideal federation would be one in which the central government collects only the revenues it needs for its own purposes and
transfers nothing to the constituent units that depend entirely on
own-source revenues for their expenditures. In reality, no such federation exists. In all OECD federations, central governments collect more
than they need for their own direct expenditures and debt repayment
and use transfers to constituent units to achieve national policy objectives (Watts 1999).

In Canada, these transfers serve at least two policy purposes. The
first is to redistribute fiscal resources from higher-income and higher-
tax-capacity regions to lower-income and lower-tax-capacity regions in
the country. The second is to set national standards or achieve national objectives by setting conditions on the transfers.

The extent to which constituent units are reliant on central government revenues is a measure of two things: the relative fiscal inca-
pacity of the constituent units, and the extent of the potential control
that can be exercised by a central government over its constituent

Table 9.2
Transfers as a percentage of constituent unit revenues in OECD federations,
2000–04

OECD federation	Percentage of constituent unit revenues (%)
Mexico	87.9
Spain	72.8
Belgium*	57.4
Austria	47.4
Australia	45.6
Germany	43.8
United States	25.6
Switzerland	24.8
Canada	12.9

Note: * Transfers to territorially based regions only (not language communities).
Source: Derived from Watts (2008, 105).

units by attaching conditions to substate transfers. In Canada, it has
often been said that provincial governments are highly reliant on federal transfers, the implication being that they are more reliant on
transfers and therefore potentially more subject to central government direction and coercion than is typical for substates in other federations. Although this statement may sound plausible, it is far from
accurate. In fact, as illustrated in table 9.2, the Canadian provinces are
the most fiscally independent constituent units in the OECD – more
fiscally independent than even the Swiss cantons – and the Government of Canada has, proportionately, the least capacity to set conditions and national standards of any OECD federation.

The word "capacity" is critical. Not all central governments take
advantage of their potential fiscal leverage by using conditional transfers. In other words, it is essential to examine the extent to which
Canada, relative to other OECD federations, relies on conditional transfers. Although transfers constitute a relatively small percentage of
provincial revenues, if the vast majority of these come in the form of
conditional transfers, then this might still support the argument that
the federal government overuses its spending power relative to other
central governments. Here again, however, the evidence does not support such an argument.

Although roughly 65% of all federal transfers can be defined as being conditional (using a very expansive definition of that term) – a midpoint among OECD countries – they nonetheless make up only 37% of provincial government revenues, one of the lowest levels in the OECD. At the same time, it should be noted that the two largest conditional transfers, the CHT and the Canada Social Transfer (CST), are actually block transfers with limited conditionality (McIntosh 2004). Of the two, the CHT is the more conditional transfer. Theoretically, the federal government has the right to deduct transfers in the event that the five criteria of the Canada Health Act are infringed, but this power has never been exercised. Instead, successive federal governments have restricted themselves to enforcing the provision on user fees and extra billing that supports the criterion of accessibility in the Canada Health Act – deducting dollar for dollar the amounts that provincial governments have permitted doctors or facilities to charge individual patients (Marchildon 2006).

It is highly debatable whether the block CHT and CST transfers are nearly as conditional as the types of social policy transfers by central governments in other federations (Ahmad 1997). In this respect, one only needs to point to the highly specific and often onerous rules and regulations that accompany the federal conditional funding of state programming in the United States.

Two calculations are shown in table 9.3, one that counts the CHT and CST as conditional transfers, and one that treats the two transfers as unconditional block transfers. The argument for the first is that there is clearly some conditionality formally attached to the two transfers, particular the CHT, given the criteria enumerated in the Canada Health Act. However, given the weakness of this formal conditionality for both transfer programs, as well as the Harper government's insistence that it intends to leave health care to the provinces, I doubt that these transfers fall into the same league as conditional transfers in other OECD federations. If this argument is accepted and the second calculation is used, then provincial governments are the most autonomous among OECD federation substates in terms of their freedom from central government imposition through the spending power. However, even when the CHT and CST are classified as conditional transfers, provincial governments are hardly outliers in terms of their reliance on conditional transfers relative to other OECD federations.

Despite this comparative evidence, it is historically accurate to say

Table 9.3
Extent of conditional transfers in OECD federations

OECD federation	Extent of conditional transfers as a proportion of federal transfers (%), 2000	OECD federation	Extent of conditional transfers as a proportion of total constituent unit revenues (%), 2000–04
United States	100.0	Mexico	48.8
Austria	78.9	Australia	45.9
Switzerland	73.1	Spain	41.9
Spain	66.1	Switzerland	38.1
Canada (includes CHT and CST)	64.9	Austria	37.4
Germany	64.5	Germany	37.0
Mexico	55.5	Canada (including CHT and CST)	37.0
Australia	40.9	United States	25.6
Belgium (communities and regions)	6.1	Belgium	4.0
		Canada (excluding CHT and CST)	3.7

Note: CHT, Canada Health Transfer; CST, Canada Social Transfer
Source: Derived from Watts (2008, 107–8)

that the Government of Canada's use of the spending power has been highly controversial in large part because of Quebec's long-standing position concerning the illegitimacy of this policy tool in areas of provincial jurisdiction, a position periodically supported by other provinces, especially Alberta (Telford 2003; Bourgault 2004). As a consequence, the historical reality of this long-standing provincial antipathy to the spending power must be balanced against the international evidence on the prevalence and use of the spending power.

With the Harper government's announcement of the changes to the CHT on 19 December 2011, we have entered a new phase of the federal government's use of the spending power in health care. However, the conditions that facilitated this change predate the Harper government. Universal hospital insurance and medical care insurance were originally implemented on the basis of shared-cost financing with relatively tight accountability for the transfer between the provincial and federal governments. This shared cost regime was replaced by a block transfer approach with looser federal-provincial accountability through established programs financing (EPF) in 1977. At the time, the federal government and most provincial governments both desired the new EPF arrangement but for different reasons (Brown 1980). Ottawa reduced its fiscal risk in terms of the future growth of the transfer while the provinces had considerably more flexibility in the use of the transfer money (Coyte and Landon 1990). One of the unforeseen consequences of the new EPF regime was the growth in user fees and extra billing in some provinces that threatened to make a mockery of the principle of universality. Less than a decade later, the federal government introduced the Canada Health Act to stop this practice. The change, however, did not affect the block nature of the EPF, which continued through subsequent iterations as the Canada Health and Social Transfer (1995–2003) and the CHT (2004–present).

The CHT and its historical paternity must represent a major challenge to the Harper government's ideology and its view of the federation. The fact that Canadians may continue to expect the Harper government to enforce a Canada Health Act that trumpets health care as a social service rather than a market commodity through transfer funding deductions to the provinces is counter to its ideological instincts. And the fact that the CHT supports a law that advances national standards or dimensions – albeit at a very high level of abstraction – is contrary to the Conservative government's view that the provinces should make decisions on publicly financed health care on their own and without "interference" or "guidance" from Ottawa. At the same time, the Harper government has been constrained by public opinion surveys that show a majority of Canadians continuing to support the principle of universal access based on need (rather than ability to pay) and the federal government playing a role to ensure that this principle is applied consistently in all provinces (Fierlbeck 2011). For example, a recent public opinion survey conducted by The Strategic Counsel for Health Canada concluded that most Canadians still "support the federal government taking a stronger leadership role in health care in a range of areas" (The Strategic Counsel 2012, 7).

Nevertheless, it must have been galling for all federal administrations over the last half century that federal health care transfers, one of the single largest spending items in the federal budget (estimated to be worth $27 billion in 2011–12), are doled out to ungrateful provincial and territorial governments for services over which Ottawa has no control and gets little credit. This is bad enough, but when you add the belief that it is inappropriate for the federal government to set (much less enforce) national standards in an area of provincial juris-diction, then you have the full measure of the Harper government's antipathy to the CHT and all that it represents. Of course, such a posi-tion is based on the assumption that health care should be a provin-cial responsibility as defined under the constitution, and it is this assumption that I will now address.

IS HEALTH EXCLUSIVELY WITHIN PROVINCIAL JURISDICTION?

Health care is not within the exclusive jurisdiction of the provinces, although this is often stated to be the case. In fact, unlike education, responsibility for which is constitutionally assigned to provincial gov-ernments, health care is not even specifically mentioned in the con-stitution. While education was a contentious issue at the time the divi-sion of powers was negotiated and written in 1864, the phrase "health care" was unknown. Moreover, activities we would recognize as com-ponents of public health care today were considered to be private or charitable activities in the 1860s. Hospital care was one such activity. Responsibility for hospitals was clearly identified and put under provincial jurisdiction – the provinces were given the power to regu-late hospitals – but this was in the context of provincial governments providing subsidies to hospitals that delivered charity care for the very poor.[2] In contrast, the control over patents – which would much later become important in terms of pharmaceutical regulation – was put under section 91 as federal jurisdiction.

The jurisdiction over almost everything else in health care must be inferred from more general wording in the constitution. Although this general reading has led most constitutional scholars to argue that the primary jurisdiction for health care lies with the provincial governments, many elements of health care outside hospital care, such as public health, remain ambiguous (Braën 2004; Leeson 2004). I would even say that the authority of the Canada Health Act, a law unilaterally passed by the Parliament of Canada, is based at least in part on this ambiguity. In fact, the Canada Health Act has never been legally contested by a provincial government on the grounds that it exceeds the federal government's powers under section 91 (Gibson 1996).

Of course, the working muscle of the Canada Health Act – the federal spending power and the ability to spend and withdraw money from the provinces – lies outside the constitution. This power has been tested and upheld in the courts. I would add that the Canada Health Act would probably survive any potential challenges concerning its constitutional legitimacy in the future because of its voluntary nature. Provinces choose whether or not to comply with the criteria, and even if they choose to comply they still have decision-making control over almost all aspects of the administration of their respective health systems. The Canada Health Act sets out five very high level national standards allowing some degree of commonality across the country even while allowing the provinces to remain in firm control of fiscal, administrative, and service delivery structures on the ground.

Since the passage of the Canada Health Act in 1984, at least two of its principles – universality and accessibility – have become an integral part of the Canadian identity. As Roy Romanow expressed it in his royal commission report on the future of health care in Canada, Canadians have come to "embrace medicare" – those medically necessary or required services covered under the Canada Health Act – "as a public good, a national symbol and a defining aspect of their citizenship" (Romanow 2002, xviii). This makes it exceedingly difficult for any federal government, whatever its views concerning the constitutional legitimacy or social policy objectives of this law, to simply repeal the Canada Health Act.

At the same time, the Canadian public has devoted far less attention to the three other principles of the Canada Health Act. To some extent, this is understandable. The principles of public administration and comprehensiveness have lost their original meaning over time and, besides, they are not under any imminent threat. All provincial governments meet the criterion of public administration simply by administering their own single-payer reimbursement systems for hospital and physician services, thereby ensuring that they are democratically accountable for financing and administering medicare in their respective provincial legislatures. In addition, provincial governments have not engaged in any major campaign to delist medicare services thereby undermining the principle of comprehensiveness.

We are presented with a very different story for the portability principle. A number of provinces no longer automatically accept medical care insurance from other provinces, particularly Quebec, putting the onus on individuals to pay upfront for physician and primary care services they receive while visiting other provinces and then recover these expenses (or a portion of them) from their home provinces. The origins of this problem stem from a decades-old dispute between Quebec and Ontario; when the government of Quebec refused to accept the Ontario tariff for services, but without federal intervention, the contagion eventually spread to other provinces. Although concerns about national unity may have prevented successive federal administrations from intervening to protect the principle of portability, this would be one area where enforcing the Canada Health Act should be consistent with the Harper government's ideology as well as its view that protecting and enhancing the economic (as opposed to the social) union is an appropriate role for the federal government. There are obvious benefits that flow from economic mobility, and any continued deterioration in portability, including the non-recognition of hospital in addition to physician billing – could impede Canadians from visiting or (much worse) moving to other parts of the country for employment.

It is not hard to see why only a federal government will be prepared to promote and protect portability as a national standard or principle. Although it is in the national interest to protect portability, it will not necessarily be in the interests of any individual province, particularly if it has a lower medicare tariff than surrounding provinces or if it tends to attract proportionately more visitors and new residents relative to other provinces. Indeed, the question of portability goes to the heart of balancing the diversity (and with it, the advantages) of ten provincial and three territorial administrative systems for medicare with the necessary unity required for Canada to remain a country with a recognizable sense of common citizenship. The economic advantage of portability should be obvious. Canadians do not select employment and place of residence on the basis of health insurance. Since they are free to select employment on other grounds, they are able to respond more quickly to demands of the marketplace.

WHAT TO DO?

Although I have argued against the two main assumptions implicit in the Harper government's position on health care, I am not advocating for a simple maintenance of the status quo. Instead, I am urging that the federal role in health care be reconfigured for the twenty-first century, and the role I am suggesting goes beyond being a national counterweight to the provincial diversity inherent in a decentralized federation. Canadians see themselves as more than simply residents living within a dual polity – federal and provincial. The majority also see themselves as citizens of a single country with a set of rights and responsibilities that are not defined by the dual territoriality of federalism (Graefe and Bourns 2009). Similar to other types of social policy, medicare is a combination of shared social rights and shared social citizenship (Béland and Lecours 2006).

In the Canadian case, the federal role should not simply be one reflecting a set of existing social rights and citizenship, but rather it should be one in which the federal government actively engages with provincial governments and the general public in a project of identity building. Medicare is an identity-building project that began in earnest in the mid-1950s and continued through the 1960s. To correct for the accountability lost as a result of the introduction of the EPF block transfer, it was further refined with the introduction of the Canada Health Act in 1984. Little has happened since that time because successive federal administrations have chosen not to build on this legacy despite the many opportunities to do so, including the first ministers' accord of 2003 (appendix 1) that followed on the heels of the Romanow commission, and the "fix for a generation" first ministers' agreement one year later.

Of course, I do not expect the current Conservative government in Ottawa to welcome these suggestions. They are written with a different administration in mind, one that may have a preference for tax-funded, universal health care, and one that is willing to have some pan-Canadian social policy threads as part of a common Canadian citizenship – a social union as well as an economic union. Admittedly, these are not assumptions shared by all political parties and government administrations.

First, I would eliminate block transfers in health care. Although they have provided some fiscal advantages to both orders of government, it is difficult not to conclude that the block transfer approach, including the CHT, has failed us as a federation, particularly in our efforts to balance unity through national standards with diversity through provincial administration (Brown 1980; McIntosh 2004). Although there are advantages to a block transfer, such transfers are not sufficiently linked to policy purpose to allow for clearer accountabilities between the two orders of government. For this reason, I would recommend a conditional cash transfer directly attached to the Canada Health Act that required withdrawals in the event that the principles of the act are being infringed. To avoid more detailed surveillance by the federal government directly, I would suggest a mechanism that is open to citizen input and complaint to encourage a more direct accountability between residents and their respective provincial governments.

The amount of the new transfer could be less than currently provided. How much less is difficult to say, but one-half of the current transfer should be more than sufficient to enforce the Canada Health Act.

Second, I would reinvest the money thus freed up to both reinforce and extend our half-century-old medicare house to ensure that public health care is more sustainable for the twenty-first century in terms of cost, quality, and access. This could be accomplished by the federal government sharing the costs of an expanded basket of universal services that the provincial governments would be responsible for administering. In exchange for federal funding, Ottawa would enact an appropriate set of national standards or principles through an extension of the Canada Health Act or, if co-payments or user fees were to attach to the new services, then through another parallel (although not identical) law.

The question to be asked is whether federal cost sharing is within the realm of the politically possible given the state of the federation today. Some provincial governments would object to the very idea of national standards accompanying transfers, particularly if those standards are unilaterally imposed and enforced by the federal government. Intergovernmental negotiation of national standards is a possibility, but the experience with intergovernmental agreements – their ambiguity, their poor accountability, and their lack of enforcement – as witnessed in the results of three health accords signed by first ministers in 2000, 2003, and 2004, does not recommend this approach (Fafard 2012).

I think there is a viable alternative. The federal government should take an ownership position in public health care by funding and administering a national pharmacare program (Marchildon 2007). There are a number of advantages to this alternative. To start with, this is the one health sector where the federal government has solid constitutional footing – in many respects stronger than that of the provincial governments. In addition, the federal government already has the machinery to regulate the market entry, the monopoly protection, and the prices of branded prescription drugs through Health Canada, the Patent Act, and the Patented Medicine Prices Review Board. I would argue that it also has the capacity, unexercised since the late 1980s, to regulate generic prescription drug prices through licensing or other means.

Given that provincial prescription drug programs have been a major cost driver of health costs since the late 1970s, a federal pharmacare program would remove an enormous cost burden from the shoulders of provincial governments. Although the fiscal liability of a pharmacare program would no doubt appear burdensome to any federal administration, the regulatory machinery is already largely in place to control cost more effectively than could ever be done at the provincial level. There are also ready examples at hand, including the federal pharmacare programs run by the central governments in Australia and New Zealand. Moreover, pharmacare would be mainly a coverage plan that would not involve the complexities of service delivery found in other health sectors. Such programs, such as the Canada Pension Plan, in part because they do not involve service delivery requiring the administration of human resources and physical facilities on the ground, are far more within the proven expertise of the federal government. Finally, pharmacare would provide a direct accountability relationship between the Government of Canada and individual Canadians, and the program could over time become a national unifier in an already highly decentralized and asymmetrical federation.

NOTES

1 I am using the word medicare to include both hospital and medical care service that are defined as "medically necessary" and therefore provided on a universal basis, free of any direct charges to the patient. On the history of the use of the word, see Marchildon (2009), and on the definition of medically necessary, see Charles et al. (1997).

2 The exact wording under section 92 is "The Establishment, Maintenance, and Management of Hospitals, Asylums, Charities and Eleemosynary Institutions in and for the Province, other than Marine Hospitals."

10

Conclusion:
Combining the Knowledge of Federalism Researchers, Health Care Researchers, and Policy Practitioners to Understand and Improve Canadian Health Care Federalism

WILLIAM LAHEY

INTRODUCTION

This book has its origins in the collaboration of most of the authors in presenting a pre-conference workshop on health care federalism at the meeting of the Canadian Association for Health Services and Policy Research that took place in Halifax in May 2011 (Canadian Association for Health Services and Policy Research 2011). At that time, just days after the re-election of the Harper Conservatives with a majority government in a national election, the focus was very much on what were generally thought to be the upcoming federal-provincial-territorial negotiations for a new intergovernmental health deal to replace the 10-Year Plan on Strengthening Health Care (appendix 2) that expires in 2014. Our objective was to understand and, we hoped, contribute to this process of negotiation through multidisciplinary analyses that combined the perspectives of individuals who approached the study of health care federalism primarily as scholars of federalism with those of individuals who approached it primarily as scholars of health care, and to supplement these perspectives with the perspectives of colleagues experi-

.enced in the world of public policy at the interface of federalism and health care.

Canada's health care federalism now seems to be at a very different kind of juncture. Through Finance Minister Jim Flaherty, the federal government has told the provinces that federal health care funding after the expiry of current federal funding commitments based on the 10-year plan will be fixed to the prevailing rate of economic growth and be distributed among the provinces on a per capita basis (Bailey and Curry 2011). The absence of any negotiation – even of advance notice – of this approach to health care financing and the disinterest in any reciprocating provincial (and territorial) commitments on health care reform signal unmistakably that the brief age of the federal-provincial-territorial health care accord as we have known it in Canadian health care federalism has come to a close, at least for now.

But what has not come to an end is the importance of federalism to Canada's health care system or, for that matter, of Canada's health care system to its federalism. In this book Fierlbeck asks if the marriage between these two fundamental Canadian institutions can be saved, but it is clear that their cohabitation at least is not in serious question. This is likely to be true even if the intention of the current federal government of Prime Minister Harper is, as it appears to be, to disentangle federal and provincial responsibilities in health care as part of a wider vision of federalism that emphasizes federal concentration on matters within exclusive federal competency. For as Fierlbeck explores in her chapter on the political dynamics of health care federalism (chapter 3), it seems likely that when this approach to federalism is applied to health care it is as much about changing Canadian health care as was the earlier accord-based approach of the Chrétien and Martin governments. Specifically, it seems likely that it is intended to create the conditions that will allow or even require provinces to make decisions that give the market a wider importance in health care governance than it already has. This outcome would align with what Fierlbeck and others, including David Haardt writing in this book (chapter 2), call the market-preserving federalism seemingly favoured by the Harper government, under which federal retrenchment in areas such as health care is combined with assertion of federal jurisdiction in economic policy domains, including financial regulation.

APPLICATIONS OF MULTIDISCIPLINARY EXAMINATION
OF AN EVOLVING HEALTH CARE FEDERALISM

Thus, multidisciplinary attention to the interaction of health care and federalism that combines the scholarship and policy experience of those who approach the interaction primarily through a broader interest in federalism and of those who do so primarily through an interest in health care remains relevant and pertinent. The health care accords of 2000 and more particularly of 2003 (appendix 1) and the 10-year plan of 2004 (appendix 2) made the operation of federalism in the governance of Canadian health care more evident but they were not the basis of health care federalism in Canada. Instead, Canada's health care federalism is based fundamentally on Canada's constitution and the divisions of governmental responsibilities it creates with respect to health and health care and on Canada's political federalism, which has shaped Canada's approach to health care governance and in turn, to some extent, been shaped by its approach to health care governance. On a continuing basis, it is these more fundamental realities, not the accord or other instrument of governance that might have been negotiated to replace the 10-year plan, that require the kind of multidisciplinary analytical collaboration that was the genesis of the collaborative work that resulted in this book.

On this deeper and more fundamental level, such multidisciplinary scholarly collaboration is crucial to understanding the ideological and political objectives that may be driving the current federal approach to health care and more specifically to health care funding. Such scholarship is also crucial to understanding the consequences that this approach may have for the evolution of the Canadian health care system. As noted above, Fierlbeck explains how an approach to federalism that is built around the disengagement of the federal government from the substance of health care governance aligns not only with a general concern for clear jurisdictional separations but also with a general concern for the role of federalism in promoting and strengthening markets and market-based answers to policy questions. As demonstrated by Haardt as well as Fierlbeck, it is crucial in this regard to understand the significant economic and policy pressures that will make it difficult for provinces to resist the additional pressure in favour of privatization that may be introduced by a decentralizing market-preserving federalism. Equally important, the two chapters by Haardt (chapters 2 and 5) demonstrate that multidisciplinary analysis of health care federalism is crucial to understanding how a decentralized health care federalism, even if it does not expand the role of market mechanisms, may prevent Canada's public health care system from realizing the advantages, including equity of access, economies of scale, and cost avoidance, that publicly financed health care systems seem generally to have over health care systems that heavily rely on private financing and management.

The multidisciplinary study of Canadian health care federalism is not, however, only important to our understanding of the consequences that a changed federalism may have for Canada's health care system. It is also pertinent to our understanding of the role that health care may play in shaping the evolution of our federalism under a paradigm that favours decentralization and that may also favour market-based health care. The impact that Canada's approach to health care has had on Canadian federalism in the past is patent: the evolution of the spending power and of the role of the federal government in social policy more generally obviously owes much to the invention in Saskatchewan of what is now called medicare across Canada. More recently, as the chapters by Fierlbeck relate (chapters 1 and 3), the concern of Canadians about the cuts to health care that were implemented by the provinces in the wake of the unilateral cuts in federal transfers that were made by the 1995 federal budget set the stage for the expensive if superficial federalism of collaborative health care governance that was heralded by two health accords and the 10-year plan between 2000 and 2004.

The history suggests that the changing of Canadian health care through market-preserving federalism will not be easy. It may indeed be the case that by linking health care transfers to economic growth and by allocating transfers on a per-capita basis, the funding model that the Harper government has announced will force the provinces (and some provinces more than others) to come to terms with their inability to continue to increase spending on health care at the rates of growth that prevailed after the 2003 accord. By connecting the level of federal funding to the level of economic growth, and by doing so with abundant notice, the model could give provinces leverage with the institutions and providers they fund that the provinces have not had under the fixed formula of "cost plus" increases that have been in place under the 10-year plan. It could therefore help to mitigate the moral hazard problem, stressed by Haardt, which arises from a system of health care governance under which the provinces fund providers and delivery agencies using federal revenue.

Nevertheless, there are reasons to think that when market-preserving federalism confronts the realities of health care governance and the commitment of Canadians to a certain kind of health care system, it is market-preserving federalism that may undergo some of the change. The provinces will obviously face resistance in making the hard choices that stable but more constrained federal funding will force upon them, and not only from those they fund. They will also face opposition from the public who will be affected by whatever limitations or restrictions on funding are placed on those who deliver services. Although the federal plan may be to let the provinces squirm in the face of this opposition, experience shows that public concern about provincial health care governance can become a political problem for the federal government. As Fierlbeck reminds us, this dynamic is a significant part of the context for the multiple health deals that Liberal administrations struck with the provinces between 2000 and 2004.

Experience also suggests that the public will expect hard provincial choices to be made within the parameters of the Canada Health Act, perhaps even in Alberta, where market-preserving federalism is most likely to resonate. There is little to indicate that the Harper government would want to be aggressive in the administration of this act. But if provincial health care governance departed as significantly from the Canada Health Act model as market-preserving federalism would seem to contemplate, the Harper government might be faced with more of a conflict between its commitment to that brand of federalism and its reelection than its unilateralism has contemplated. As I emphasize in chapter 4, the fidelity of governments to the act has always depended at least as much on its popularity with voters as with the act's formal regulatory effect. But that being said, there are also limits, as I point out, to the law's "softness." A federal government that is too tolerant of provincial disregard for the act's core elements cannot be sure that public concern would not be validated and reinforced by judicial intervention. Besides, as Marchildon observes in chapter 9, a federal government that is determined to strengthen and solidify the economic union may come to appreciate the positive contribution that the Canada Health Act, specifically the program criterion of portability, makes to that objective.

The point is that while there is no doubt that Canada's health care federalism is about to be changed by a new and distinct approach to federalism that implies less attention to health care in the processes of federalism, there can also be little doubt that this new and distinct approach to federalism is bound to evolve as it unavoidably confronts the complexities of health care governance in a country that defines itself as much by its approach to health care as it does by its federalism. In that context, sustained multidisciplinary analysis of health care federalism will not only contribute to our understanding of how federalism could and does change health care governance. It will also contribute to our understanding of how the dynamics and forces of health care governance could influence and change federalism, notwithstanding the apparent desire of the Harper government to save federalism (in purer form) from health care.

Finally, the possibility of a new round of intergovernmental discussions on health care reform cannot be discounted entirely. As Fierlbeck and I both consider, there is the possibility that provinces and territories may collaborate, through the Council of the Federation or otherwise, to try to fill some of the pan-Canadian void that will be left in the governance of Canada's health care system to the extent that the federal government is successful in extricating itself from the field, difficult as that may be. This has, at least, been the suggestion of some of the provincial premiers after the provinces received the federal government's non-negotiated (and non-negotiable) statement on how it would handle health care transfers after the expiry of the 10-year plan (Meissner 2012; Scoffield 2012).

Alternatively or in addition, the same forces that might make it difficult for the federal government to stay away from health care and its problems may pull the federal government back into health care discussions with the provinces or alternatively into intergovernmental discussions on other subjects that unavoidably lead to discussions of health care. These forces may be reinforced by any number of events or combinations of events that are not directly about health care but that could make health care an issue that cannot be entirely excluded from the intergovernmental agenda.

One of these events could be the reelection of a sovereignist government in Quebec, should it lead to a national unity crisis and a powerful political dynamic in favour of nation building. Another might be growing pressure for federal engagement with the provinces on federalism's broader fiscal framework. This pressure is already being driven by dissatisfaction with the equalization system relative to the country's economic structure (MacKinnon 2011). It could also be pushed by the scale at which spending pressures are being placed on the provinces by decisions in a range of federal areas of responsibility, including income security for seniors, penal policy, and the federal government's own health care functions (Cheadle 2012). The Harper government – or its successors – may be able to withstand the pressure for a day of reckoning with the provinces on these accumulating pressures. But it is also possible that it may not be able to withstand that pressure, especially if it is combined with pressures relative to health care spending and if it crystallizes into political pressure not just from braying provinces but from voters affected by provincial decisions that voters trace to the federal government.

If intergovernmental discussions do come, it is now fairly clear that it is highly unlikely that their objective will be to achieve anything like a new 10-Year Plan to Strengthen Health Care, at least in the short term. That would imply a continuing role for the federal government in the general business of health care governance that is highly at odds with the Harper government's general approach to federal-provincial relations. What is more likely, perhaps, is that discussions will take place that are focused on specific structural changes that increase the capacity of governments within their distinct jurisdictional spheres to contribute to effective health care governance.

Like the negotiation of the broader kind of framework originally contemplated when most of the authors involved in this book started their collaboration on health care federalism, this kind of more focused intergovernmental discussion could be informed by a multi-disciplinary collaboration that brings together expertise in both federalism and health care and the perspectives of both scholars and those experienced in policy-making. Indeed, this book has already begun the process of applying that kind of analysis to the new realities of Canada's health care federalism. Here, I provide four examples of how the analysis provided in this book could both challenge and inform the evolution of Canadian health care federalism as it transitions from a phase of co-governance based on soft law accords to an approach that stresses the distinctness of federal and provincial responsibilities and a more limited ongoing federal role in the governance of health care at the provincial level.

The first example is the proposal of Boessenkool for a transfer of the revenue from the goods and services tax (GST) to the provinces, with federal tax administration retained, as a fixed substitute for much of the funding that would otherwise come to the provinces through discretionary annual grants (see chapter 8). Clearly, this proposal reflects a policy preference for structural changes in health care federalism that would give both levels of government greater fiscal certainty relative to the cost of health care, that would minimize discretionary federal intermeddling in a provincial sphere of jurisdiction, and that would give the provinces greater freedom to run their health care systems as they see fit. But it also responds to a structural problem with the status quo that David Haardt, who concludes that all of health care should be a federal responsibility, also emphasizes – the moral hazard that arises when provinces fund health care using federal dollars. Thus, while the GST revenue transfer envisaged by Boessenkool is not embraced by Marchildon, who like Haardt argues for greater federal leadership in health care and who (also like Haardt) questions the constitutional correctness of the view that health care is entirely provincial, it is not rejected by him either (chapter 9).

Another example is Marchildon's reiteration of the proposal, also mentioned by Haardt and Lahey, which has been put forward by others, including the provinces, for the initiation of a federal pharmacare program that would largely or entirely supplant the ones currently run by the provinces. This obviously would move the balance in Canadian health care federalism significantly toward the federal government, even though it would probably include a funded "opt out" provision for non-participating provinces. This explains Marchildon's view that the proposal has no prospects for acceptance in the current context. But as Marchildon notes, a federal pharmacare program could arguably be enacted on the basis of unquestioned federal jurisdiction in respect of drugs and therefore without calling into question general provincial jurisdiction over health care governance more broadly. Meanwhile, a federal pharmacare program would have several significant benefits for the quality of Canada's health care system. Depending on how it was done, it would at a stroke make Canada's system more equitable in terms of access to necessary health services. It would remove significant financial pressure from the provinces in the area of health care spending that has the fastest rate of growth. This would alleviate the economic risks that Canada (not just the provinces) face owing to the steady growth in the proportion of provincial spending that must be dedicated to health care, a point stressed by Haardt.

At the same time, like the GST proposal of Boessenkool, a federal pharmacare program would mitigate the core problem of moral hazard that is created by the current system that gives significant control of sources of revenue to one level of governance and much of the control over the spending on health care to the other level of governance. Marchildon's proposal reminds us that this problem is not only amendable to solutions that move control of sources of revenue to the provinces but also to solutions that move responsibility for areas of spending to the federal government. Another commonality is that Marchildon's proposal, like that of Boessenkool, would contribute to a disentangling and rationalization of federal and provincial jurisdictions in respect of health care. It would therefore be consistent with a health care federalism that is more structurally clear.

A third example that would also qualify as a structural change is the development and implementation of a more sophisticated system for measuring and reporting on health system performance, particularly on the interrelated imperatives of quality and productivity. The debate in Canada over whether the provinces should be subject to or free from accountability to the federal government for the quality of their management of health care arguably misses two essential points. The first is that although governments unquestionably govern health care, even if they delegate much of that responsibility to the market, they do not really manage health care, even when they largely opt for public financing and public management (Lahey 2010). Instead, they rely on health care providers and health system administrators to manage health care. The second point is that Canada is arguably behind other countries in subjecting its health care system (or systems) to accountability for performance through processes of evaluation and reporting that are administered by arm's-length agencies that are independent of both government and the organizations and providers that are mandated (or allowed) by government to deliver health care services.

In this book, I argue in chapter 4 that the modest progress made in this direction under the 2003 health accord and the 10-year plan of 2004 is progress that should be built upon at a pan-Canadian level. As explained by Levy and Sobolev in chapter 7, this would be a complex and multifaceted undertaking owing to the difficulties inherent in measuring the performance of health systems in any constitutional context, never mind that of a decentralized federalism. But doing it nevertheless may be crucial if Canadians are to have a health care system that functions – and that can be shown to function – at or above international standards. This may be the reality even if governmental roles and responsibilities relative to health care are rationalized and clarified in ways that better align powers and financial and other incentives with effective health care governance. It will more certainly be the reality if these clarifications and alignments are not achieved and implemented. Moreover, if meaningful processes of independent arm's-length accountability through measurement, evaluation, and reporting could be instituted, they might facilitate the emergence of a health care federalism that was less about accountability between governments and more about the distinct accountability of both levels of government to Canadians, subject to their respective jurisdictional mandates. Admittedly, such processes would seem to run contrary to the apparent animosity of the current federal government to third-party oversight and accountability (May 2012). But they might also align with and even support a federalism that emphasizes role differentiation and clarity and accountability for the making of hard decisions.

The final example is that of needs-based health human resources planning in a pan-Canadian context, as explored in this book by Tomblin Murphy (see chapter 6). As she explains, health human resource planning that considers the full range of options for meeting future patient needs will be increasingly foundational to the sustainability of health care systems and to their capacity to deliver the services that citizens will reasonably expect. It cannot, however, be optimally done if confined to subnational efforts, a point that is particularly strongly pressed by Haardt. This is due to the reality that health human resources are produced and deployed within national or at least regional markets and not merely within provincial markets. This is a good thing. It does, however, mean that the functioning of these national and regional markets without common or at least consistent approaches by provincial health care systems allows some provinces to benefit at the expense of others. Moreover, it means that all provinces suffer from the degree of leverage the functioning of these national and regional markets gives to provider groups to ensure the primacy of their interests in health human resources planning and associated decision-making.

To date, recognition of the common provincial (and territorial) interest in cooperative approaches to health human resources planning has not been strong enough to produce a robust pan-Canadian approach or process. But it has been strong enough, as Tomblin Murphy relates, to support continuing intergovernmental work on the issue at both the regional and national levels. This continuing progress has been made when most of the continuing intergovernmental collaboration envisaged by the 2003 health accord and the 10-year plan has evaporated. This may suggest that meaningful outcomes could be realistically expected in health human resources planning from intergovernmental processes that are largely provincial and territorial. The federal contribution could be focused on providing policy support in clear areas of associated federal jurisdiction (such as immigration policy). This potential for effective interprovincial (and territorial) collaboration may be harnessed if health human resources planning on the intergovernmental level is done, as Tomblin Murphy argues it must be if it is to be done effectively at any level of governance, by a collaborative process that includes providers.

In addition, both the proposal for continuing and more serious attention to performance measurement, evaluation, and reporting at the system level and the proposal for more serious efforts in pan-Canadian health human resources planning would require completion of an integrated system of electronic health record systems, something envisaged by the 2003 accord and the 10-year plan. This is a point made both by Levy and Sobolev and by Tomblin Murphy. Such a system may also be essential or at least very helpful to a federal pharmacare program and it would undoubtedly contribute to nationwide improvement in many other aspects of health system governance, as stressed in this book by both Fierlbeck and Haardt. Continuing and ideally increased federal leadership in the area of electronic health records would, like Marchildon's proposal for a federal pharmacare program, be consistent with a federalism paradigm that limited federal intrusion into general health care governance. It would be consistent with the role that the federal government plays in creating and maintaining other kinds of national infrastructure. It would also, like the program criterion of portability from the Canada Health Act, support the expansion and operation of the economic union dimensions of market-preserving federalism.

If adopted and implemented, these examples of proposals for improvement in the interaction of federal governance and the governance of health care in the current Canadian context may or may not result in better federalism or better health care. Similarly, individually or collectively, they may or may not be capable of gaining traction in the current situation of limited federal government engagement with the health care file. These are questions that can only be answered by further analysis and ultimately by those who make and implement policy. The point being made here is that these examples illustrate the kinds of proposals that need to be identified, developed, and critiqued on a continuing basis if the ongoing and unavoidable interaction of federalism and health care is to be informed by evolving knowledge as to what could be done – as well as to what should not be done – if Canadians are to benefit from more optimal governance in their federalism and in their health care.

FUTURE WORK

This continuing work is work for many hands. It can clearly be taken up and organized in many different and equally valid and useful ways. It is, more specifically, work that can be usefully advanced by federalism and health care researchers working separately in their distinct disciplines and areas of specialization, with or without collaboration with those who have worked in the policy process at the interface of federalism and health care. At a minimum, however, we believe that this book shows that a multidisciplinary collaboration that embraces experts in federalism and experts in health care as well as practitioners of health care federalism has an important and distinct contribution to make. In fact, our hope is that this book shows that this kind of collaboration has an essential contribution to make on an ongoing basis.

This is the basis on which many of those who have contributed to this book are continuing to collaborate, with others, in examining the functioning of Canada's health care federalism. Building on this book, that collaboration is currently examining, with research funding provided by the Canadian Institutes of Health Research, the question of whether there are ways of rethinking the manner in which federal-provincial relations are conducted in the field of health care that can improve the capacity of both orders of government to provide effective, sustainable, and accountable health care across Canada. More precisely, the question being examined is whether recently established and newly emerging approaches to governance, including as applied in Europe and as variously labelled "soft," "collaborative," or "experimental" or simply as "new" governance, can be applied in Canada (or applied more effectively in Canada) to overcome what has often been the intransigent relations of health care federalism in Canada.

In some ways, these approaches can be said, especially because of their reliance on soft governance, to have things in common with the style of health care federalism associated with the health accords of 2000 and 2003 and the 10-year plan of 2004. Others have equated "new governance" in the health care context with privatization and the commodification of health care (Newdick 2008). Yet, at the same time, what is interesting about these approaches from the perspective of the current juncture in Canadian health care federalism is that they have been applied in Europe to achieve coordinated approaches to health care governance while respecting the European constitutional reality that health care is a matter of national jurisdiction. Indeed, these approaches have been characterized as "a machine for learning from diversity" that transforms jurisdictional autonomy from being an obstacle to achieving alignment on policy issues "into an asset for achieving it" (Sabel and Zeitlin 2008). They may therefore provide guidance for how Canadians might align the functioning of their federalism with the vertical and horizontal coordination and alignment that is a prerequisite for seamless, efficient, and sustainable delivery of effective health care services.

Whatever the lessons that we will learn from the European experience or from the concepts of "new governance" more broadly, the focus of the continuing collaboration among those who have contributed to this book will be on the more comprehensive understanding of Canada's health care federalism that we believe can be achieved if it is studied through collaboration between federalism and health care researchers from multiple disciplines with colleagues experienced in the intergovernmental process. It will also be on producing ideas for making Canada's health care federalism more effective for and responsive and accountable to the vast majority of Canadians who clearly identify at least as strongly with their country's largely national approach to health care as they do with its federalism.

APPENDICES

Text of the First Ministers' Accord on Health Care Renewal, 2003 (First Ministers of Canada 2003)

In September 2000, First Ministers agreed on a vision, principles and action plan for health system renewal. Building from this agreement, all governments have taken measures to improve the quality, accessibility and sustainability of our public health care system and all have implemented important reforms. Federal and provincial/territorial governments have also commissioned a number of task forces and studies that reflect the views of Canadians. These studies reflect a great convergence on the value of our publicly funded health system, the need for reform, and on the priorities for reform: particularly primary health care, home care, catastrophic drug coverage, access to diagnostic/medical equipment and information technology and an electronic health record.

Canadians want a sustainable health care system that provides timely access to quality health services. They recognize that reform is essential, and they support new public investments targeted to achieve this goal.

This Accord sets out an action plan for reform that reflects a renewed commitment by governments to work in partnership with each other, with providers, and with Canadians in shaping the future of our public health care system.

A COMMITMENT TO CANADIANS

Canadian values are reflected in the five principles of public health insurance: Universality, Accessibility, Portability, Comprehensiveness and Public Administration. First Ministers reaffirm their commitment to these principles. They also commit to enhancing the transparency and accountability of our health care system while ensuring that health care remains affordable.

Drawing from this foundation, First Ministers view this Accord as a covenant which will help to ensure that:

- all Canadians have timely access to health services on the basis of need, not ability to pay, regardless of where they live or move in Canada;.
- the health care services available to Canadians are of high quality, effective, patient-centred and safe; and
- our health care system is sustainable and affordable and will be here for Canadians and their children in the future.

First Ministers believe that the initiatives set out in this Accord will result in real and lasting change. The ultimate purpose of this Accord is to ensure that Canadians:

- have access to a health care provider 24 hours a day, 7 days a week;
- have timely access to diagnostic procedures and treatments;
- do not have to repeat their health histories or undergo the same tests for every provider they see;
- have access to quality home and community care services;
- have access to the drugs they need without undue financial hardship;
- are able to access quality care no matter where they live; and
- see their health care system as efficient, responsive and adapting to their changing needs, and those of their families and communities now, and in the future.

All governments have made significant investments in health care since the First Ministers' agreement of September 2000. First Ministers agree that public health care in Canada requires more money, but that money alone will not fix the system. While all jurisdictions are making progress on health reform, First Ministers agree that significant new investments must address immediate cost pressures and the reforms necessary to achieve timely access to quality care in a sustainable manner. The federal government will continue to work with territorial governments to address their unique challenges.

A PLAN FOR CHANGE: A NEW HEALTH REFORM FUND FOR
PRIMARY HEALTH CARE, HOME CARE AND CATASTROPHIC
DRUG COVERAGE

First Ministers agree that additional investments in primary health care, home care and catastrophic drug coverage are needed for a long-term sustainable public health care system in Canada. The federal government will create a 5-year Health Reform Fund which will transfer resources to the provinces and territories to address these three priorities. Recognizing that provinces and territories are at differing stages of reforms in these areas, the Fund will provide the provinces and territories the necessary flexibility to achieve the objectives set out below. Premiers and Territorial Leaders agree to use the Health Reform Fund to achieve these objectives. Therefore, these funds to be transferred to the provinces and territories will be available for any of the programs described within the Health Reform Fund, at their discretion. Achievement of the objectives of the Health Reform Fund by a province or territory will allow use of any residual fiscal resources in the Fund for other priority areas of their own health system.

The Government of Canada will establish a new long-term Canada Health Transfer (CHT) by March 31, 2004. It will include the portion of the current CHST (both cash and tax points) corresponding to the current proportion of health expenditures in provincial social spending supported by this federal transfer. In establishing the CHT, the federal government will ensure predictable annual increases in health transfers.

Subject to a review of progress toward achieving the agreed-upon reforms and following a First Ministers' Meeting, by March 31, 2008, the federal government will ensure that the level of funding provided through the Health Reform Fund is also integrated into the CHT.

Primary Health Care:
Ensuring Access to the Appropriate Health Provider When Needed

The key to efficient, timely, quality care is primary health care reform. First Ministers agree that the core building blocks of an effective primary health care system are improved continuity and coordination of care, early detection and action, better information on needs and outcomes, and new and stronger incentives to ensure that new approaches to care are swiftly adopted and here to stay.

First Ministers agree that the ultimate goal of primary health care reform is to provide all Canadians, wherever they live, with access to an appropriate health care provider, 24 hours a day, 7 days a week. Towards this goal, First Ministers agree to immediately accelerate primary health care initiatives and to make significant annual progress so that citizens routinely receive needed care from multi-disciplinary primary health care organizations or teams. First Ministers agree to the goal of ensuring that at least 50% of their residents have access to an appropriate health care provider, 24 hours a day, 7 days a week, as soon as possible and that this target be fully met within 8 years. First Ministers agree that each jurisdiction will publicly set out its own multi-year targets for verifiable progress towards achieving this objective.

Home Care for Canadians

Improving access to a basket of services in the home and community will improve the quality of life of many Canadians by allowing them to stay in their home or recover at home. First Ministers direct Health Ministers to determine by September 30, 2003, the minimum services to be provided. Such services provided in the home can be more appropriate and less expensive than acute hospital care. To this end, First Ministers agree to provide first dollar coverage for this basket of services for short-term acute home care, including acute community mental health, and end-of-life care. First Ministers agree that access to these services will be based on assessed need and that, by 2006, available services could include nursing/professional services, pharmaceuticals and medical equipment/supplies, support for essential personal care needs, and assessment of client needs and case management. The Government of Canada will complement these efforts with a compassionate care benefit through the Employment Insurance Program and job protection through the Canada Labour Code, for those who need to temporarily leave their job to care for a gravely ill or dying child, parent or spouse.

Catastrophic Drug Coverage and Pharmaceuticals Management

First Ministers agree that no Canadian should suffer undue financial hardship for needed drug therapy. Accordingly, as an integral component of these reforms, First Ministers will take measures, by the end of

2005/06, to ensure that Canadians, wherever they live, have reasonable access to catastrophic drug coverage.

As a priority, First Ministers agree to further collaborate to promote optimal drug use, best practices in drug prescription and better manage the costs of all drugs including generic drugs, to ensure that drugs are safe, effective and accessible in a timely and cost-effective fashion.

Reporting

First Ministers agree to prepare an annual public report to their citizens on each of the above three areas commencing in 2004. They further agree to use comparable indicators and to develop the necessary data infrastructure for these reports. This reporting will inform Canadians on progress achieved and key outcomes. It will also inform Canadians on current programs and expenditures, providing a baseline against which new investments can be tracked, as well as on service levels and outcomes.

A PLAN FOR CHANGE: DIAGNOSTIC/MEDICAL EQUIPMENT FUND

Enhancing the availability of publicly funded diagnostic care and treatment services is critical to reducing waiting times and ensuring the quality of our health care system. To this end, First Ministers agree to make significant new investments, including support for specialized staff training and equipment, which improve access to publicly funded diagnostic services. The Government of Canada will establish a Diagnostic/Medical Equipment Fund for that purpose.

Commencing in 2004, First Ministers agree to report to their citizens on an annual basis on enhancements to diagnostic and medical equipment and services, using comparable indicators, and to develop the necessary data infrastructure for these reports. This reporting will inform Canadians on progress achieved and key outcomes. It will also inform Canadians on current programs and expenditures, providing a baseline against which new investments can be tracked, as well as on service levels and outcomes.

A PLAN FOR CHANGE: INFORMATION TECHNOLOGY
AND AN ELECTRONIC HEALTH RECORD

Improving the accessibility and quality of information is critical to quality care, patient safety and sustainability, particularly for Canadians who live in rural and remote areas. Better use of information technology can also result in better utilization of resources. First Ministers agree to place priority on the implementation of electronic health records and the further development of telehealth applications which are critical to care in rural and remote areas. The Government of Canada will provide additional support for Canada Health Infoway to achieve this objective. First Ministers are also committed to the appropriate protection of personal information in building a national system of electronic health records.

Canada Health Infoway will report to the Canadian public and to the members of Infoway, who are Deputy Ministers of Health of federal/provincial/territorial governments, on an annual basis on its progress in implementing these initiatives. This reporting will inform Canadians on current programs, investment expenditures and milestones.

ADDITIONAL REFORM INITIATIVES

The adoption of innovations and the sharing of best practices by health care providers and managers is critical to making health care more efficient and improving its quality. First Ministers commit to accelerate collaborative work on priority issues with respect to patient safety, health human resources, technology assessment, innovation and research, and healthy living. The federal government is committed to providing funding in support of this work.

Building from this, First Ministers direct Health Ministers to work on the following:

Patient Safety

The implementation of a national strategy for improving patient safety is critical. Health Ministers will take leadership in implementing the recommendations of the National Steering Committee on Patient Safety.

Health Human Resources

Appropriate planning and management of health human resources is key to ensuring that Canadians have access to the health providers they need, now and in the future. Collaborative strategies are to be undertaken to strengthen the evidence base for national planning, promote inter-disciplinary provider education, improve recruitment and retention, and ensure the supply of needed health providers (including nurse practitioners, pharmacists, and diagnostic technologists).

Technology Assessment

Managing new technologies and treatments is critical to ensuring that our health system remains relevant to the evolving needs of Canadians. Health Ministers are directed to develop, by September 2004, a comprehensive strategy for technology assessment which assesses the impact of new technology and provides advice on how to maximize its effective utilization in the future.

Innovation and Research

Applied research and knowledge transfer are essential to improving access and the quality of care. The work of academic health centres is vital in developing new approaches for the collection of information and evidence needed to improve care.

Healthy Canadians

An effective health system requires a balance between individual responsibility for personal health and our collective responsibility for the health system. Coordinated approaches are necessary to deal with the issue of obesity, promote physical fitness and improve public and environmental health. First Ministers direct Health Ministers to continue their work on healthy living strategies and other initiatives to reduce disparities in health status. First Ministers further recognize that immunization is a key intervention for disease prevention. They direct Health Ministers to pursue a National Immunization Strategy.

ABORIGINAL HEALTH

First Ministers recognize that addressing the serious challenges that face the health of Aboriginal Canadians will require dedicated effort. To this end, the federal government is committed to enhancing its funding and working collaboratively with other governments and Aboriginal peoples to meet the objectives set out in this Accord including the priorities established in the Health Reform Fund. Governments will work together to address the gap in health status between Aboriginal and non-Aboriginal Canadians through better integration of health services.

First Ministers direct Health Ministers to consult with Aboriginal peoples on the development of a comparable Aboriginal Health Reporting Framework. They further agree to consult with Aboriginal peoples in this effort, to use comparable indicators, and to develop the necessary data infrastructure. This reporting will inform Canadians on progress achieved and key outcomes. It will also inform Canadians on current programs and expenditures, providing a baseline against which new investments can be tracked, as well as on service levels and outcomes.

REPORTING TO CANADIANS ON CHANGE

First Ministers agree that Canadians are entitled to better and more fully comparable information on the timeliness and quality of health care services. Enhanced accountability to Canadians and improved performance reporting are essential to reassuring Canadians that reforms are occurring. To this end, First Ministers agree that:

- each jurisdiction will report to its constituents on its use of all health care dollars spent on an annual basis;
- each jurisdiction will continue to provide comprehensive and regular public reporting on the health programs and services it delivers as well as on health system performance, health outcomes and health status;
- these reports will include the indicators set out in the September 2000 communique as well as additional comparable indicators, to be developed by Health Ministers, on the themes of quality, access, system efficiency and effectiveness based on Annex A of this Accord; and

• jurisdictions will develop the necessary data infrastructure and collect the data needed for quality reporting.

This will enable the development of nationally comparable information for Canadians on the themes of access, quality, system efficiency and effectiveness and on reform priorities and objectives set out in this Accord.

First Ministers recognize that Canadians want to be part of the implementation of this Accord. Accordingly, they agree to establish a Health Council to monitor and make annual public reports on the implementation of the Accord, particularly its accountability and transparency provisions. The Health Council will publicly report through federal/provincial/territorial Ministers of Health and will include representatives of both orders of government, experts and the public. To fulfill its mandate, the Council will draw upon consultations and relevant reports, including governments' reports, the work of the Federal/Provincial/Territorial Advisory Committee on Governance and Accountability and the Canadian Institute for Health Information (CIHI). Health Ministers will establish the Council within three months. Quebec's Council on Health and Welfare, with a new mandate, will collaborate with the Health Council.

ANNEX A TO ACCORD:
PERFORMANCE INDICATORS

First Ministers direct Health Ministers to develop further indicators to supplement the work undertaken in follow-up to the September 2000 Communique. This work is to be completed by September 2003, following review by experts and stakeholders, to ensure these new indicators measure progress on achieving the reforms set out in this Accord and meet the following objectives:

• Timely Access: the measurement of access to essential services across the country as well as waiting times;
• Quality: the measurement of quality of health care services across the country, including patient safety, patient satisfaction and health outcomes;
• Sustainability: including measurements of the state of health human resources, equipment, information systems and value for money from the system; and

• Health Status and Wellness.

Ministers are to consider the following:

Timely Access Indicators

ACCESS TO HEALTH CARE PROVIDERS/SERVICES
• % of population having a regular family doctor (FMM 2000)
• % of doctors accepting new patients
• number of multi-disciplinary primary health care organizations or teams by region (rural/urban)
• % of population having access to 24/7 primary care provider (e.g, nurse practitioner, doctor)/telehealth/online health information
• % of population routinely receiving needed care from a multi-disciplinary primary health care organization or team
• % of population with public coverage of core set of home care services

WAIT TIMES/VOLUME MEASURES FOR
• radiation therapy for breast and prostate cancer, cardiac bypass surgery, hip and knee replacement surgery (FMM 2000)
• referral to specialists for cancers (lung, prostate, breast, colo-rectal), heart and stroke
• emergency rooms from entry to discharge (seasonally adjusted)
• diagnostic tests (MRI, CT)
• from referral to provision of first home care service
• waiting period before being eligible for public coverage of home care services in another jurisdiction
• proportion of services/facilities linked to a centralized (provincial/regional) wait list management system for selected cancers and surgeries, referral to specialists, emergency rooms and diagnostic tests (all of the above wait time indicators)

CATASTROPHIC DRUG COVERAGE
• to be developed

Quality Indicators

PATIENT SAFETY

- reported medical error/events (e.g., disease surveillance, adverse drug reactions) – to be determined by proposed Institute on Patient Safety

PATIENT SATISFACTION (FMM 2000)

- overall health care services
- hospital care
- physician care
- community-based health care
- telehealth/online information

HEALTH OUTCOMES

- readmissions for selected conditions
- AMI, pneumonia (FMM 2000)
- congestive heart failure, GI haemorrhage
- mortality rate for cancers (FMM 2000)
- survival rate for cancers (FMM 2000)

Sustainability (Efficiency and Effectiveness) Indicators

HEALTH HUMAN RESOURCES

- age distribution of practicing providers by area of specialty
- number of providers (by specialty) leaving/entering the system each year
- a 10-year rolling forecast of providers expected to enter system (trained in Canada, incoming from other countries)

EQUIPMENT

- number and types of equipment installed
- number of diagnostic professionals to operate equipment
- volume flow/wait times for MRI, CT (covered under access indicators)

INFORMATION SYSTEMS

- progress on building information systems
- degree of standardization of information collected and shared for evidence-based decision-making

- degree of technology utilization based on evidence

VALUE FOR MONEY – QUALITATIVE INDICATORS PRIMARILY
- annual health reports on plans and priorities reported by every jurisdiction
- expenditures linked to reform areas (link inputs to outputs)
- lessons learned and best practices shared within and between provinces/territories
- comparisons of productivity measures

HEALTH STATUS AND WELLNESS
- % of Canadians engaged in physical activities
- % of Canadians with recommended Body Mass Index (BMI)
- Potential years of life lost (PYLL)
- Disability-Free Life Expectancy (DFLE)
- Cost of Illness

Nothing in this document shall be construed to derogate from the respective governments' jurisdictions. This Accord shall be interpreted in full respect of each government's jurisdiction.

Text of the 10-Year Plan to Strengthen Health Care, 2004 (First Ministers of Canada 2004)

September 16, 2004

In recent years, through an ongoing dialogue between governments, patients, health care providers and Canadians more generally, a deep and broad consensus has emerged on a shared agenda for renewal of health care in Canada. This agenda is focused on ensuring that Canadians have access to the care they need, when they need it.

Foremost on this agenda is the need to make timely access to quality care a reality for all Canadians. First Ministers remain committed to the dual objectives of better management of wait times and the measurable reduction of wait times where they are longer than medically acceptable.

First Ministers also recognize that improving access to care and reducing wait times will require cooperation among governments; the participation of health care providers and patients; and strategic investments in areas such as: increasing the supply of health professionals (e.g. doctors, nurses and pharmacists); effective community based services, including home care; a pharmaceuticals strategy; effective health promotion and disease prevention, and adequate financial resources.

Building on the renewal agenda set out by the First Ministers' meeting held in February 2003 and the related investments, significant progress has been made and numerous efforts are underway throughout Canada and across jurisdictions to make health care more responsive and sustainable. First Ministers remain committed to achieving results, recognizing that making health care sustainable and able to adapt to the ever-changing needs of Canadians, will take time, sustained commitment and adequate resources.

First Ministers agree that access to timely care across Canada is our biggest concern and a national priority. First Ministers have come together and agreed on an action plan based on the following principles:

- universality, accessibility, portability, comprehensiveness, and public administration;
- access to medically necessary health services based on need, not ability to pay;
- reforms focused on the needs of patients to ensure that all Canadians have access to the health care services they need, when they need them;
- collaboration between all governments, working together in common purpose to meet the evolving health care needs of Canadians;
- advancement through the sharing of best practices;
- continued accountability and provision of information to make progress transparent to citizens; and
- jurisdictional flexibility.

Recognizing that an asymmetrical federalism allows for the existence of specific agreements for any province, First Ministers also agreed that a separate communiqué be released to reflect the arrangements between the Government of Canada and the Government of Québec regarding the interpretation and the implementation of the present communiqué. The funding provided by the federal government will be used by the government of Québec to implement its own plan aiming, notably, at ensuring access to quality care in a timely manner and at reducing waiting times.

In addition, all governments have agreed to work together on the important matter of Aboriginal health, as set out in a separate communiqué.

REDUCING WAIT TIMES AND IMPROVING ACCESS

All jurisdictions have taken concrete steps to address wait times. Building on this, First Ministers commit to achieve meaningful reductions in wait times in priority areas such as cancer, heart, diagnostic imaging, joint replacements, and sight restoration by March 31, 2007, recognizing the different starting points, priorities, and strategies across jurisdictions.

The Wait Times Reduction Fund will augment existing provincial and territorial investments and assist jurisdictions in their diverse initiatives to reduce wait times. This Fund will primarily be used for jurisdictional priorities such as training and hiring more health professionals, clearing backlogs, building capacity for regional centres of excellence, expanding appropriate ambulatory and community care programs and/or tools to manage wait times.

First Ministers agree to collect and provide meaningful information to Canadians on progress made in reducing wait times, as follows:

• Each jurisdiction agrees to establish comparable indicators of access to health care professionals, diagnostic and treatment procedures with a report to their citizens to be developed by all jurisdictions by December 31, 2005.
• Evidence-based benchmarks for medically acceptable wait times starting with cancer, heart, diagnostic imaging procedures, joint replacements, and sight restoration will be established by December 31, 2005 through a process to be developed by Federal, Provincial and Territorial Ministers of Health.
• Multi-year targets to achieve priority benchmarks will be established by each jurisdiction by December 31, 2007.
• Provinces and territories will report annually to their citizens on their progress in meeting their multi-year wait time targets.

The Canadian Institute for Health Information will report on progress on wait times across jurisdictions.

STRATEGIC HEALTH HUMAN RESOURCE (HHR) ACTION PLANS

There is a need to increase supply of health care professionals in Canada, including doctors, nurses, pharmacists and technologists. These shortages are particularly acute in some parts of the country.

As part of efforts to reduce wait times, First Ministers agree to continue and accelerate their work on Health Human Resources action plans and/or initiatives to ensure an adequate supply and appropriate mix of health care professionals. These plans and initiatives will build on current work in the area of health labour relations, interdisciplinary training, investments in post-secondary education, and credentialing of health professionals. Recognizing the important contribution of health care providers in facilitating reforms, First Ministers commit to involving them in their work in this area. To facilitate better planning and management of HHR, First Ministers acknowledge the need to foster closer collaboration among health, post-secondary education and labour market sectors.

Federal, Provincial and Territorial governments agree to increase the supply of health professionals, based on their assessment of the gaps and to make their action plans public, including targets for the training, recruitment and retention of professionals by December 31, 2005. Federal, Provincial and Territorial governments will make these commitments public and regularly report on progress.

The federal government commits to:

- accelerate and expand the assessment and integration of internationally trained health care graduates for participating governments;
- targeted efforts in support of Aboriginal communities and Official Languages Minority Communities to increase the supply of health care professionals for these communities;
- measures to reduce the financial burden on students in specific health education programs; and
- participate in health human resource planning with interested jurisdictions.

HOME CARE

Home care is an essential part of modern, integrated and patient-centered health care. Improving access to home and community care services will improve the quality of life for many Canadians by allowing them to be cared for or recover at home. Services provided in the home can be more appropriate and less expensive than acute hospital care. Greater use of home and community care services can reduce wait times for acute hospital beds by making beds available for those who are more acutely ill, can provide choices for end-of-life care, and be an effective option for some patients with chronic mental health concerns.

All governments have recognized the value of home care as a cost-effective means of delivering services and are developing home care services to prevent or follow hospitalization.

First Ministers agree to provide first dollar coverage by 2006 for certain home care services, based on assessed need, specifically to include:

- short-term acute home care for two-week provision of case management, intravenous medications related to the discharge diagnosis, nursing and personal care;
- short-term acute community mental health home care for two-week provision of case management and crisis response services; and
- end-of-life care for case management, nursing, palliative-specific pharmaceuticals and personal care at the end of life.

Each jurisdiction will develop a plan for the staged implementation of these services, and report annually to its citizens on progress in implementing home care services. First Ministers task their Health Ministers to explore next steps to fulfill the home care commitment and report to First Ministers by December 31, 2006.

PRIMARY CARE REFORM

Timely access to family and community care through primary health care reform is a high priority for all jurisdictions. Significant progress is underway in all jurisdictions to meet the objective of 50% of Canadians having 24/7 access to multidisciplinary teams by 2011. Building on this progress, First Ministers agree to establish a best practices network to share information and find solutions to barriers to progress in primary health care reform such as scope of practice. First Ministers agree to regularly report on progress.

Electronic health records and telehealth are key to health system renewal, particularly for Canadians who live in rural and remote areas. Recognizing the significant investment that has been made and achievements to date, First Ministers agree to accelerate the development and implementation of the electronic health record, including e-prescribing. To this end, First Ministers commit to work with Canada Health Infoway to realize the vision of the electronic health record through an ambitious plan and associated investment. First Ministers have also asked for acceleration of efforts on telehealth to improve access for remote and rural communities.

ACCESS TO CARE IN THE NORTH

Access to family and community-based health care services is a particular challenge in Northern communities, where the system's capacity to provide timely, health care services to a remote population can be limited. The federal government has agreed to help to address the unique challenges facing the development and delivery of health care services in the North on a priority basis, including the costs of medical transportation as follows:

- The federal government proposes to increase funding to the Territories totaling $150 million over 5 years through a Territorial Health Access Fund, targeted at facilitating long-term health reforms, and establish a federal/territorial working group to support the management of the fund, and additional direct funding for medical transportation costs.
- Recognizing the enormous potential of the North, the Government of Canada and the Territories will jointly develop a vision for the North.

NATIONAL PHARMACEUTICALS STRATEGY

The founders of Medicare a half-century ago established the principle of equity of access to hospitals and doctors' services for all Canadians. First Ministers agree that no Canadians should suffer undue financial hardship in accessing needed drug therapies. Affordable access to drugs is fundamental to equitable health outcomes for all our citizens.

First Ministers direct Health Ministers to establish a Ministerial Task Force to develop and implement the national pharmaceuticals strategy and report on progress by June 30, 2006. The strategy will include the following actions:

- develop, assess and cost options for catastrophic pharmaceutical coverage;
- establish a common National Drug Formulary for participating jurisdictions based on safety and cost effectiveness;
- accelerate access to breakthrough drugs for unmet health needs through improvements to the drug approval process;
- strengthen evaluation of real-world drug safety and effectiveness;

- pursue purchasing strategies to obtain best prices for Canadians for drugs and vaccines;
- enhance action to influence the prescribing behaviour of health care professionals so that drugs are used only when needed and the right drug is used for the right problem;
- broaden the practice of e-prescribing through accelerated development and deployment of the Electronic Health Record;
- accelerate access to non-patented drugs and achieve international parity on prices of non-patented drugs; and
- enhance analysis of cost drivers and cost-effectiveness, including best practices in drug plan policies.

[It is understood that Quebec will maintain its own pharmacare program.]

PREVENTION, PROMOTION AND PUBLIC HEALTH

All governments recognize that public health efforts on health promotion, disease and injury prevention are critical to achieving better health outcomes for Canadians and contributing to the long-term sustainability of medicare by reducing pressure on the health care system. In particular, managing chronic disease more effectively maintains health status for individuals and counters a growing trend of increasing disease burden. For example, recent federal investments in diabetes, hepatitis C and HIV-AIDS have provided important resources to patients and professionals for preventing and managing these life-threatening diseases.

In recognition of the importance of the healthy development of children, there has been extensive collaboration by governments, in recent years, through the Early Childhood Development initiative.

First Ministers recognize the progress that has been made by all jurisdictions to strengthen Canada's public health system, including the creation of the new Public Health Agency of Canada. All governments commit to further collaboration and cooperation in developing coordinated responses to infectious disease outbreaks and other public health emergencies through the new Public Health Network.

The federal government also commits to building on recent investments in immunization through ongoing investments for needed vaccines, which are recognized as the single most cost-effective investment in public health, through the National Immunization Strategy. This Strategy will provide new immunization coverage for Canadian children.

In addition, governments commit to accelerate work on a pan-Canadian Public Health Strategy. For the first time, governments will set goals and targets for improving the health status of Canadians through a collaborative process with experts. The Strategy will include efforts to address common risk factors, such as physical inactivity, and integrated disease strategies. First Ministers commit to working across sectors through initiatives such as Healthy Schools.

HEALTH INNOVATION

A strong, modern health care system is a cornerstone of a healthy economy. Investments in health system innovation through science, technology and research help to strengthen health care as well as our competitiveness and productivity. Investments in science, technology and research are necessary to develop new, more cost-effective approaches and to facilitate and accelerate the adoption and evaluation of new models of health protection and chronic disease management.

Recognizing the progress that has been made, the federal government commits to continued investments to sustain activities in support of health innovation.

ACCOUNTABILITY AND REPORTING TO CITIZENS

All governments agree to report to their residents on health system performance including the elements set out in this communiqué. Governments agree to seek advice from experts and health providers on the most appropriate indicators to measures of health system performance.

All funding arrangements require that jurisdictions comply with the reporting provisions of this communiqué.

First Ministers of jurisdictions participating in the Health Council agree that the Council prepare an annual report to all Canadians, on the health status of Canadians and health outcomes. The Council will report on progress of elements set out in this communiqué.

DISPUTE AVOIDANCE AND RESOLUTION

By inclusion in this communiqué, governments formalize the agreement reached on dispute avoidance and resolution with regard to the Canada Health Act in an exchange of letters in April 2002

Bibliography

LEGAL REFERENCES

A.-G. N.S. v. A.-G. Can. (Nova Scotia Inter-delegation) [1951] S.C.R. 31.
Auton (Guardian ad litem of) v. British Columbia (Attorney General) [2004] 3 S.C.R. 657.
Canada (Attorney General) v. Inuit Tapirisat of Canada [1980] 2 S.C.R. 735.
Canada (Attorney General) v. PHS Community Services Society [2011] S.C.R. 44.
Canadian Environmental Law Assn. v. Canada (Minister of the Environment) [1999] 3. F.C. 564.
Canadian Federation of Agriculture v. A.-G. Quebec [1951] A.C. 179.
Chaoulli v. Quebec (Attorney General) [2005] 1 S.C.R. 791.
Constitution Act, 1867 (U.K.), 30 & 31 Vict., c. 3, reprinted in R.S.C., 1985, App. II, No. 5.
Eldridge v. British Columbia (Attorney General) [1997] 3 S.C.R. 624.
Food and Drugs Act, R.S.C., 1985, c. F-27.
Knox Contracting Ltd. v. Canada [1990] 2 S.C.R. 338, 348.
NIL/TU,O Child and Family Services Society v. B.C. Government and Service Employees' Union [2010] 2 S.C.R. 696.
P.E.I. Marketing Board v. Willis [1952] S.C.R. 392.
R. v. Hauser [1979] 1 S.C.R. 984, 1026 (Per Dickson J.)
Reference re Assisted Human Reproduction Act [2010] 3 S.C.R. 457.
Reference re Canada Assistance Plan (B.C.) [1991] 2 S.C.R. 525.
Reference re Secession of Quebec [1998] 2 S.C.R. 217.
Reference re Securities Act [2011] 3 S.C.R. 837.
Reference re Validity of Section 5(a) of the Dairy Industry Act, 1949 (The Margarine Reference) [1949] S.C.R. 1, 50 (per Rand J.).

Schneider v. The Queen [1982] 2 S.C.R. 112.

SECONDARY SOURCES

Abraham, J., and P. Karaca-Mandic. 2011. *What affects medical loss ratios in the individual market?* Presentation at the Academy Health Annual Research Meeting, Seattle, WA, 13 June 2011. http://www.academyhealth.org/files/2011/monday/abraham.pdf.

Adam, M.-A. 2008. The spending power, co-operative federalism and Section 94. *Queen's Law Journal* 34:175.

Advisory Committee on Health Delivery and Human Resources (ACHDHR). 2007. *A framework for collaborative pan-Canadian health human resources planning.* Rev ed. Ottawa: Health Canada.

Advisory Panel on Fiscal Imbalance. 2006. *Reconciling the irreconcilable: Addressing Canada's fiscal imbalance.* Ottawa: Council of the Federation. http://www.councilofthefederation.ca/pdfs/Report_Fiscalim_Mar3106 .pdf.

Ahmad, E. 1997. Intergovernmental transfers – an international perspective. In *Financing decentralized expenditures: An international comparison of grants*, ed. E. Ahmad, 1–17. Cheltenham, UK: Edward Elgar.

Alkin, M. 2004. *Evaluation roots: Tracing theorists' views and influences.* Thousand Oaks, CA: Sage.

Anderson, L., and T. Findlay. 2010. Does public reporting measure up? Federalism, accountability, and child-care policy in Canada. *Canadian Public Administration* 53(3):417–38.

Atkinson, T. 2002. Social inclusion and the European Union. *Journal of Common Market Studies* 40(4):625–43.

Auditor General Canada. 2008. *Report of the Auditor General of Canada.* Ottawa. http://www.oag-bvg.gc.ca/internet/English/parl_oag_200812_e _31776.html.

Ayers, I., and J. Braithwaite. 1992. *Responsive regulation: Transcending the deregulation debate.* Oxford: Oxford University Press.

Bailey, I., and B. Curry. 2011. In surprise move, Flaherty lays out spending plans until 2024. *Globe and Mail*, 19 December. http://www.theglobeand mail.com/news/politics/in-surprise-move-flaherty-lays-out-health-spending-plans-til-2024/article4247851/

Bakvis, H., G. Baier, and D. Brown. 2009. *Contested federalism: Certainty and ambiguity in the Canadian federation.* Toronto: Oxford University Press Canada.

Baldwin, R., and J. Black. 2008. Really responsive regulation. *Modern Law Review* 71(1):59–94.

Banting, K., and R. Broadway. 2004. Defining the sharing community: the federal role in health care. In *Money, politics, and health care: Reconstructing the federal-provincial partnership*, ed. H. Lazar and F. St-Hillaire, 1–77. Montreal: Institute for Research on Public Policy.

Barua, B., M. Rovere, and B.J. Skinner. 2011. *Waiting your turn: Wait times for health care in Canada – 2011 report.* Calgary: Fraser Institute. http://www.fraserinstitute.org/uploadedFiles/fraser-ca/Content/research-news/research/publications/waiting-your-turn-2011.pdf.

Battista, R.N., B. Cote, M.J. Hodge, and D. Husereau. 2009. Health technology assessment in Canada. *International Journal of Technology Assessment in Health Care* 25(Suppl 1):53–60.

Bégin, M. 2002. *Revisiting the* Canada Health Act *(1984): What are the impediments to change?* Speech given to the Institute for Research on Public Policy, Ottawa, 20 February.

Béland, D., and A. Lecours. 2006. Substate nationalism and the welfare state: Québec and Canadian federalism. *Nations and Nationalism* 12(1):77–96.

Bell, S. 2011. Do we really need a new 'constructivist institutionalism' to explain institutional change? *British Journal of Political Science* 41(4):883–906.

Berger, E. 1996. Don't distort flaws in Canada health care. *New York Times,* 22 December, D8. http://www.nytimes.com/1996/12/22/opinion/l-don-t-distort-flaws-in-canada-health-care-854344.html.

Biggs, M. 1996. *Building blocks for Canada's new Social Union.* Ottawa: Canadian Policy Research Networks.

Birch, S., G. Kephart, L. O'Brien-Pallas, G. Tomblin Murphy, R. Alder, A. MacKenzie, et al. 2005. *Atlantic Health Human Resources Planning Study.* Mississauga: Med-Emerg.

Birch, S, G. Kephart, G. Tomblin Murphy, L. O'Brien-Pallas, R. Alder, and A. MacKenzie. 2007. Human resources planning and the production of health: A needs-based analytical framework. *Canadian Public Policy* 33(Suppl):S1–S16.

Birch, S., G. Lavis, B. Markham, C. Woodward, and L. O'Brien-Pallas. 1994. *Nursing requirements for Ontario over the next twenty years: Development and application of estimation methods.* Report commissioned by the Ontario Nursing Human Resources Data Centre. Hamilton: McMaster University.

Birch, S., L. O'Brien-Pallas, C. Alksnis, G. Tomblin Murphy, and D. Thomson. 2003. Beyond demographic change in human resources planning:

An extended framework and application to nursing. *Journal of Health Services Research and Policy* 8(4):225–9.

Bird, R.M. 2005. Taxing sales twice: International experience with multilevel sales taxes. *State Tax Notes* 37(11). http://www.rotman.utoronto.ca/iib /ITP0607.pdf.

Bladen, V.W. 1935. The economics of federalism. *The Canadian Journal of Economics and Political Science* 1(3):348–51.

Blyth, M. 2002. *Great transformations: Economic ideas and institutional change in the twentieth century*. Cambridge, UK: Cambridge University Press.

Bobinski, M.A. 1990. Unhealthy federalism: barriers to increasing health care access for the uninsured. *U.C. Davis Law Review* 24(2):255–348.

Boessenkool, K. 1996. *The illusion of equality: provincial distribution of the Canada Health and Social Transfer*. Toronto: C.D. Howe Institute.

– 1997. *Clearly Canadian: Improving equity and accountability in an overarching equalization program*. Toronto: CD Howe Institute.

– 2001. Ottawa must get off the health care pulpit. *National Post*, 17 November, 1: A13.

– 2008. Unleash consumer spending with a temporary GST cut. *Toronto* Star, 27 November. http://www.thestar.com/Opinion/article/544260.

– 2010. *Fixing the fiscal imbalance: Turning the GST over to the provinces in exchange for lower transfers*. SPP Research Papers 3, no. 10. Calgary: University of Calgary School of Public Policy.

Boothe, P., and D. Hermanutz. 1999. *Simply sharing: An interprovincial equalization scheme for Canada*. Toronto: C.D. Howe Institute.

Boudon, R. 2003. Beyond rational choice theory. *Annual Review of Sociology* 29:1–21.

Bourgault, J. 2004. Quebec's role in Canadian federal-provincial relations' In *Canada: The state of the federation 2002: Reconsidering the institutions of Canadian federalism*, ed. J.P. Meekison, M. Telford, and H. Lazar, 341–76. Kingston: McGill-Queen's University Press for the Institute of Intergovernmental Relations.

Braën, A. 2004. Health and the distribution of powers in Canada. In *The governance of health care in Canada*, ed. T. McIntosh, P.-G. Forest, and G.P. Marchildon, 25–49. Toronto: University of Toronto Press.

Braun, D. 2006. Between market-preserving federalism and intergovernmental coordination: The case of Australia. *Swiss Political Science Review* 12(2):1–36.

Brøchner, J., J. Jensen, P. Svensson, and P.B. Sørensen. 2006. *The dilemmas of tax coordination in the enlarged European Union*. CESifo Working Paper

No. 1859. Munich: CESifo Group. http://www.econ.ku.dk/pbs/diverse filer/EU tax coordination.pdf

Brown, D. 2003. Getting things done in the federation: Do we need new rules for an old game? In *Constructive and co-operative federalism? A Series of commentaries on the Council of the Federation*, ed. D. Brown and F. St-Hillaire. Kingston, ON: Institute of Intergovernmental Relations, School of Policy Studies, Queen's University. http://www.queensu.ca/iigr/working/CouncilFederation/FedEN/1.pdf.BROWN

Brown, M.C. 1980. The implications of established program finance for national health insurance. *Canadian Public Policy* 6(3):521–32.

Brownlee, M. 2011. Provincial borders thwarting MDs. *Globe and Mail*, 2 August, A7.

Buettner, T. 2002. Fiscal federalism and interstate risk sharing: empirical evidence from Germany. *Economics Letters* 74:195–202.

Burelle, A. 2003. The Council of the Federation: From a defensive to a partnership approach? In *Constructive and co-operative federalism? A series of commentaries on the Council of the Federation*, ed. D. Brown and F. St-Hillaire. Kingston, ON: Institute of Intergovernmental Relations, School of Policy Studies, Queen's University. http://www.irpp.org/miscpubs/archive/federation/burelle.pdf.

Cai, H., and D. Treisman. 2004. State corroding federalism. *Journal of Public Economics* 88:819–43.

Cameron, D.R. 1994. Half-eaten carrot, bent stick: decentralization in an era of fiscal restraint. *Canadian Public Administration* 37(3):431–44.

Cameron, D. 1997. Assessing ACCESS. In *Accessing ACCESS: Towards a new social union*, ed. D.R. Cameron, A. Burelle, K. Swinton, P. Leslie, D. Milne, R. Gibbins, et al., 3–11. Kingston, ON: Institute of Intergovernment Relations, Queen's University. http://www.queensu.ca/iigr/pub/archive/books/AssessingAccess-TowardsaNewSocialUnion.pdf.

Cameron, D.R., A. Burelle, K. Swinton, P. Leslie, D. Milne, R. Gibbins, et al. 1997. *Accessing ACCESS: Towards a new social union*. Kingston, ON: Institute of Intergovernment Relations, Queen's University. http://www.queensu.ca/iigr/pub/archive/books/AssessingAccess-TowardsaNewSocial Union.pdf.

Cameron, D.R., and J. McCrea-Logie. 2004. Cooperation and dispute resolution in Canadian health care. In *Money, politics, and health care*, ed. H. Lazar and F. St. Hillaire, 80–134. Montreal and Kingston: Institute for Research in Public Policy and Institute of Intergovernmental Relations.

Canada Department of Finance. 2007. *Budget plan 2007: Aspire to a stronger,*

safer, better Canada. Ottawa: Department of Finance. http://www.budget
.gc.ca/2007/pdf/bp2007e.pdf

Canadian Association for Health Services and Policy Research. 2011. *Renewing federalism, improving health care: Can this marriage be saved?* Conference program for the 2011 Annual CAHSPR Conference, Halifax, NS, 9–12 May. http://www.cahspr.ca/sites/default/files/imce/CAHSPR-Post-Conference-Program-2011.pdf

Canadian Health Human Resources Network (CHHRN). 2012. *Canadian Health Human Resources Network*. http://www.hhr-rhs.ca/.

Canadian Institute for Health Information (CIHI). 2010a. *Health care in Canada 2010*. Ottawa: CIHI.

– 2010b. Have health card, will travel: out-of-province/-territory patients. *Analysis in Brief*, March. Ottawa: CIHI.
https://secure.cihi.ca/free_products/out_of_province_aib_201003_e.pdf

– 2010c. *National health expenditure trends, 1975 to 2010*. Ottawa: CIHI.
http://secure.cihi.ca/cihiweb/products/NHEX_Trends_Report_2010_final
_ENG_web.pdf.

– 2010d. *Health indicators 2010*. Ottawa: CIHI. https://secure.cihi.ca/estore/
productFamily.htm?pf=PFC1435.

– 2011a. *National health expenditure trends, 1975 to 2011*. Ottawa: CIHI.
https://secure.cihi.ca/free_products/nhex_trends_report_2011_en.pdf.

– 2011b. *Wait times in Canada – A comparison by province*. Ottawa: CIHI.
http://secure.cihi.ca/cihiweb/products/Wait_times_tables_2011_en.pdf.

– 2012a. *Health indicators 2012*. Ottawa: CIHI. https://secure.cihi.ca/free
_products/health_indicators_2012_en.pdf.

– 2012b. *Wait times in Canada – a summary, 2012*. Ottawa: CIHI.
https://secure.cihi.ca/free_products/WaitTimesSummary2012_EN.pdf

Chan, B., G.M. Anderson, and M.-E. Thériault. 1998. Fee code creep among general practitioners and family physicians in Ontario: Why does the ratio of intermediate to minor assessments keep climbing? *CMAJ* 158(6):749–54.

Charles, C., J. Lomas, M. Vanda, G. Bhatia, and V.A. Vincent. 1997. Medical necessity in Canadian health policy: four meanings and … a funeral. *Milbank Quarterly* 75(3):365–94.

Cheadle, B. 2012. Budget Officer: Limiting house arrest will cost more, convict less. *Chronicle Herald*, 29 February. http://thechronicleherald.ca/
canada/68381-budget-officer-limiting-house-arrest-will-cost-more-convict-fewer.

Choudhry, S. 1996. The enforcement of the *Canada Health Act*. *McGill Law Journal* 41(2):461.

Choudhry, S. 2002. Recasting social Canada: A reconsideration of federal jurisdiction over social policy. *University of Toronto Law Journal* 52:163.

Commission on Fiscal Imbalance. 2002. *A new division of Canada's financial resources.* Quebec, QC: Government of Quebec.

– 2002a. *Pharmacare in Canada.* Discussion paper produced by the Canadian Health Services Research Foundation. http://www.chsrf.ca/Libraries/ Romonow_Commission_ENGLISH/Discussion_Paper_Pharmacare_in_C anada.sflb.ashx.

Courchene, T. 1995. *Redistributing money and power: A guide to the Canada Health and Social Transfer.* Toronto: C.D. Howe Institute.

– 2004. Pan-Canadian provincialism – the new federalism and the old Constitution. *Policy Options* (November):20–8.

– 2006. Variations on the federalism theme. *Policy Options* (September):46–54.

– 2008. Reflections on the federal spending power: Practices, principles, perspectives. *Queen's Law Journal,* 34(2):75–124.

– 2010. Intergovernmental transfers and Canadian values: Retrospect and prospect. *Policy Options* (May):32–40.

Coyte, P.C., and S. Landon. 1990. Cost-sharing and block-funding in a federal system: A demand systems approach. *Canadian Journal of Economics* 23(4):817–38.

Crivelli, L., M. Filippini, and I. Mosca. 2006. Federalism and regional health care expenditures: An empirical analysis for the Swiss cantons. *Health Economics* 15:535–41.

Curry, B., H. Scoffield, and T. Perkins. 2012. Feds warn provinces: Get in line. *Globe and Mail,* 24 February, A1, A4.

Davis, K., C. Schoen, and K. Stremikis. 2010. *Mirror, mirror, on the wall: How the performance of the US health care system compares internationally (2010 update).* New York: The Commonwealth Fund. http://www.common wealthfund.org/~/media/Files/Publications/Fund%20Report/2010/Jun/ 1400_Davis_Mirror_Mirror_on_the_wall_2010.pdf.

Decter, M. 2000. First ministers' meeting communiqué on health: Provincial health reform joined by federal health dollars. *Healthcare Quarterly* 4(1):20–3.

Department of Justice. No date. *Consolidation of Constitution Acts, 1867 to 1982.* http://laws.justice.gc.ca/eng/Const/PRINT_E.PDF.

Department of Justice. 2011. *Consolidation, Canada Health Act,* R.S.C., 1985, c. C-6, current to 8 August 2011. http://lois-laws.justice.gc.ca/PDF/ C-6.pdf.

Donahue, P.J. 1998. Federalism and the financing of health care in Canada and Switzerland: Lessons for health care reform in the United States. *Boston College International & Comparative Law Review* 21(2):385–435.

Elson, S. 2006. The evolution of health system governance in Canada and Ontario. *Law and Governance* 10(2):9–12.

Emery, H. 2010. *Understanding the political economy of the evolution and future of single-payer public health insurance in Canada.* Calgary: School of Public Policy.

Evans, D.B., T.T. Edejer, J. Lauer, J. Frenk, and C.J.L. Murray. 2001. Measuring quality: From the system to the provider. *International Journal for Quality in Health Care* 13:439–46.

Expert Panel on Equalization and Territorial Formula Financing. 2006. *Achieving a national purpose: Putting equalization back on track.* Ottawa: Department of Finance.

Facal, J. 2005. *Social policy and intergovernmental relations in Canada: Understanding the failure of* SUFA *from a Quebec perspective.* Policy paper no. 32. Regina: Saskatchewan Institute of Public Policy, University of Regina.

Fafard, P. 2013. Intergovernmental accountability and health care: Reflections on the recent Canadian experience. In *Overpromising and underperforming? Understanding new intergovernmental accountability regimes,* ed. L. White, P. Graefe, and J. Simmons, 31–55. Toronto: University of Toronto Press.

Falkner, G. 2011. Introduction: The EU's decision traps and their exits. In *The European Union's decision traps: Comparing policies,* ed. G. Falkner, 1–17. Oxford: Oxford University Press.

Fierlbeck, K. 2011. *Health care in Canada: A citizen's guide to policy and politics.* Toronto: University of Toronto Press.

First Ministers of Canada. 2003. *2003 First Ministers' Accord on Health care Renewal.* Ottawa. http://www.hc-sc.gc.ca/hcs-sss/delivery-prestation/fpt collab/2003accord/index-eng.php.

First Ministers of Canada. 2004. *A 10-Year Plan to Strengthen Health Care, September 16, 2004.* Ottawa. http://www.hc-sc.gc.ca/hcs-sss/delivery-presta-tion/fptcollab/2004-fmm-rpm/index-eng.php.

Fitzpatrick M. 2010. Bernier suggests scrapping Canada Health Transfer. *National Post,* 13 October.

Ford, C. 2008. New governance, compliance, and principle-based securities regulation. *American Business Law Journal* 45(1):1–59.

Fredriksson, M., P. Blomqvist, and U. Winblad. 2011. Conflict and compliance in Swedish health care governance: Soft law in the "shadow of hierarchy." *Scandinavian Political Studies* 35(1):48–70.

Gibson, D. 1996. The *Canada Health Act* and the constitution. *Health Law Journal* 4:1–33.

Goeree R., L. Levin, K. Chandra, J.M. Bowen, G. Blackhouse, J.E. Tarride, et al. 2009. Health technology assessment and primary data collection for reducing uncertainty in decision making. *Journal of the American College of Radiology* 6:332–42.

Gordon, R.H. 1983. An optimal taxation approach to fiscal federalism. *The Quarterly Journal of Economics* 98(4):567–86.

Graefe, P., and A. Bourns. 2009. The gradual defederalization of Canadian health policy. *Publius: The Journal of Federalism* 39(1):187–209.

Gunningham, N. 2009. Environmental law, regulation and governance: Shifting architectures. *Journal of Environmental Law* 21(2):179–212, 198.

Gunningham, N., P. Grabosky, and D. Sinclair. 1998. *Smart regulation: Designing environmental policy*. Oxford: Clarendon University Press.

Haardt, D. 2012. *Healthcare expenditure, population, and population density across Canada*. Unpublished manuscript.

Hamlin, A.P. 1991. Decentralization, competition and the efficiency of federalism. *The Economic Record* 67(3):193–204.

Harmes, A. 2007. The political economy of open federalism. *Canadian Journal of Political Science* 40(2):417–37.

Harrison, K., ed. 2006. *Racing to the bottom? Provincial interdependence in the Canadian federation*. Vancouver: UBC Press.

Hay, C. 2004. Ideas, interests, and institutions in the comparative political economy of great transformations. *Review of International Political Economy* 11:204–26.

Health Council of Canada. 2008. *Rekindling reform: Health care renewal in Canada, 2003–2008*. Toronto: Health Council of Canada. http://www.healthcouncilcanada.ca/docs/rpts/2008/HCC%205YRPLAN%20(WEB)_FA.pdf.

– 2011. *Progress report 2011: Health care renewal in Canada*. Ottawa: Health Council of Canada. http://www.healthcouncilcanada.ca/tree/2.45-2011Progress_ENG.pdf

Health Technology Assessment Task Group on behalf of the Federal/Provincial/Territorial Advisory Committee on Information and Emerging Technologies. 2004. *Technology strategy 1.0*. Ottawa: Health Canada. http://www.hc-sc.gc.ca/hcs-sss/pubs/ehealth-esante/2004-tech-strateg/index-eng.php

Hébert, P., and M. Stanbrook. 2010. The federal government's abandonment of health. *CMAJ* 182(18):E809.

Hogg, P. 2007. *Constitutional law of Canada*, 5th ed. (supplemented). Toronto: Carswell/Thomson Reuters.

Hutton J., C. McGrath, J.M. Frybourg, M. Tremblay, E. Bramley-Harker, and

C. Henshall. 2006. Framework for describing and classifying decision-making systems using technology assessment to determine the reimbursement of health technologies (fourth hurdle systems). *International Journal of Technology Assessment in Health Care* 22:10–8.

Ibrahim, J.E. 2001. Performance indicators from all perspectives. *International Journal for Quality in Health Care* 13:431–2.

International and Intergovernmental Relations. 2004. *Report of the MLA Committee on Strengthening Alberta's Role in Confederation*. Edmonton: Government of Alberta.

Ip, I., and J. Mintz. 1992. *Dividing the spoils: The federal-provincial allocation of taxing powers*. Toronto: CD Howe Institute.

Jackman, M. 1996. The constitutional basis for federal regulation of health. *Health Law Review* 15(2):3.

– 2000. Constitutional jurisdiction over health in Canada. *Health Law Journal* 8:95.

Jacob, R., and M. McGregor. 1993. Assessing the impact of health technology assessment. *International Journal of Technology Assessment in Health Care* 13:68–80.

Jerome-Forget, M. 2002. *A question of priorities, equity and accountability*. Ottawa: Centre for Research and Information on Canada.

Jordan, J. 2009. Federalism and health care cost containment in comparative perspective. *Publius* 39(1):164–86.

Keen, M.J., and C. Kotsogiannis. 2002. Does federalism lead to excessively high taxes? *The American Economic Review* 92(1):363–70.

Kennett, S. 1998. *Securing the Social Union: A commentary on the decentralized approach*. Kingston: Institute of Intergovernmental Relations.

Kephart, G., S. Birch, G. Tomblin Murphy, L. O'Brien-Pallas, and A. MacKenzie. 2005. *Health human resources planning simulation model*. Mississauga: Med-Emerg.

Kirby, M.J.L. 2002. *The health of Canadians – The federal role, final report on the state of the health care system in Canada. Vol. 6: Recommendations for reform*. http://www.parl.gc.ca/37/2/parlbus/commbus/senate/com-e/soci-e/rep-e/repoct02vol6-e.pdf.

Klazinga, N., K. Stronks, D. Delnoij, and A. Verhoeff. 2001. Indicators without a cause. Reflections on the development and use of indicators in health care from a public health perspective. *International Journal for Quality in Health Care* 13:433–8.

Kneebone, R. 2008. *National subsidization policy and its implications for Western Canada*. Calgary: Canada West Foundation.

– 2012. *How you pay determines what you get: Alternative financing options as a determinant of publicly funded health care in Canada*. SPP Research Paper, vol. 5, issue 20. Calgary: School of Public Policy, University of Calgary. http://www.policyschool.ucalgary.ca/sites/default/files/research/r-kneebone-althealthpayfinal.pdf.

Kneebone, R., and K. McKenzie. 1999. *Past (in)discretions: Canadian federal and provincial fiscal policy*. Toronto: Centre for Public Management, University of Toronto Press.

Kong, H. 2008. The spending power, constitutional interpretation and legal pragmatism. *Queen's Law Journal* 34:305.

Lafortune, L., L. Farand, I. Mondou, C. Sicotte, and R. Battista. 2008. Assessing the performance of health technology assessment organizations: a framework. *Internatiopnal Journal of Technology Assessment in Health Care* 24:76–86.

Lahey, W. 2010. New governance regulation and managerial accountability for performance in Canada's health care systems. In *Grand challenges in health law and policy*, ed. R.P. Kouri and C. Régis, 243–78. Cowansville, QC: Thomson Reuters.

– 2011. Medicare and the law: Contours of an evolving relationship. In *Canadian health law and policy*, 4th ed., ed. J. Downie, T. Caulfield, and C. Flood, 1, 50–2. Toronto: Lexis Nexis.

Lajoie, A. 2008. Current exercises of the "federal spending power": What does the constitution say about them? *Queen's Law Journal* 34:141.

Lazar, H. 2000. The Social Union Framework Agreement: Lost opportunity or new beginning? Working paper 3. Kingston: Institute of Intergovernmental Relations, School of Policy Studies, Queen's University. http://www.queensu.ca/sps/publications/workingpapers/03.pdf.

– 2003. Managing interdependencies in the Canadian Federation: Lessons from the Social Union Framework Agreement. In *Constructive and cooperative federalism? A series of commentaries on the Council of the Federation*, ed. D. Brown and F. St-Hillaire. Kingston: Institute of Intergovernmental Relations, School of Policy Studies, Queen's University. http://www.irpp.org/miscpubs/archive/federation/lazar.pdf.

– 2008. The spending power and the Harper government. *Queen's Law Journal* 34(75):125–40.

Lazar, H., F. St-Hillaire, and J.F. Tremblay. 2004. Vertical fiscal imbalance: myth or reality? In *Money, politics, and health care: Reconstructing the federal-provincial partnership*, ed. H. Lazar and F. St-Hillaire, 135–87. Montreal: Institute for Research on Public Policy.

Leblanc, D. 2012. Budget to upend RCMP health care. *Globe and Mail*, 21 May. http://www.theglobeandmail.com/news/politics/budget-bill-to-upend-rcmp-health-care/article4198164/.

Leeson, H. 2004. Constitutional jurisdiction over health and health care services in Canada. In *The governance of health care in Canada*, ed. T. McIntosh, P-G. Forest, and G.P. Marchildon, 50–82. Toronto: University of Toronto Press.

Levin, L., R. Goeree, N. Sikich, B. Jorgenson, M.C. Brouwers, T. Easty, et al. 2007. Establishing a comprehensive continuum from an evidentiary base to policy development for health technologies: the Ontario experience. *International Journal of Technology Assessment in Health Care* 23:299–309.

Levy, A.R. 2005. Categorizing outcomes of health care delivery. *Clinical & Investigative Medicine* 28:347–50.

Levy, A.R.., and M. McGregor. 1995. How has extracorporeal shock-wave lithotripsy changed the treatment of urinary stones in Quebec? *CMAJ* 153:1729–36.

Levy, A.R., M. Terashima, and A. Travers. 2010. Should geographic analyses guide the creation of regionalized care models for ST-segment elevation myocardial infarction? *Open Medicine* 1:e22–e25.

Lewis, S. 2002. The bog, the fog, the future: 5 strategies for renewing federalism in health care. *CMAJ* 166(11):1421–2.

Lindner, J., and B. Rittberger. 2003. The creation, interpretation and contestation of institutions – revisiting historical institutionalism. *Journal of Common Market Studies* 41(3): 445–73.

MacIntosh, C. 2006. Jurisdictional roulette: Constitutional and structural barriers to Aboriginal access to health. In *Just medicare: What's in, what's out, how we decide*, ed. C.M. Flood, 193–215. Toronto: University of Toronto Press.

MacKinnon, D. 2011. *Dollars & sense: A case for modernizing Canada's transfer agreements*. Toronto: Ontario Chamber of Commerce. http://www.occ.on.ca/assets/Fiscal-Imbalance_final-electronic1.pdf.

MacKinnon, N., and I. Ip. 2009. The National Pharmaceuticals Strategy: Rest in peace, revive, or renew? *CMAJ* 180(8): 801–3.

Manitoba Department of Finance. 1999. *A renewed fiscal partnership to support Canada's Social Union*, Budget paper C. Winnipeg: Government of Manitoba. www.gov.mb.ca/finance/pdf/budget1999/fiscal.pdf.

Manitoba Minister of Health and Healthy Living. 2004. *Manitoba's comparable health indicators report*. Winnipeg.

Marchildon, G.P. 1995. Fin de siècle Canada: The federal government in retreat. In *Disintegration or transformation: The crisis of the state in advanced industrial countries*, ed. P. McCarthy and E. Jones, 133–51. New York: St. Martin's Press.

– 2003. The Health Council of Canada proposal in light of the Council of the Federation. In *Constructive and co-operative federalism? A series of commentaries on the Council of the Federation*, ed. D. Brown and F. St-Hillaire. Kingston: Institute of Intergovernmental Relations, School of Policy Studies, Queen's University. http://www.irpp.org/miscpubs/archive /federation/marchildon.pdf.

– 2006. *Health systems in transition: Canada*. Toronto: University of Toronto Press.

– 2007. Pharmacare: prescription for an ailing federation? In *Medicare: Facts, myths, problems, promise*, ed. B. Campbell and G.P. Marchildon, 268–84. Toronto: Lorimer.

– 2009. The policy history of Canadian Medicare. *Canadian Bulletin of Medical History* 26(2):247–60.

Mather, G. 2010. *Is soft law taking over? The perils and benefits of non-traditional legislation*. Switzerland: Progress Foundation. http://www.progress foundation.ch/PDF/referate/220_Referat%20Graham%20Mather_20.10 .2010.pdf.

May, K. 2012. Legal expert backs parliamentary budget officer in fight for data on cuts. *Ottawa Citizen*, 18 June. http://www.ottawacitizen.com/news /Legal+expert+backs+parliamentary+budget+officer+fight+data+cuts/6799 433/story.html.

McGregor, M., and J.M. Brophy. 2005. End-user involvement in health technology assessment (HTA) development: a way to increase impact. *International Journal of Technology Assessment in Health Care* 21:263–7.

McIntosh, T. 2004. Intergovernmental relations, social policy and federal transfers after Romanow. *Canadian Public Administration* 47(1):27–51.

McKenzie, K. 2005. *Reflections on the political economy of fiscal federalism in Canada*. Working paper. Toronto: C.D. Howe Institute.

Meekison, P. 2003. Council of the Federation: An idea whose time has come. In *Constructive and co-operative federalism? A series of commentaries on the Council of the Federation*, ed. D. Brown and F. St-Hillaire. Kingston: Institute of Intergovernmental Relations, School of Policy Studies, Queen's University. http://www.irpp.org/miscpubs/archive/federation /meekison.pdf.

Meissner, D. 2012. Premiers skip Ottawa, form own health working group. *Chronicle Herald*, 17 January. http://thechronicleherald.ca/canada/53005-premiers-skip-ottawa-form-own-health-working-group.

Mendes, E. 2008. Building firewalls and deconstructing Canada by hobbling the federal spending power: The rise of the Harper doctrine. *Queen's Law Journal* 34(1):225–48.

Mintz, J. 2009. Ontario's bold move to create jobs and growth. *School of Public Policy Communiqué* 1(4). Calgary: School of Public Policy, University of Calgary.

Mintz, J., R.D. Brown, J.S. Cowan, B. Dahlby, A.R. Lanthier, W. Lefebvre, et al. 1997. *Report of the Technical Committee on Business Taxation*. Ottawa: Department of Finance. 11.3–11.4.

Mintz, J., and M. Smart. 2002. *Why tax point transfers will strengthen Canada*. Ottawa: Centre for Research and Information on Canada.

Montinola, G., Y. Qian, and B. Weingast. 1995. Federalism, Chinese-style: The political basis for economic success in China. *World Politics* 48(October):50–81.

Mosca, I. 2007. Decentralization as a determinant of health care expenditure: Empirical analysis for OECD countries. *Applied Economics Letters* 14(7):511–5.

Murray, C.J.L., and A.D. Lopez. 1996. *The global burden of disease: A comprehensive assessment of mortality and disability from diseases, injuries and risk factors in 1990 and projected to 2020*. Report no. 1. Cambridge, MA: Harvard School of Public Health/WHO/World Bank.

Nassiri, A., and L. Rochaix. 2006. Revisiting physicians' financial incentives in Quebec: A panel system approach. *Health Economics* 15(1):49–64.

Nathan, R.P. 2005. Federalism and health policy. *Health Affairs* 24(6):1458–66.

Newdick, C. 2008. Preserving social citizenship in health care markets: There could be trouble ahead. *McGill Journal of Law and Health* 2:93.

Newman, D. 2011. Changing division of powers doctrine and the emergent principle of subsidiarity. *Saskatchewan Law Review* 74:21–31.

Noel, A. 2000. General study of the framework agreement. In *The Canadian Social Union without Quebec*, ed. A.-G. Gagnon and H. Segal, 9–36. Montreal: Institute for Research on Public Policy.

O'Brien-Pallas, L., and A. Baumann. 2000. Toward evidence-based policy decisions: A case study of nursing health human resources in Ontario, Canada. *Nursing Inquiry* 7(4):248–57.

O'Brien-Pallas L., S. Birch, A. Baumann, and G. Tomblin Murphy. 2001a. Integrating workforce planning, human resources, and service planning. *Human Resources for Health Development Journal* 5:1–15.

O'Brien-Pallas, L., G. Tomblin Murphy, S. Birch, and A. Baumann. 2001b. A Framework for Collaborative Pan-Canadian Health Human Resources Planning. In *Future development of information to support the management of nursing resources: Recommendations*, 6. Ottawa: Canadian Institute for Health Information.

O'Brien-Pallas, L., G. Tomblin Murphy, S. Birch, and A. Baumann. 2005. Appendix: Example of a conceptual model For HHR planning. In *A framework for collaborative pan-Canadian health human resources planning*, 29–36. Ottawa: Federal/Provincial/Territorial Advisory Committee on Health Delivery and Human Resources.

Organisation for Economic Co-operation and Development (OECD). 2011. OECD *health data 2011*. http://www.oecd.org/document/16/0,3343,en_2649 _34631_2085200_1_1_1_1,00.html.

Osbourne, D., and T. Gaebler. 1992. *Reinventing government*. Lexington, MA: Addison-Wesley.

Parker, C. 1999. *Just lawyers: Regulation and access to justice*. Oxford: Oxford University Press.

– 2002. *The open corporation: Self-regulation and democracy*. Melbourne: Cambridge University Press.

Petretto, A. 2000. On the cost-benefit of the regionalisation of the National Health Service. *Economics of Governance* 1:213–32.

Petter, A. 1989. Federalism and the myth of the spending power. *Canadian Bar Review* 68:448–79.

Picard, A. 2009. Canadians back "public solutions" to improve care, poll finds. *Globe and Mail*, 14 August. http://www.nanosresearch.com/news /in_the_news/Globe%20and%20Mail%20August%2014%202009.pdf.

– 2011. It's time to find a cure for the problem of how doctors are paid. *Globe and Mail*, 28 April.

Premont, M.-C. 2007. Wait-time guarantees for health services: An analysis of Quebec's reaction to the *Chaoulli* Supreme Court decision. *Health Law Journal* 15:43.

Provincial and Territorial Finance Ministers. 2001. *Addressing the fiscal imbalance: Report of provincial and territorial finance ministers*, prepared for discussion at the 2001 Annual Premiers Conference, Victoria, BC, 1–3 August.

Qian, Y., and G. Roland. 1998. Federalism and the soft budget constraint. *American Economic Review* 88(5):1143–62.

Qian, Y., and B. Weingast. 1997. Federalism as a commitment to preserving market incentives. *Journal of Economic Perspectives* 11(4):83–92.

Rae, B. 2003. Some personal reflections on the Council of the Federation. In *Constructive and co-operative federalism? A series of commentaries on the Council of the Federation*, ed. D. Brown and F. St-Hillaire. Kingston: Institute of Intergovernmental Relations, School of Policy Studies, Queen's

University. http://www.queensu.ca/iigr/working/CouncilFederation
/FedEN/12.pdf

Raftery J., P. Roderick, and A. Stevens. 2005. Potential use of routine
databases in health technology assessment. *Health Technology Assessment*
9:i–iv.

Requejo, F. 2010. Federalism and democracy: The case of minority nations –
a federalist deficit. In *Federal democracies*, ed. M. Burgess and A. Gagnon,
175–98. London and New York: Routledge.

Rettig, R.A. 1994. Medical innovation duels cost containment. *Health Affairs*
13(3):7–27.

Ribstein, L., and B. Kobayashi. 2006. *The economics of federalism.* Illinois Law
& Economics Working Paper no. LE06-001, George Mason University
Law & Economics Research Paper no. 06-15. http://papers.ssrn.com
/sol3/papers.cfm?abstract_id=875626.

Rice, T. 2009. *The economics of health reconsidered,* 3rd ed. Chicago: Health
Administration Press.

Rico, A., and J. Costa-Font. 2005. Power rather than path dependency? The
dynamics of institutional change under health care federalism. *Journal of
Health Politics, Policy and Law* 30(1–2):231–52.

Roberts, D. 2011. The EPA: The Tea Party's next target. *The Guardian*, 3
August. http://www.guardian.co.uk/commentifree/cifamerica/2011/aug
/03/epa-republicans-tea-party.

Roberts M.J., W. Hsiao, P. Berman, and M. Reich. 2008. *Getting health reform
right – A guide to improving performance and equity.* Oxford, UK: Oxford
University Press.

Robson, W.B.P. 1997. *Ottawa's incredible disappearing act: Canadians pay billions more than in tax than the budget shows and the gap is growing.* Toronto:
C.D. Howe Institute.

Rodden, J. 2002. The dilemma of fiscal federalism: Grants and fiscal performance around the world. *American Journal of Political Science*
46(3):670–87.

Rode, M., and M. Rushton. 2004. Increasing provincial revenues for health
care. In *The fiscal sustainability of health care in Canada*, ed. G.P.
Marchildon, T. McIntosh, and P.-G. Forest, 199–319. Toronto: University
of Toronto Press.

Romanow, R. 2002. *Building on values: The future of health care in Canada.
Final report.* Saskatoon: Commission on the Future of Health Care in
Canada.

Roos, L.L., S. Gupta, R.A. Soodeen, and L. Jebamani. 2005. Data quality in an information-rich environment: Canada as an example. *Canadian Journal on Aging* 24(Suppl):153–70.

Roski, J., and R. Gregory. 2001. Performance measurement for ambulatory care: Moving towards a new agenda. *International Journal for Quality in Health Care* 13:447–53.

Ryan, Claude. 2003. Quebec and interprovincial discussion and consultation. In *Constructive and co-operative federalism? A series of commentaries on the Council of the Federation*, ed. D. Brown and F. St-Hillaire. Kingston: Institute of Intergovernmental Relations, School of Policy Studies, Queen's University. http://www.irpp.org/miscpubs/archive/federation/ryan.pdf.

Sabel, C., and J. Zeitlin. 2008. Learning from difference: The new architecture of experimentalist governance in the EU. *European Law Journal* 14(3):271.

Sabel, C., and J. Zeitlin, eds. 2010. *Experimentalist governance in the European Union.* Oxford: Oxford University Press.

Saltman, R.B. 2008. Decentralization, re-centralization, and future European health policy. *European Journal of Public Health* 18(2):104–6.

Sand, I.-J. 1998. Understanding the new forms of governance: Mutually interdependent, reflexive, destablised and competing institutions. *European Law Journal* 4(3):271–93.

Saulnier, M., S. Shortt, and E. Gruenwoldt. 2004. *The taming of the queue: Toward a cure for health care.* Ottawa: Canadian Medical Association and Canadian Nurses Association. http://www.rehabmed.ualberta.ca/spa/LTC_Waitlists/tame.pdf.

Scharpf, F.W. 1988. The joint-decision trap: Lessons from German federalism and European integration. *Public Administration* 66(Autumn):239–78.

– 1997. Balancing positive and negative integration: The regulatory options for Europe. Max Planck Institute for the Study of Societies Working Paper 97/8.

– 2001. European governance: Common concerns vs. the challenge of diversity. Max Planck Institute for the Study of Societies Working Paper 01/6.

– 2002. The European social model: Coping with the challenges of diversity. *Journal of Common Market Studies* 40(4):645–70.

– 2006. The joint-decision trap revisited. *Journal of Common Market Studies* 44(4):845–64.

– 2009. The double asymmetry of European integration, or why the EU cannot be a social market economy. Max Planck Institute for the Study of Societies Working Paper 09/12.

Schmidt, V. 2008. Discursive institutionalism: The explanatory power of ideas and discourse. *Annual Review of Political Science* 11:303–26.

– 2010. Taking ideas and discourse seriously: explaining change through discursive institutionalism as the fourth "new institutionalism." *European Political Science Review* 2:1–25.

Scoffield, H. 2012. Provinces ready and willing to fill health-care void left by feds: Brad Wall. *Canadian Press*, 18 April. http://ca.news.yahoo.com /provinces-ready-willing-fill-health-care-void-left-182458956.html.

Segal, L., K. Dalziel, and T. Bolton. 2008. A work force model to support the adoption of best practice care in chronic diseases – a missing piece in clinical guideline implementation. *Implementation Science* 3:35.

Shepherd, R.P. 2012. In search of a balanced Canadian federal evaluation function: Getting to relevance. *Canadian Journal of Program Evaluation* 26:1–45.

Singh, D., H. Lalani, B. Kralj, E. Newman, J. Goodyear, D. Hellyer, et al. 2010. *Ontario population needs-based physician simulation model*. Toronto: Ontario Ministry of Health and Long-Term Care.

Skinner, B.J., and M. Rovere. 2011. Without some privatization, medicare will collapse. *National Post*, 19 April. http://fullcomment.nationalpost .com/2011/04/19/brett-j-skinner-and-mark-rovere-without-some-privatiza- tion-medicare-will-collapse/. [The study itself is available at http://www .fraserinstitute.org/research-news/display.aspx?id=17414]

Smart, M. 2005. *Federal transfers: Principles, practice, and prospects*. C.D. Howe Institute Working Paper (September). Toronto: C.D. Howe Institute.

Smart, M., and R. Bird. 2006. *The GST cut and fiscal imbalance*. Toronto: Inter- national Tax Program, Rotman School of Management.

Snowdon, A., K. Schnarr, A. Hussein, and C. Alessi. *Measuring what matters: The cost vs. values of health care*. London, ON: Ivey International Centre for Health Innovation. http://sites.ivey.ca/healthinnovation/thought- leadership/white-papers/measuring-what-matters-the-cost-vs-values-of- health-care-november-2012/.

Sobolev, B., V. Sanchez, and L. Kuramoto. 2012. *Health care evaluation using computer simulation: Concepts, methods and applications*. New York: Springer.

Sossin, L. 2003. Discretion unbound: Reconciling the charter and soft law. *Canadian Public Administration* 45:465–89.

– 2004. The politics of soft law: How judicial review influences bureaucrat- ic decision-making in Canada. In *Judicial review and bureaucratic impact: International and inter-disciplinary perspectives*, ed. S. Halliday and M. Her- togh, 129–60. London: Cambridge University Press.

Sossin, L., and C. Smith. 2003. Hard choices and soft law: Ethical codes, policy guidelines and the role of the courts in regulating government. *Alberta Law Review* 40:867–93.

Statistics Canada. 2009. *Provincial and territorial general government revenue and expenditures, by province and territory.* Ottawa: Statistics Canada. http://www40.statcan.ca/l01/cst01/govt08a-eng.htm.

Sternman, J. (2000). *Business dynamics, systems thinking and modeling for a complex world.* Toronto: McGraw-Hill.

Stevenson, G. 2006. *Fiscal federalism and the burden of history. Conference on Fiscal Federalism and the Future of Canada.* Kingston: Institute of Intergovernmental Relations, School of Policy Studies, Queen's University. http://www.queensu.ca/iigr/working/fiscalImb/Stevenson.pdf.

The Strategic Counsel. 2012. *Canadians' attitudes toward the health care system: A report to Health Canada.* Toronto: The Strategic Counsel.

Suissa, S., D. Henry, P. Caetano, C.R. Dormuth, P. Ernst, B. Hemmelgarn, et al. 2012. CNODES: The Canadian Network for Observational Drug Effect Studies. *Open Medicine* 2012;6(4)e134.

Telford, H. 2003. The federal spending power in Canada: nation-building or nation-destroying. *Publius* 33(1):23–44.

Tomblin Murphy, G., R. Alder, A. MacKenzie, and J. Rigby. 2010a. *Model of care initiative in Nova Scotia (MOCINS): Final evaluation report. Report to the Nova Scotia Department of Health.* Halifax: WHO/PAHO Collaborating Centre on Health Workforce Planning and Research, Dalhousie University. http://www.gov.ns.ca/health/mocins/docs/mocins-evaluation-report.pdf.

Tomblin Murphy, G., R. Alder, C. Pelletier, and A. MacKenzie. 2007a. *Simulation modeling for health human resources strategy development in Nova Scotia: Registered nurses report.* Halifax: Nova Scotia Department of Health.

Tomblin Murphy, G., R. Alder, C. Pelletier and A. MacKenzie. 2007b. *Simulation modeling for health human Resources strategy development in Nova Scotia: Family physician report.* Halifax: Nova Scotia Department of Health.

Tomblin Murphy, G., R. Alder, C. Pelletier, and A. MacKenzie. 2008. *Simulation modeling for health human resources strategy development in Nova Scotia: Medical radiation technologist report.* Halifax: Nova Scotia Department of Health.

Tomblin Murphy, G., R. Alder, S. Tomblin, A. MacKenzie, J. Rigby, C. Pauley, et al. 2010b. *WHO/PAHO Collaborating Centre on Health Workforce Planning and Research: International Consortium on Needs-Based Health Human Resources Planning: Final report. Report to the HHR Planning Unit, Health Canada.* Halifax: WHO/PAHO Collaborating Centre on Health Workforce Planning and Research, Dalhousie University.

Tomblin Murphy, G., S. Birch, R. Alder, A. MacKenzie, and L. Lethbridge. 2009a. *Needs-based health human resources planning for nurses in Ontario.* Toronto: Ontario Ministry of Health and Long-Term Care.

Tomblin Murphy, G., S. Birch, R. Alder, A. MacKenzie, L. Lethbridge, L. Little, et al. 2009b. *Tested solutions for eliminated Canada's registered nurse shortage.* Ottawa: Canadian Nurses Association.

Tomblin Murphy, G., S. Birch, and A. MacKenzie. 2007c. *The challenge of linking needs to provider requirements.* Ottawa: Canadian Medical Association.

Tomblin Murphy, G., S. Birch, A. MacKenzie, R. Alder, L. Lethbridge, and L. Little. 2012. Eliminating the shortage of registered nurses in Canada: An exercise in applied needs-based planning. *Health Policy* 105:192–202.

Tomblin Murphy, G., G. Kephart, L. Lethbridge, L. O'Brien-Pallas, and S. Birch. 2009c. Planning for what? Challenging the assumptions of health human resource planning. *Health Policy* 92(2):225–33.

Tomblin Murphy, G., A. MacKenzie, R. Alder, S. Birch, G. Kephart, and L. O'Brien-Pallas. 2009d. An applied simulation model for estimating the supply of and requirements for registered nurses based on population health needs. *Policy, Politics & Nursing Practice* 10(4):240–51.

Tomblin Murphy, G., and L. O'Brien-Pallas. 2006. Appendix: Example of a conceptual model for HHR planning. In *A framework for collaborative pan-Canadian health human resources planning,* ed. Health Canada, 29–36. Ottawa: Federal/Provincial/Territorial Advisory Committee on Health Delivery and Human Resources (ACHDHR).

Tömmel, I., and A. Verdun. 2009. *Innovative governance in the European Union: The politics of multilevel policymaking.* Boulder: Lynne Rienner.

Tremblay, A. 2000. The federal spending power. In *The Canadian Social Union without Quebec,* ed. A.-G. Gagnon and H. Segal, 155–88. Montreal: Institute for Research on Public Policy.

Trubek, D., D.P. Cottrell, and M. Nance. 2006. Soft law, hard law and European integration: Towards a theory of hybridity. In *Law and new governance in the EU and the US,* ed. G. de Burca and J. Scott. Oxford: Hart Publishing.

Trubek, D., and L. Trubek. 2007. New governance and legal regulation: Complimentarity, rivalry, or transformation. *Columbia Journal of European Law* 13:542.

Trubek, L. 2006. New governance and soft law in health care reform. *Indiana Health Law Review* 3:137.

Tu, J.V., J. Bowen, M. Chiu, D.T. Ko, P.C. Austin, Y. He, et al. 2007. Effectiveness and safety of drug-eluting stents in Ontario. *New England Journal of Medicine* 357:1393–402.

Vancouver Island Health Authority (VIHA). 2009. *Care delivery model redesign (CDMR) – phase 1 implementation project plan*. Victoria: VIHA.

Velasco, G.M., A. Gerhardus, J.A. Rottingen, and R. Busse. 2010. Developing health technology assessment to address health care system needs. *Health Policy* 94:196–202.

Waddams, S.M. 2005. *The law of contracts*, 5th ed., 461–8. Toronto: Canada Law Book Inc.

Wait Time Alliance. 2012. *Shedding light on Canadians' total wait times in Canada: Report card on wait times in Canada*. Ottawa: Wait Time Alliance. http://www.waittimealliance.ca/media/2012reportcard/WTA2012-report card_e.pdf.

Watson, W. 1999. How the budget is made: An interview with Scott Clark Deputy Minister of Finance. *Policy Options* (January/February):14–15. http://www.irpp.org/po/archive/jan99/clark.pdf.

Watts, R.L. 1999. *The spending power in federal systems: A comparative study*. Kingston: Institute of Intergovernmental Relations.

– 2008. *Comparing federal systems*, 3rd ed. Kingston: McGill-Queen's University Press for the Institute of Intergovernmental Relations.

Weingast, B. 1995. The economic role of political institutions: Market-preserving federalism and economic development. *Journal of Law, Economics, and Organization* 11(1):1–31.

– 2005. The performance and stability of federalism: An institutional perspective. In *Handbook of new institutional economics*, ed. C. Ménard and M.M. Shirley, 149–72. Dordrecht: Springer.

Weintraub, W.S., M.V. Grau-Sepulveda, J.M. Weiss, S.M. O'Brien, E.D. Peterson, P. Kolm, et al. 2012. Comparative effectiveness of revascularization strategies. *New England Journal of Medicine* 366:1467–76.

Wilson, K. 2000. Health care, federalism and the new Social Union. *CMAJ* 162(8):1171–4.

Woolhandler, S., T. Campbell, and D.U. Himmelstein. 2003. Costs of health care administration in the United States and Canada. *New England Journal of Medicine* 349(8):768–75.

Contributors

KEN BOESSENKOOL   An executive fellow at the School of Public Policy at the University of Calgary, Ken Boessenkool was national practice director of public affairs at Hill & Knowlton and also served as general manager for Alberta. Before that, Ken was senior policy advisor and senior strategist to Conservative Party of Canada leader Stephen Harper. He played senior strategic roles in the 2004, 2006, and 2011 national Conservative election campaigns. He has served in senior policy and strategic roles on the winning side of three national leadership races. He has also worked on leadership campaigns in Alberta and Ontario.

KATHERINE FIERLBECK   Katherine Fierlbeck is professor of political science at Dalhousie University. She works in the areas of political theory and public policy. A graduate of the University of Alberta (BA Hon, Killam postdoctoral fellowship), York University (MA), and Cambridge University (PhD), her books include *Globalizing Democracy* (Manchester University Press 1998, 2nd edition 2008); *The Development of Political Thought in Canada* (University of Toronto Press/ Broadview 2005); *Political Thought in Canada: An Intellectual History* (University of Toronto Press/Broadview, 2006), and *Health Care in Canada* (University of Toronto Press 2011). She is a member of the European Union Centre of Excellence and is currently researching European health care federalism.

DAVID HAARDT   David Haardt is an assistant professor in the School of Health Administration at Dalhousie University. He received his undergraduate degree from Johannes Kepler University in Linz, Austria, and his PhD in economics from the University of Essex in England. Before joining Dalhousie University, he spent two years as a postdoctoral fellow in the Department of Economics at McMaster University, where he was a member of the Social Sciences and Humanities Research Council-funded research program on the social and economic dimension of an aging population. Much of his research is related to the link between older men and women's employment and health, including cognitive functioning. He is also interested in economic evaluation and health care reform.

WILLIAM LAHEY William Lahey is associate professor, Schulich School of Law, Dalhousie Health Law Institute, and Faculty of Health Professions, Dalhousie University. He is a graduate of Mount Allison University (BA), of the University of Oxford (BA Juris), and of the University of Toronto (LLM). He was clerk to Mr. Justice La Forest, Supreme Court of Canada, 1989–90. He has written on the law of the Canadian health care system, administrative law, professional regulation, environmental regulation, and Canadian constitutional history. He has practised law in the private sector and in the Nova Scotia public service and has held a number of leadership positions in the Nova Scotia public service, including assistant deputy minister of health (1998–2001) and deputy minister of environment and labour (2004–07), the latter while on leave from Dalhousie Law School.

ADRIAN R. LEVY Adrian Levy is professor and head, Department of Community Health and Epidemiology, at Dalhousie University and a district chief in the Capital District Health Authority. He holds a PhD from McGill University (epidemiology) and did postgraduate training at McMaster University (economic evaluation). In the early 1990s, he worked on the secretariat of the Conseil d'Évaluation des Technologies de la Santé du Québec. After completing his postdoctoral fellowship, he joined the faculty of the University of British Columbia (UBC) in July 2000. During nine years at UBC, he held BC Michael Smith Foundation for Health Research Scholar and Senior Scholar awards and a Canadian Institutes of Health Research New Investigator award. His academic interests are in health services research and include epidemiology, performance measurement in health care, health technology assessment, and access to care.

GREG MARCHILDON   Canada Research Chair at the Johnson-Shoyama Graduate School of Public Policy, Greg Marchildon received his doctorate from the London School of Economics and Political Science and spent five years at Johns Hopkins University in Washington, DC. His academic pedigree was among the reasons Marchildon was asked to serve as executive director of the Commission on the Future of Health Care in Canada, chaired by the Hon. Roy Romanow, QC, in 2001 His most recent books include *Making Medicare: New Perspectives on the History of Medicare in Canada* and the WHO's updated *Health Systems in Transition: Canada.*

GAIL TOMBLIN MURPHY   Gail Tomblin Murphy (RN, PhD) is a professor in the School of Nursing, Faculty of Health Professions, and in the Department of Community Health and Epidemiology, Faculty of Medicine, Dalhousie University. She is a co-investigator at the Nursing Research Unit at the University of Toronto. She is also the director of the newly designated WHO Collaborating Centre on Health Workforce Planning and Research, located at Dalhousie University.

BORIS G. SOBOLEV   Boris Sobolev is a full professor and Canada Research Chair at the UBC School of Public and Population Health. Since 2002, he has served as a senior scientist at the Centre for Clinical Epidemiology and Evaluation. His research interests include factors influencing access to care, methodology for analysis of waiting times, risk of adverse events while awaiting elective surgery, and the use of simulation experiments in policy evaluation.

Index

welfare state, 5, 174
West Virginia, 33
who Collaborating Centre on
  Health Workforce Planning and
  Research, 253

World Health Organization, 253
World Trade Organization, 17
World War II, 174